The Illustrated Columcille

JOHN MARSDEN

Translation by John Gregory
Photography by Geoff Green

MACMILLAN

For Sister T.

ACKNOWLEDGEMENTS

I must first of all acknowledge the contribution of my two colleagues to this book. The idea of *The Illustrated Columcille* first emerged from conversations with John Gregory in the course of our work on *The Illustrated Bede*, and I am again greatly indebted to him for the skill and scholarship he has applied to his translation of Adamnan. I am no less indebted to Geoff Green for his camera-work and for sharing with me the 'grey martyrdom' of the weather forecasts for the western seaboard.

Geoff and I gratefully acknowledge the generous co-operation of the Dean of Down, the Iona Cathedral Trust and Historic Scotland in allowing photography of properties in their care. I am similarly grateful to the British Library; Trinity College, Dublin; the Royal Irish Academy; the Stiftsbibliothek, St Gallen; and the Stadtbibliothek, Schaffhausen, for permission to reproduce manuscript materials from their collections; and to the Scottish Academic Press, Edinburgh, for their kind permission to include the extracts from Alexander Carmichael's *Carmina Gadelica*.

I must also thank Mr Attie MacKechnie of Iona Cathedral and Dr René Specht of the Stadtbibliothek, Schaffhausen, for their especial co-operation; Mrs Ingrid Date and Mrs Frieda Faulkner for their help with German translation and correspondence; Mr Michael Robson for his guidance on the language and lore of the Gael; and Miss Clare Gallagher who went before me into Donegal.

It only remains to add that the opinions, interpretations and speculations involved in *The Illustrated Columcille* remain the responsibility of its author.

JM

Introduction copyright © John Marsden 1991
Translation copyright © John Gregory 1991

First published 1991 by
MACMILLAN LONDON LIMITED
Cavaye Place London SW10 9PG
and Basingstoke

Associated companies in Auckland, Delhi, Dublin, Gaborone, Hamburg, Harare, Hong Kong, Johannesburg, Kuala Lumpur, Lagos, Manzini, Melbourne, Mexico City, Nairobi, New York, Singapore and Tokyo

A CIP catalogue record for this book is available from the British Library

ISBN 0-333-52985-5

Designed by Robert Updegraff
Typeset by Wyvern Typesetting Ltd, Bristol
Printed in Singapore

CONTENTS

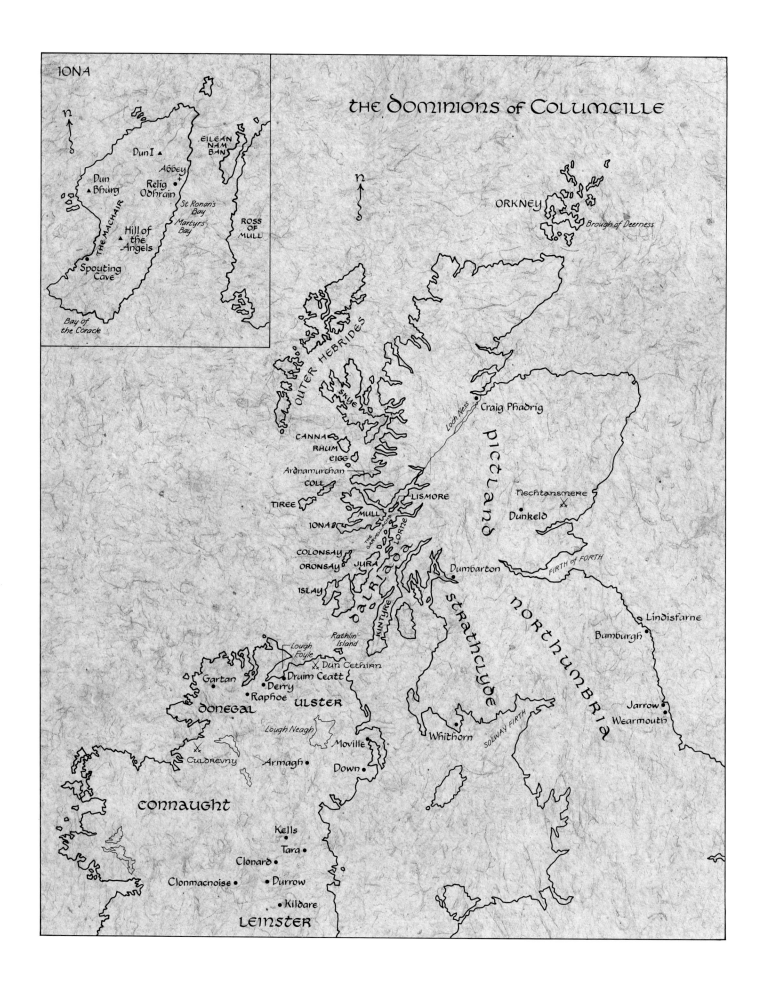

IONA

n

Dun I ▲

Dun
Bhuirg ▲

THE MACHAIR

EILEAN
NAM
BAN

Abbey

Relig
Odhrain

St Ronan's
Bay

Martyrs
Bay

ROSS
OF
MULL

Hill of
the
Angels ▲

Spouting
Cave

Bay of
the Coracle

THE DOMINIONS OF COLUMCILLE

n

ORKNEY

Brough of Deerness

OUTER HEBRIDES

SKYE

Loch Ness

Craig Phadrig

PICTLAND

CANNA

RHUM

EIGG

Ardnamurchan

COLL

LISMORE

Nechtansmere

Dunkeld

TIREE

MULL

IONA

THE GARVELLACHS

LORNE

COLONSAY

ORONSAY

JURA

DALRIADA

FIRTH OF FORTH

Dumbarton

STRATHCLYDE

NORTHUMBRIA

ISLAY

KINTYRE

Lindisfarne

Bamburgh

Rathlin
Island

Lough
Foyle

Dun Cethirn

Druim Ceatt

SOLWAY FIRTH

Jarrow

Wearmouth

Gartan

Derry

Raphoe

ULSTER

Whithorn

DONEGAL

Lough Neagh

Moville

Culdrevny

Armagh

Down

CONNAUGHT

Kells

Tara

Clonard

Clonmacnoise

Durrow

Kildare

LEINSTER

Preface

The vast and various bibliography that has accumulated around the man known to the world by the Latin name of Columba and to the Gael by his given name of Columcille pays tribute to the extraordinary fascination he has exerted through fourteen centuries since his death.

Much of that literature has a discernible polemic quality – claiming Columcille for the land of his birth, for the highlands and islands of his maturity, for the ancient Celtic faith, even for an astonishing spectrum of latter-day evangelical and ideological worthy causes – which bears testimony to a charisma seemingly quite impervious to the erosions of the centuries.

The Illustrated Columcille sets out with no conscious ideological or polemic intent. It sets out simply to offer a new translation of the earliest and most authoritative *Life of Columba*, accompanied by introductory explorations of the rich seam of history and biography to be found woven into its hagiographical narrative and illustrated with the manuscript art that evokes his time and the landscapes that evoke his world.

This book grew out of my involvement, in company with the same two colleagues, in a similar project concerned with the life and writings of the Venerable Bede. It remains one of history's more intriguing synchronicities that Adamnan must certainly have met the young Bede in the monastery at Jarrow on his visits to Northumbria in 686 and 688, and it cannot be without significance that he began to write his great *Life of Columba* shortly after his return from those visits.

In the world-view of Adamnan's time, the kingdoms of Ireland, of Scottish Dalriada, of Pictland and of Northumbria were the four focal points of a complex and symbiotic inter-relationship. At least two, and possibly three, Anglo-Saxon kings of Northumbria were educated on Iona. A fourth is said to lie interred in its earth. It was an Irish monk from Iona who founded the monastery on Lindisfarne which inspired Northumbria's golden age, and it was that monastery's scriptorium which gave birth to the manuscript masterworks of the Columban tradition.

'His grace in Iona without stain,/And his soul in Derry', begins the ancient quatrain on the full habitation of Columcille and few would dispute that time-honoured prophecy. Should these pages reveal any measure of Northumbrian perspective unusual in the Columban bibliography, they do so only to reclaim something of the legacy of Bede's Northumbria for the Celtic dominion of Columcille.

JM

THE NINTH ABBOT OF IONA

He shall receive his name from my name.
He shall make a law for women,
from the noble, widespread Ictian sea hither.
He shall be learned without defect.
He shall attract half the language of envy,
for he will ordain a great law.
A sapling who will wrest the sovereignty of Tara from Finnachta,
over Tara he shall not assume power.
Thirty years in abbotship shall
Adamnan, of high and illustrious renown, be.

Columcille's foretelling of Adamnan

The year AD 685 marked a sea change in the history of the northern kingdoms of these islands. On 20 June in that year a battle was fought at Dunnichen Moss beside Nechtansmere in Forfar, where the Pictish warriors of Brude mac-Bile inflicted a savage defeat on the invading army of Egfrith of Northumbria. Riagal of Bangor's verses on the conflict are preserved in the *Chronicles of the Picts and Scots*:

> This day Bruide fights a battle for the land of his grandfather
> This day the son of Ossa was killed in battle with green swords,
> Although he did penance, he shall lie in Hi after his death:
> This day the son of Ossa was killed, who had the black drink.

Thus fell in battle the last in a line of warrior-kings who had ruled at Bamburgh since 547. Egfrith – the name can be translated from Anglo-Saxon as 'sword's edge' – was the grandson of Aethelfrith who had crushed the Scots of Dalriada at Degsastan and unified the kingdom of Northumbria between the Humber and the Forth. In 671, Egfrith had succeeded to that kingdom from which his father, Oswy, had ruled over all Britain as *Bretwalda*. In the first years of his reign he himself had thrown back a Pictish invasion, filling two rivers with the slain, and when Wulfhere of Mercia marched against Northumbria in 674 Egfrith repulsed him in battle. But ten years later Egfrith despatched his own invasion force to raid and plunder Ireland's plain of Brega. The *Annals of the Four Masters* record:

> The devastation of Magh-Breagh, both churches and territories, by the Saxons, in the month of June and they carried off with them many hostages from every place which they left, throughout Magh-Breagh, together with many other spoils, and afterwards went to their ships.

The motive for Egfrith's attack is nowhere clearly indicated, although the *Annals of Clonmacnoise* blame it on 'the alliance of the Irish with the Britons'. He may have been prompted by the men of Leinster to attack the domain of the High King Finnachta of the southern Ui-Neill. He may even have been provoked by Irish support for his illegitimate half-brother Aldfrith, the offspring of Oswy and an Irish princess.

Whatever the motive, Egfrith's Irish adventure was undertaken against the earnest advice of Northumbria's ecclesiastical worthies, according to Bede in his *Historia Ecclesiastica*. Bede goes on to suggest that divine rage against Egfrith's assault on 'a harmless race which had always been most friendly to the English' brought about his defeat and death at Dunnichen Moss. Bede's *Life of Cuthbert* quotes that saint's prophecy of the successor to the childless Egfrith:

> 'Do you see how many islands there are in this great wide sea? It would be easy for God to provide for himself a man from one of these to put in charge of the kingdom of the English.'

Cuthbert's prophecy was fulfilled when Aldfrith came to Bamburgh – probably from Iona, possibly from Ireland – in 685 to succeed his half-brother as king of a Northumbria greatly reduced in its dominion by Pictish incursion. Whether as a consequence of a natural inclination or of his education by Irish monks, Aldfrith proved a ruler of a very different mettle to that of his forebears. He was a man of the book rather than the blade and his succession seems to have come about at the urging of the powerful ecclesiastical counsellors on Lindisfarne. A monarch of conciliatory disposition and half Irish by blood, it was to Aldfrith that Finnachta appealed for the restoration of the five dozen Irish hostages carried off by Egfrith and his chosen emissary was Adamnan mac-Ronan, the ninth abbot of Iona. The Old Irish *Life* of Adamnan, the *Betha Adamanain*, provides a characteristically colourful account of his arrival in Aldfrith's kingdom:

> The north Saxons went to Erin and plundered Magh Bregh as far as Bealach-duin; and they carried with them a great prey of men and women. The men of Erin besought of Adamnan to go in quest of the captives to Saxonland. Adamnan went to demand the prisoners, and put in at Tracht-Romra. The strand is long, and the flood rapid; as rapid that if the best steed in Saxonland, ridden by the best horseman, were to start from the edge of the tide when the tide begins to flow, he could only bring his rider ashore by swimming, so extensive is the strand and so impetuous is the tide. The Saxons now were unwilling to permit Adamnan to land upon the shore. Put your currachs to the shore, said Adamnan to his people, for both their land and sea are obedient to God, and nothing can be done without God's permission. The clerics did as they were told. Adamnan drew a circle with his crozier around the currachs, and God rendered the strand firm under their currachs, and he formed a high wall of sea about them, so that the place where they were was an island, and the sea went to her limits past it, and did them no injury. When the Saxons had observed this very great miracle, they trembled for fear of Adamnan, and they gave him his full demand. Adamnan's demand was that a complete restoration of the captives should be made to him, and that no Saxon should ever again go on a predatory expedition to Erin; and Adamnan brought back all the captives.

Those familiar with the unpredictable tidal flow on the sands of the Solway Firth – which is almost certainly the landing place rendered in Irish as *Tracht-Romra* – will find the reported circumstances of Adamnan's landfall rather less miraculous than did the author of the *Betha Adamanain*. None the less, whether by miracle or diplomacy, the ninth abbot of Iona successfully liberated his captive compatriots and the *Annals of Ulster* for AD 687 confirm that 'Adamnan brought back sixty captives to Ireland'.

At the beginning of his seventh decade, Adamnan, intimate of monarchs and ecclesiastical power in three kingdoms, was soon to embark on the great work by which his place in history is assured. Some two years after his diplomatic mission in Northumbria, he was to set down the *Life* of his ancestral kinsman and renowned predecessor, Columcille of Iona.

'He shall receive his name from my name', begins the prophecy attributed to Columcille and translated from a medieval Brussels manuscript by Dr William Reeves. The fulfilment of that prophecy is one of the few precise certainties we have of the birth and parentage of Adamnan, descending by his father through six generations from Columcille's grandfather, Fergus, son of Niall of the Nine Hostages. The *Martyrology of Donegal* identifies Adamnan's father as 'Ronan, of the race of Conal Gulban, son of Niall' and thus places Adamnan in the line of the northern Ui-Neill which bore Columcille himself as its greatest son. His grandfather was Tinne, a chieftain of Donegal, and, in at least one medieval text, Adamnan is surnamed *ua-Tinne*, 'grandson of Tinne', instead of *mac-Ronan*, 'son of Ronan'.

'His mother was of the race of Enna . . . Ronat was her name', records the *Martyrology*. Her family's territory would have lain between Lough Foyle and Lough Swilly, where the monastery at Raphoe, though traditionally founded by Columcille, was dedicated to Adamnan.

His place of birth is nowhere recorded, but it was almost certainly in his father's homeland of south-west Donegal and probably near Drumholm, where the church is prominent amongst those dedicated to Adamnan. His date of birth is recorded by the *Annals of Ulster* at 623 and by the *Annals of Tighernach* at 624. The *Annals of Ulster* are now known to record dates at one year before the actual event throughout this period, so both annalists, in fact, agree on 624. The annals cast a shadow of doubt on their own date for his birth when they record his death at 704 and state his age as variously seventy-six and seventy-seven, which would place the year of his birth around 628.

Adamnan was certainly a monastic name and has, on occasion, been interpreted as a diminutive of Adam. A. O. Anderson proposes that Adomnanus was his own Latinisation from the Old Irish form of *A'domnan*, which translates as 'man of great dread' and corresponds prophetically with many aspects of his personality recorded in the Old Irish *Betha Adamanain*.

The earliest manuscripts of Adamnan's works spell his name as 'Adomnan' and so it was written down to the tenth century and occasionally afterwards. In the Old Irish period, 'a' was substituted for 'o' and 'Adamnan' became the usual spelling thereafter, with the exception of those occasions where Adamnan is known by the more recent alternative form of 'St Eunan'.

A form of Adamnan was the name under which he entered upon his monastic education in the foundation of St Ernan at Drumholm. The *Martyrology of Donegal* records Ernan's death in the year 640 and identifies him as the 'son of the brother of Columbkille'. After Drumholm, Adamnan went on to pursue his education in Meath, very possibly at the esteemed seminary of Clonard.

From this period of his life comes an anecdote found in the *Life of Finnachta Fledach*, describing the first encounter of Adamnan with the king whom he later served as emissary to Northumbria. The story casts Adamnan in the traditional role of the 'poor scholar', sharing humble lodging and meagre larder with his fellows. Each day it was the task of one of the novice monks to fetch a supply of milk from the dairy in a communally owned stone pitcher. Journeying back to the monastery with his burden, the young Adamnan found himself in the path of a company of galloping horsemen. As he leapt out of the way of the pounding hoofs, he slipped and fell to the ground, with his milk pitcher shattered on the stones. The leader of the horsemen, who reined up to offer apologies and compensation, proved to be Finnachta mac-Dunchada, a chieftain of the southern Ui-Neill. When Adamnan expressed his distress at having lost the brothers' milk and broken a vessel that he could ill afford to replace, Finnachta promised his personal protection and provided a sumptuous feast for the scholar-monks by way of reparation. Adamnan's abbot rewarded Finnachta's generosity with a prophecy recorded in *MacFirbis' Fragmentary Annals*:

'The man who has given this banquet will be High King of Ireland, and Adamnan will be the head of piety and wisdom in Ireland, and he will be Finnachta's confessor, and Finnachta will be in great prosperity until he gives offence to Adamnan.'

As is so often the case with such foretelling, its fulfilment is conveniently borne out in the annals when they record how Finnachta slew Cennfaeled on the battlefield and succeeded to the throne of the *Ard Ri* or High King at Tara in 675. Adamnan – whose career between his student years and his succession to the abbacy of Iona in 679 is a matter of some speculation – had clearly retained enough of Finnachta's esteem to serve as his emissary to Northumbria in 686. The two men remained close until 692, when their rival blood-lines of the northern and southern Ui-Neill proved stronger than mere friendship.

'In the land of the Saxons'

Dawn from the shore of Lindisfarne, 'a second Iona among the English'.

There is an apt footnote to the *Betha*'s anecdote in that Finnachta is often identified in the annals as *Finnachta Fledach*. The name translates as 'Finnachta of the Feastings'.

The first certain date in Adamnan's chronology is the year 679 when he was appointed abbot on Iona. The prophecy of his service as *anmchara* or spiritual counsellor to Finnachta is at least partly confirmed by his mission to Northumbria. He may well have been at Tara for a period between 675 and 679 and there is also the possibility that he entered the monastery of Cloncha on the Inishowen peninsula after his time in Meath. Some authorities assume that Adamnan went to Iona very early in his monastic career, even as early as 650, yet the evidence of his own writings indicates that he had no personal acquaintance with any abbot of Iona earlier than his immediate predecessor, Failbe, who succeeded to the abbacy in 669. He may have joined the Iona community around the time of Failbe's succession and possibly as heir apparent to the abbacy, or he may have met Failbe in Ireland. His own standing as spiritual counsellor to the *Ard Ri* – if such he became – would have provided eminent qualification for his succession to the esteemed office of abbot on 'the island of Columcille', and yet it would hardly seem that Adamnan mac-Ronan had need of any such further qualification.

He was of Columcille's line and came from Columcille's own country. He had begun his education there with Columcille's nephew, before moving on to the seminary at Clonard, traditionally the school of the Apostles of Ireland. He was the confidant, counsellor and emissary of kings, as Columcille himself had often been. Decades after Adamnan's death, an epigram penned by Alcuin of York was to rank him amongst the greatest names of Irish sanctity:

> Patrick, Ciaran, glory of the Irish race,
> And Columba, Comgall and Adomnan,
> Illustrious fathers, teachers of conduct and life,
> By these prayers may their devotion help us all.

The eulogistic prologue to the *Fis Adamnain*, an account of Adamnan's great vision of heaven and hell which certainly derives from a date very much closer to his own lifetime than the earliest surviving medieval manuscript, acclaims him as 'the High Scholar of the Western World', but by the time he became abbot of Iona in his mid-fifties, Adamnan had apparently yet to write any book of his own.

His first surviving written work was occasioned by an unexpected visitor to the monastery in the early years of his abbacy, when a ship ran foul of the Atlantic gales of Scotland's western seaboard and foundered on rocks close to Iona. Among the survivors was a distinguished passenger *en route* from the eastern Mediterranean. Bede takes up the story in the fifth book of his *Historia Ecclesiastica*, explaining how Adamnan

wrote a book about the holy places which has been of great value to many readers, and for which he used information dictated to him by Arculf, a bishop of Gaul, who had gone to Jerusalem to visit the holy places. Arculf had travelled all over the promised land, and had also been to Damascus, Constantinople, Alexandria and many islands of the sea; and on his voyage home he was driven off course by a violent storm on to the west coast of Britain. After many adventures, he came to the said servant of Christ, Adamnan, and was found to be learned in the scriptures and well acquainted with the holy places. He was very gladly welcomed by Adamnan, and listened to even more gladly, to the extent that Adamnan was quick to commit to writing whatever he testified to having seen in the holy places worthy of record. And, as I have said, he compiled a work of value to many people, and especially to those who live far away from the places where the patriarchs and prophets were, and who know of them only what they have learned from books.

We are left in no doubt that one such grateful reader was Bede himself, who had travelled no further than Lindisfarne when he drew on Adamnan's text to inform two chapters of his own *Historia*.

Bede's characteristically informative contribution brings Adamnan's story up to the year 686, when he came as Finnachta's ambassador to the court of Aldfrith. The fact that Adamnan already knew Aldfrith well is borne out by his choice of peace-offering to the Northumbrian king: no less than a copy of his own transcription of Arculf's travels, known still as *De Locis Sanctis* – 'Concerning the Holy Places'. Bede offers further provenance when he adds that 'Adamnan presented this book to King Aldfrith, and through his generosity it was circulated for lesser folk to read'. Aldfrith, naturally, deposited a volume of such importance in the great library of his kingdom at the monastery at Wearmouth/Jarrow, where it was certainly added to the reading list of the young Bede.

The son, albeit out of wedlock, of Fina, daughter of a High King of the Cenel Eogain, and Oswy, future 'king of the Saxons', Aldfrith is known to the eighth-century Irish writer Oengus, and in the later Irish annals, as *Flann Fina*, which name translates as 'Blood of the Wine'. He was renowned for his learning in both Ireland and England, and might even have been responsible for the first transcription of *Beowulf*. The similarities scholars have detected between that masterpiece of Anglo-Saxon narrative verse and Irish heroic sagas might well support such a link with Aldfrith. His connection with Adamnan is far better documented. Aldfrith is noted in *MacFirbis' Annals* as 'the illustrious wise man, the foster-son of Adamnan', and elsewhere as '*alumnus Adamnan*'. Born to a princess of the northern Ui-Neill, Aldfrith was certainly entrusted at some point in his youth to Adamnan. There is also evidence that he gained his early education from the Irish monks at Malmesbury, and the later abbot-chronicler William of Malmesbury records how

> though the elder brother, he had been deemed by the nobility unworthy of the government from his illegitimacy . . . and had retired to Ireland, either through compulsion or indignation. In this place, safe from the persecution of his brother, he had from his ample leisure become deeply versed in literature, and had enriched his mind with every kind of learning.

There is nowhere any certain indication that Aldfrith had been educated on Iona, apart from a brief reference found in the 'anonymous' *Life of Cuthbert*, where the Lindisfarne author recalls that, at the time of St Cuthbert's prophecy of the succession, Aldfrith 'was then on the island which they call Ii'.

Aldfrith's precise point of departure for Northumbria in 686 and the place and time of his last previous acquaintance with Adamnan remain less than certain, but the ninth abbot of Iona certainly still knew his former student well enough to choose a book as a suitable tribute. Bede records that 'the author was sent back to his own land enriched by many gifts'. Amongst those gifts, of course, were the sixty Irish captives carried off by the late and largely unlamented Egfrith and brought back to Ireland by Adamnan in 687.

Between Adamnan's arrival in Northumbria in 686 and his return to Ireland with the liberated hostages, he paid a visit to Bede's monastery at Jarrow, despite the hazard of travel through a kingdom in the grip of plague. Adamnan was apparently greatly impressed by what he found in that monastery, because in the following year he returned again to Jarrow. It is important to mention here that the dual foundation of St Peter and St Paul at Wearmouth/Jarrow – founded by Benedict Biscop in the early 670s – was one of the great centres of learning in Western Europe. Its library and scriptorium were unrivalled in England and it was there that Bede wrote and researched the first history of England to be written by an Englishman. On one or both of his visits, Adamnan would certainly have met the teenage Bede, who was already clearly recognised as a monastic student of outstanding qualities.

'This day the son of Ossa was killed in battle'

RIAGAL OF BANGOR

Portraying Pictish and Anglo-Saxon warriors in battle, the seventh-century Pictish symbol stone at Aberlemno near Forfar stands just six miles from the battlefield of Nechtansmere.

On his second visit in 688, Adamnan apparently spent at least a year in Jarrow, and left behind a favourable impression. 'He was a good and wise man with an excellent knowledge of the scriptures,' recalled Bede, writing some forty years later. Yet, it seems, a fractious point of discussion between Adamnan and Ceolfrith, the abbot at Jarrow, was the same controversy which had been debated at Whitby over twenty years earlier.

The Council of Whitby – summoned in 664 by Aldfrith's father, King Oswy – had resolved, at least for the supremely powerful kingdom of Northumbria, the long-standing debate over the proper dating of the festival of Easter and the correspondingly proper 'crown of thorns' form of the monastic tonsure. In the year 541, the Synod of Orleans had set out a system for the precise dating of Easter in the Church calendar. A papal edict had been issued to inform the whole Church of the new orthodoxy, but somehow that edict had not reached Ireland and thus when Colum-cille established Iona the earlier governance of Easter was retained as the orthodoxy of the Columban order. Thus when Aidan came from Iona to found the monastery on Lindisfarne in 635, the Celtic calendar came with him. Only in 664, when the Northumbrian king took a Kentish queen educated in the Augustinian tradition of the Roman orthodoxy, did the ecclesiastical controversy demand resolution. At St Hild's foundation at Whitby, Wilfrid of Hexham – polished, authoritarian, and enthused by his continental travels – carried the day for the Roman calendar and the Roman tonsure. Bishop Colman of Lindisfarne suffered humiliating defeat in that debate and even more humiliating slurs on the monastic tradition of Columcille's Iona. In consequence, he left Northumbria to return, in company with all Lindisfarne's Irish monks and a number of English brothers, to Iona.

By the time of Adamnan's visit to Jarrow, the Roman orthodoxy was everywhere accepted. The south of Ireland had followed Northumbria soon after the Whitby decision. Only the monasteries in the north of Ireland, the homeland of Columcille and of Adamnan, held tenaciously to the Celtic tradition and Adamnan, for all his fulsomely acknowledged virtue and wisdom, found himself subjected to the full force of the Roman argument at Jarrow, where his Celtic tonsure met with the utmost disapproval as the crown of Simon the Magus, the mark of the druid.

In a letter of guidance on monastic rules offered to the Pictish King Nechtan in 710, Ceolfrith recalled his encounters with Adamnan some two decades earlier:

> In the course of some conversation, I said to him: 'I beseech you, holy brother, you who believe that you will win the crown of life that knows no end, why do you bear on your head a crown designed with ends, a fashion which contradicts your faith? And if you seek the company of blessed Peter, why do you copy the form of tonsure which he cursed, instead of showing that even now you love with all your heart the fashion of him with whom you desire to live in bliss for ever?' He replied: 'You must be in no doubt, my beloved brother, that although in the custom of my country I wear the tonsure of Simon, yet I loathe and reject with all my heart the wickedness of simony; and I desire to follow in the footsteps of the most blessed chief of the apostles, as far as my frailty permits.' I replied: 'I truly believe that it is so; but it would be a sign that you and your people accept in your inmost hearts the teachings of the apostle Peter, if you also adhered in your outward appearance to what you know to be his teaching.'

MacFirbis' Annals – always highly coloured and, in this case, deriving from and elaborating on Bede – suggest that Adamnan was forcibly tonsured at Jarrow and compelled to adopt the Roman orthodoxy, but this seems at the least extremely unlikely. Adamnan was, none the less, made fully aware of the extent to which adherence to the Celtic tradition had isolated Iona from the wider Christian world. Adamnan, certainly a man of great political wisdom, would have been all too well aware of the implications of that situation not only for his own monastery, but for the universal standing of his beloved Columcille and the whole Columban tradition.

There is no question but that the visits to Northumbria marked a watershed in the life and work of Adamnan. When he returned to Iona, he proposed to his community that they adopt the Roman orthodoxies and, in the intransigent tradition of Colman of Lindisfarne, they sternly resisted any such thing. Bede would have us believe that Adamnan was so alienated from the Iona brothers that he soon returned to Ireland, leaving Iona as a Celtic backwater until it finally acceded to the Roman orthodoxy in 716. Bede – always, at least formally, the passionate advocate of the Roman rules – is here at his least reliable. More recent studies of the Celtic–Roman divide suggest that the whole question was taken much more seriously in Bede's Northumbria than elsewhere – although it does remain difficult to imagine an abbot and his monastic *familia* celebrating Easter on different weekends. Whatever discord there may have been upon Adamnan's return, and indeed such discord was prophesied by Columcille, he remained in office as abbot of Iona until the end of his days, although it is far from certain that he was permanently resident on the island between 692 and 697.

He was certainly on Iona in 693 when the Pictish King Brude mac-Bile, who had triumphed at Dunnichen Moss eight years earlier, was carried to Iona to lie in the burial ground of the Relig Odhrain. The Old Irish *Life of Adamnan* records how the body of Bruide, son of Bile, king of the Cruithnigh, was brought to Ia, and his death was sorrowful and grievous to Adamnan, and he desired that the body of Bruide should be brought to him.

The Irish annals specifically state that Adamnan 'returned' to Ireland on two occasions, first in 692 and finally in 697. We might reasonably assume that he was 'returning' from Iona, although there is evidence that he might have spent extensive periods in the kingdom of the Picts to the east of the 'Spine of Britain'. He clearly maintained excellent relations with the Pictish royal house and there are dedications to Adamnan to be found throughout Pictland, notably in Aberdeenshire, Forfar and Banff. Alexander Carmichael's collection of the lyric lore of the Gael, *Carmina Gadelica*, identifies a *Srath Adhamhnain*, Strath Adamnan, in Glen Dochart on Tayside and a *Crois Adhamhnain*, Adamnan's Cross, on the island of North Uist in the Outer Hebrides. Always a diplomat, it would have been entirely characteristic of the Roman-inclined Adamnan to have retained his abbacy of the Columban *familia* whilst ensuring his own absence from the monastery on Iona during the paschal season. Extensive travels throughout the highlands and islands may well have served to accomplish just such a diplomatic stratagem.

By 697, Adamnan was into his seventies and effectively 'retired' to Ireland until the year 704, when a premonition of his own passing prompted his return to Iona that he might die on the holy island of Columcille. He left Ireland in the summer – very probably after the Easter festival – of that year and died on 23 September.

The *Annals of the Four Masters* record his obituary:

Adamnan, son of Ronan, abbot of Ia-Coluim-Cille, died on the 23rd of September, after having been twenty-six years in the abbacy, and after the seventy-seventh year of his age. Adamnan was a good man, according to the testimony of St Beda.

The eighth-century *Annales Cambriae* of Nennius link his passing with that of Aldfrith of Northumbria in their entry for the year 704:

Aldfrith, king of the Saxons died.
The sleep of Adomnan.

In the years between his return to Iona from Northumbria and his last journey to that island in the year of his death, Adamnan entered into the annals on two occasions.

'A sapling who will wrest the sovereignty of Tara from Finnachta', promises Columcille's foretelling and such Adamnan became in the year 692 when the long-standing association between the abbot and the High King was irrevocably breached in synod on the hill of Tara. The controversy centred on the ancient tradition of the *boruma*, the annual cattle-tribute paid since the time of Tuathal by the men of Leinster to the Ui-Neill of the north. Finnachta Fledach's remission of this *Boruma Laigan* would have been largely at the expense of Adamnan's own people and thus prompted his fierce opposition to Finnachta's proposal. The royal attitude to the monastic *paruchia* of Columcille held a more ominous importance for Adamnan as abbot of Iona than as a son of the Ui-Neill. Finnachta increasingly favoured the foundations of Patrick, Finnian and Ciaran, even to the extent of awarding them special privileges denied to those of the Columban dominion. Adamnan was so provoked by the royal intent that he drew down a prophetic curse – recorded in the *Betha Adamanain* – on the king whom he had so long served as *anmchara*: 'The life of the king who made this proclamation shall be short; he shall fall by fratricide; and there shall be no king of his race for ever.'

The annals record the fulfilment of the curse of Adamnan when they chronicle the death of Finnachta Fledach by his cousin's hand in 695. After him the succession to the High Kingship passed from Tara and from Finnachta's race of the southern Ui-Neill to Columcille's own people, the Ui-Neill of the north.

Five years later, in the centenary year of the death of Columcille, Adamnan returned again to Ireland where he further fulfilled Columcille's foretelling. 'He shall make a law for women, from the widespread Ictian sea hither', and so he did when the *Cain Adamnain* was proclaimed at the Synod of Birr in 697. 'Adamnan's Law' exempted women, children and clergy from taking any part in warfare. It amounted to no less than a social revolution in late seventh-century Ireland, where 'the work which the best of women had to do was to go to battle and battlefield, encounter and camping, fighting and hosting, wounding and slaying'. Adamnan – according to the Old Irish *Life* – had witnessed the horrific mutilation of women on the battlefield at an early age, most probably on visits to the territory of his mother's family which often served as the killing ground in dynastic rivalries.

It says much for the dominion of Adamnan's authority that his law held for Scottish Dalriada and for Pictland as well as for the Irish mainland and that the penalties for its transgression were to be paid over to the Columban monasteries under Adamnan's abbacy.

Behind these events of 697 looms the apocalyptic shadow of 'Adamnan's Vision', the *Fis Adamnain*. The earliest surviving text of this Dante-esque odyssey through heaven and hell – transcribed from an earlier manuscript into the *Book of the Dun Cow*, which dates from 1103 – does not itself claim to be written by Adamnan and is certainly apocryphal, but it does nevertheless provide an indication of the awesome standing of his later years. The opening lines of the *Fis Adamnain* offer an impressive example:

> To Adamnan ua Tinne, the High Scholar of the Western World, were revealed the things which are here recorded; for his soul departed from out of his body on the feast of John the Baptist, and was conveyed to the celestial realm, where the heavenly angels are, and to Hell, with its rabble-rout.

Adamnan traditionally experienced his vision on the eve of the great synod at Birr, thus reinforcing his authority in the debate and also providing timely divine inspiration for the Law of Adamnan which that assembly was about to ordain. The *Fis Adamnain* foreshadows the portrait pages of the Book of Kells as clearly as it echoes the angelic visions of Columcille himself. By the year 697, Adamnan was the pre-eminent authority on the life, works and wonders of his great predecessor, and, more than ever before, the keeper of the Columban flame.

Between Adamnan's return from the second visit to Northumbria and his last return to Ireland in 697, he had composed the work by which he is best remembered, the three books setting out in turn the prophecies, miracles and visions of Columcille – the *Vita Columbae*. An entry in the *Annals of Boyle* at 692 tells how 'Adamnan came to Ireland and brought the evangel with him', which might certainly suggest that he had already completed the *Vita Columbae* by that year and carried it with him when he came to confront the High King Finnachta at Tara. That suggestion would date the authorship of the *Vita* quite precisely to the four years between 688 and 692. Thirteen centuries on it remains the earliest surviving documentary record of its subject and the major source for the life and times of one of the most remarkable personalities of the early Christian world.

There was an earlier *Life* written by the seventh abbot of Iona, Cummene Ailbe, who died ten years before Adamnan succeeded to the abbacy. Dorbbene, the scribe of the earliest surviving Adamnan manuscript, inserted an extract from this *liber de virtutibus sancti Columbae* into Adamnan's text, but no manuscript of the Cummene work has survived. A text purporting to be the lost Cummene which came to light in John Colgan's *Triadis Thaumaturgae* of 1647 has been shown to be no more than a shorter recension of Adamnan, written in Flanders or northern France as late as the twelfth century.

'Whoever reads these books of Columba's miracles, may he pray to God for me, Dorbbene. . . .'

The colophon naming Dorbbene as the scribe of the 'A' manuscript is the evidence which confirms that document as the earliest and most authoritative text of Adamnan's *Vita Columbae*.

The name Dorbbene is rare in the Irish records, so much so that only one man of that name is identified in the annals in connection with Iona. The *Annals of Ulster* record his obituary at 713:

> Dorbeni obtained the chair of Ia,
> and having spent five months in the primacy,
> died on Saturday, the fifth of the Kalends of November.

The *Annals of Tighernach* confirm precisely those events at that date and so also do the *Annals of the Four Masters* in a concise entry at 713:

> St Dorbene Fota, abbot of Iona,
> died on the 28th of October.

The 'fifth of the kalends of November' – 28 October – did fall on a Saturday in 713 and the martyrologies provide their own confirmation when they enter the feast of Dorbbene on that date. The *Martyrology of Tallaght* in the Brussels manuscript of the *Book of Leinster* enters 'Dorbene, abbot of Iona' under 28 October, as does the *Martyrology of Donegal* which adds that Dorbbene was 'Altaine's son'. The twelfth-century *Martyrology of Gorman* places *Dorbene seng* – 'slender Dorbene' – under the same date and adds the note 'abbot of Iona of Columcille: he was of the kindred of Conall Gulban'.

All of which serves to confirm the scribe of the 'A' manuscript as a close contemporary of Adamnan, who followed him in the abbacy of Iona in the few months before his own death just nine years after Adamnan's passing. Thus the 'A' manuscript was transcribed, probably from Adamnan's original and possibly in Adamnan's own lifetime, in the scriptorium on Iona.

The Dorbbene manuscript is today in the Stadtbibliothek at Schaffhausen in Switzerland. It is written on a goatskin parchment in a heavy hand peculiar to Irish calligraphy and less rounded than that of the Books of Kells and Durrow. The manuscript was taken to Germany, probably by Iona monks who joined the Irish monastic emigration which followed the Viking onslaught of the early ninth century, and found its way to the monastery at Reichenau, which attracted a sizeable Irish community during the abbacy of the former dean of the monastery of St Gall, Walafrid Strabo, in the 840s. It was at Reichenau that the manuscript was discovered by the Jesuit Stephen White in 1621 and his transcription was used for the Columban hagiographies in Colgan's *Triadis Thaumaturgae* of 1647 and the Bollandist *Acta Sanctorum* of 1698. The travels of Dorbbene's manuscript after 1621 are unclear, but Dr René Specht, the librarian at Schaffhausen, suggests that it might have been purchased by the library around the year 1757, when the monastery was dissolved.

Dorbbene precedes his colophon with a paragraph adjuring 'all those who wish to copy these books . . . that after carefully copying them they compare them with the exemplar from which they have written and amend them with all possible care'. The *Book of Leinster* version of the celebrated epic of Cuchulainn, the *Tain Bo Cuailnge*, ends with a blessing 'on all who shall memorise the Tain in this form and not put any other form upon it'.

It is at least curious that the monastic scribe on Iona should conclude his transcription of Adamnan's *Vita Columbae* in so similar a style to the bards of the ancient heroic tradition.

The Dorbbene colophon: f. 136ᵃ.

Adamnan Vita Columbae, *Stadtbibliothek, Schaffhausen: Generalia 1.*

l au clib: magiſ ac magiſ glo
rificant In menſis publimat
honorib: qui ept benedictur
In saecula amen

Ob ſecro eos quicumq;
uolucrint hos diſcribe
re libellos Immo potiuſ ad
iuro ph xpm iudicem ſecu
lorum ut poſt quam deſ
criben diſcripſerint con
ferant & ſubi elbrt cū om
ni dilitgenta ad exempl
ar unde ſcraxerunt &
hanc quoq; ad iuracionem
hoc In loco ſub ſcribant.

The Old Irish *Life*, the *Betha Coluim Cille*, was written no earlier than the tenth century. It certainly draws heavily on Adamnan yet is structured in a chronological 'cradle-to-grave' sequence as a work of biography as opposed to hagiography, incorporating much material from Irish tradition which Adamnan chooses to omit or to discredit, even if he was aware of it at all. The Adamnan *Life* was written on Iona and drew on Iona sources, while the *Betha* is emphatically Irish-centred even to the extent of relocating some of Adamnan's stories from a Scottish to an Irish setting. All the Old Irish *Lives* of saints habitually insert historical personalities into stock anecdotal narratives, as does the often bizarre *Betha Adamanain*. The *Betha Coluim Cille* does have sufficient Columban legend on which to draw without needing to resort to the stock-in-trade of the vernacular hagiographer. It cannot be so totally discounted as some modern scholarship would imply, and on more occasions than one might even be shown to throw intriguing and often revealing sidelights on Adamnan.

The encyclopedic compendium of Columban material assembled by Manus O'Donnell in the sixteenth century, his *Betha Colaim Chille*, is a work of undeniable interest and no little value, but it was set down a full millennium after Columcille and owes at least as much to an accumulation of legend, anecdote and apocrypha as to any attempt at historical record, meanwhile heavily smudging any dividing lines between.

Adamnan's *Vita Columbae* remains the primary source *non pareil*. Here was an abbot of Iona, regarded in his own time as 'the High Scholar of the Western World', born of the same lineage as Columcille and inspired throughout his life by the Columban tradition, drawing on pre-eminent primary sources, both textual and oral, to set down the life of his great predecessor. The provenance of the text of his *Vita Columbae* is itself remarkable. The manuscript now in the library at Schaffhausen in Switzerland and known as the 'A' manuscript was transcribed, almost certainly from Adamnan's original and within nine years of his death, on Iona by the scribe Dorbbene. There is a second and partly variant 'B' text, of which the earliest example, now in the British Library, is known as the 'B1' manuscript. This is a transcription – probably made in the scriptorium at Durham in the second half of the twelfth century – of a text closely similar to the 'A' manuscript but including some marginal material not found in Dorbbene's manuscript, notably a list of the names of the twelve men who first accompanied Columcille to Iona. One hypothetical explanation of the two apparently authentic yet slightly variant forms is the possibility that Adamnan carried one manuscript back to Ireland when he returned for the last seven years of his life in 697, leaving another manuscript in the monastery on Iona. Thus it is suggested that he might, whilst in Ireland, have added the variant material to his original draft to produce the 'B' version. There is also the alternative possibility that the 'B' text variations were the work of scribes adding to Adamnan's original, just as Dorbbene made his own identifiable additions, principally the extract from the earlier Cummene *Life*, to his transcription.

To the modern reader the abundance of miracle, fulfilled prophecy and divine vision in Adamnan's pages might seem – as it might also in Bede – to be a cornucopia from an age encrusted at least as much by superstition as inspired by faith. Such is the prerogative of the modern reader, but prophecies, miracles and visions were then, indeed still are, no more than a question of the reality perceived through the prism of human imagining. What remains remarkable in Adamnan's text is a rich and reliable seam of history and biography to be found only a little way below the hagiographical surface.

William Reeves, who made the outstanding annotated translation of the *Vita Columbae* of the last century, describes it as 'an inestimable literary relic of the Irish Church: perhaps, with all its defects, the most valuable monument of that institution which has escaped the ravages of time'. After thirteen centuries this masterwork of the ninth abbot of Iona endures – pre-eminent amongst the vast Columban bibliography – as the first and the last word on the life and times of Columcille.

INTRODUCTION

COLUMCILLE IN HIS TIME

A manchild shall be born of his race,
He will be a sage, a prophet, a poet,
A beloved lamp, pure, clear,
Who will utter no falsehood

Patrick's foretelling of Columcille

Although it remains the outstanding primary source for all subsequent Columban researches, the Adamnan *Life* corresponds barely at all to any modern concept of biography. Consequently, a biographical and historical introduction to Columcille in his time might serve some of the purpose of a modern 'reading light' on a seventh-century narrative.

The quest for the birth of Columcille in the documentary record reveals the Irish annals at their customary variance. The *Annals of Ulster* at 518 record

the birth of Colum Cille,
on the same day in which Buite, son of Bronach, slept.

The same annals record 'Colum Cille was born' under the year 522. Because the *Annals of Ulster* date events at one full year in arrears throughout this period, those dates can be amended to 519 and 523. The *Annals of Tighernach* offer the date of 520 and the *Annals of the Four Masters* the year 521.

Adamnan's testimony leads to the calculation of the year 521 as the most likely date of birth. He states that Columcille came to Scotland from Ireland in 563 – 'in the second year after the battle of Cul-drebene, in the forty-second year of his age', and that his 'pilgrimage' to Scotland extended over thirty-four years until his death 'on the night of Sunday', 9 June 597. All the annals concur with Adamnan on 9 June and that day was indeed a Sunday in the year 597. Adamnan tells us that Columcille died in his seventy-sixth year and the calendar of saints enters the death of St Buite – on the same day as the birth of Columcille according to the *Annals of Ulster* – on 7 December. Those two dates together place the birth of Columcille on 7 December in the year 521.

Although modern chronological research discredits the claim, tradition has long held that 7 December was a Thursday in 521 and Thursday has long been 'Columba's Day', a day of good omen throughout the islands of Scotland's western seaboard. Alexander Carmichael's *Carmina Gadelica* includes Gaelic verses in celebration of the 'Thursday of Columcille benign':

Day to send sheep to prosperity,
Day to send cow on calf,
Day to put the web in the warp.

Day to put currach on the brine,
Day to place the staff to the flag,
Day to bear, day to die,
Day to hunt the heights.

'*Gortan now is the place in which he was born*'

BETHA COLUIM CILLE

'St Columbkille's Stone', traditionally the saint's 'birth-flag', at Gartan, Donegal.

There is a curious synchronicity in that Thursday is also 'Thor's day' in the mythic calendar of the northern world. The tradition of the isles is a blend of the Gaelic and the Norse, and the place of Columcille in the old Celtic Church provides a bright echo of Thor, lord of the thunder, in the mythos of the northmen.

The Old Irish *Life of Columcille* – the *Betha Coluim Cille* – provides the earliest identification of his place of birth: 'Gortan, now, is the name of the place in which he was born', and Manus O'Donnell quotes lines attributed to St Mura to the same effect:

> He was born at Gartan by his consent;
> And he was nursed at Cill-nic-Neoin;
> And the son of goodness was baptised,
> At Tulach Dubhglaise of God.

No Latin hagiographies identify Columcille's birthplace, but Donegal tradition certainly confirms the Old Irish *Life*'s location. Ten miles from Letterkenny, numerous place-names around Gartan Lough bear the name of Columcille. A ruined church bears the ancient Columban dedication of 'St Columbkille's Chapel'. Stone crosses and a holy well stand nearby and a little way to the south at Laknacoo is 'St Columbkille's Stone', long claimed to be the flagstone on which he was born.

Of his family and lineage, we have the clear testimony of Adamnan's second preface: 'Saint Columba . . . was born of noble parents, his father being Fedilmith, son of Fergus, and his mother Ethne, whose father's name is mac-Naue in Irish'. Fedilmith mac-Fergus was in direct line of descent from Conall Gulban, and thus of the line of the Cenel Conaill, the powerful northern clan of the race of the Ui-Neill, descendants of *Niall Noigiallach*, Niall of the Nine Hostages, who reigned as *Ard Ri* at Tara through a quarter of a century until 405. Standing in the shadowy territory between historical record and heroic myth, Niall – dynast, warlord and slave-raider – was the most celebrated of the High Kings of ancient Irish legend. In an age when the holding of hostages – usually the sons of kings – established right of tribute, the eulogies of the bards boasted that Niall of the Nine Hostages held dominion over the kingdoms of Ireland – the *Ulaid* of Ulster, the *Connachta* of Connaught, the *Lagin* of Leinster, the *Mumin* of Munster and the Pictish *Cruithne* – and also over the Britons, the Picts, the Saxons and the Gauls. Those bardic claims may have been no more than an extravagant apologia for Niall's successful slave-trading, but history would not deny that his sons allied themselves into the two dynasties of the *Ui-Neill*, 'the descendants of Niall' – those of his first wife into that of the south and those of his second into that of the north – who became fierce rivals through succeeding centuries.

Of Eogain and Conall, the sons of Niall who seized the north of Ireland, it was Conall Gulban who forged the kingdom of Donegal and accepted baptism into the Christian faith – traditionally when St Patrick himself inscribed the sign of the cross on his battle-shield. From Conall comes the place-name Tirconnel, 'the Land of Conall', and his line passed into Ireland's history as the *Cenel Conaill*. As the rising power of the northern Ui-Neill claimed more and more 'sword-land' in the north of Ireland, so their warlords succeeded to the High Kingship. First the line of Eogain, the *Cenel Eogain*, claimed the throne at Tara when Muirchertach mac-Erca became the *Ard Ri* after the victory of his alliance on the battlefield of Ocha in 482. He loomed over the dynastic power struggles for half a century, but was succeeded on his death by Diarmit mac-Cerbaill when Tara passed to the southern Ui-Neill in 532. The northern and southern Ui-Neill thus became rivals for the High Kingship which passed between them through five hundred years. On the death of Diarmit, Tara passed back to the Cenel Eogain until Ainmure – or Ainmire – of the Cenel Conaill succeeded in 566.

When Columcille was born the son of Fedilmith, he was born into a royal line and, had he followed in the mould of his forebears, may well himself have entered the annals as a High King. Adamnan records the first indication that Columcille of the line of Niall was to follow his own extraordinary destiny when he tells of Columcille's mother's vision of a cloak of wondrous colours which passed out of her hands to cover the hills of the horizon and the islands beyond. Adamnan names Columcille's mother as Ethne – or Eithne – the daughter of mac-Naue. He tells us no more than that, but later documentary records identify her as the daughter of a provincial king of the Ui-Bairrche in the province of Leinster, who himself claimed descent from the High King Cathair Mor, legendary forebear of the Lagin.

The offspring of two royal blood-lines, Columcille was baptised – according to the Old Irish *Life* – by the presbyter 'Cruithnechan, son of Cellachan, the illustrious priest'. The name with which he was baptised remains a matter of some speculation. His original name – according to the *Martyrology* of Oengus compiled in the early ninth century – was Crimthann, meaning 'the fox'. The name Columcille – in its various forms – was almost certainly a monastic name. Oengus calls him 'Columb cille the lustrous', and Bede writes of 'this Columba called Columcelli by some, a name compounded from "cella" and "Columb" '. Notker Balbulus suggests 'he was called Columkille among his people, because he was the institutor, founder and ruler of many cells, that is, monasteries or churches'. The *Leabhar Brac* – the fourteenth-century 'Speckled Book' – offers its own explanation:

Cille, because of the frequency of his coming *from the cell* in which he used to read his psalms to meet neighbouring children. And what they used to say among themselves was, Has our little Colum come today from the cell. . . .

As was the custom for the sons of noble families, Columcille began his schooling in the care of a foster-father. The fact that the priest Cruithnecan was chosen for the task, rather than a nobleman of the laity, suggests that young Columcille was early intended for the Church. So it was that his earliest education was conducted in the monastic tradition and probably at Temple Douglas, or *Tulach Dubhglaise* in the Irish. Interestingly, the name 'Cruithnecan' suggests his tutor was of the *Cruithne*, the Picts of Ireland. The Picts – from the Latin *Picti*, 'the painted men', as the Roman historians described them – were a similar Celtic stock to the Irish Gael but differentiated principally by their language. The Gael alone spoke a variant form known as 'Q-Celtic' while the Cruithne – like the Celtic peoples of England, Scotland and Wales – spoke the form known as 'P-Celtic'. It may well be that Columcille's early acquaintance with a tutor of Pictish stock laid some foundation for his remarkable encounter with the overlord of the Picts of Scotland four decades on.

Adamnan refers fleetingly in his second book to the involvement of a 'Finnian' in Columcille's scriptural studies, while the Irish sources offer a fuller – if less reliable – account of his monastic education under the guidance of two 'Finnians'. The first of these, certainly the one mentioned by Adamnan, was St Finnian of Moville. A famous scholar and teacher, he had been educated in St Ninian's foundation of Candida Casa at Whithorn in Galloway before returning to Ireland to found his own monasteries at Dromin in Louth and at Moville in County Down. It was in this Finnian's foundation of Moville at the head of Strangford Lough that Columcille would have been ordained deacon before the age of twenty, at which time the Old Irish *Life* suggests he entered the seminary of St Finnian at Clonard in Meath.

Between his periods of study with the two Finnians, Columcille passed some time in his mother's country of Leinster studying under the tutelage of the Christian bard Gemman. The bards, or *filidh*, were an élite class who enjoyed the prestigious standing of a 'fourth estate' in ancient Ireland, as the keepers of the flame of history and legend of a proud Celtic warrior civilisation enshrined in their heroic sagas and battle poetry. The Irish tradition of Columcille makes much of his poetic achievements, despite the Columban attribution of all surviving examples being at best very tenuous. There are many sides to the persona of Columcille, amongst them something of bardic accomplishment and allegiance which was to have its own bearing on the convention of Druim Ceatt and which might well be traced back to the teaching of Gemman.

At this point in his monastic education, the Old Irish *Life* suggests Columcille prepared for the priesthood in the great seminary of Finnian of Clonard. Finnian, a famed teacher known as the 'Father of Saints', died in 550 and must certainly have been a man of advanced years when Columcille entered his monastery. He was born and educated in Leinster – according to a tenth-century *Life* – before crossing the Irish Sea to Wales where he studied in the monastic tradition of St David and the historian Gildas, then returned to Ireland with a company of Welsh monks to found Clonard.

Had Columcille studied with the two Finnians, his learning would have placed him at the centre of the two great monastic traditions of his time, in that he was educated both at Moville with its allegiance through St Ninian's Candida Casa to St Martin of Tours and at Clonard under the influence of the saints of Wales.

However, it is possible to take Adamnan quite literally as offering evidence of Columcille studying with only one St Finnian. A note in Maire Herbert's *Iona, Kells and Derry* suggests that the Old Irish biographer was drawing on two regional interpretations of the identity of Adamnan's variously named *Findbarr/Finnio*, the northern adaptation claiming Columcille as a pupil of the Finnian of Moville and the

Clonard adaptation claiming him for the school of its own 'local' Finnian. Chronological probability would suggest Finnian of Moville, who lived until 579, as the most likely tutor of the two, and would also accord with the later incident of the *Cathach* psalter. The connection with Finnian of Clonard may even be an unhistorical attempt to offer provenance for Columcille's inclusion in the company of the 'Twelve Apostles of Ireland' – amongst them Ciaran of Clonmacnoise, Brenden of Birr, Brenden 'the Navigator' of Clonfert, and Cainnech of Aghaboe – all traditionally, if not necessarily historically, trained by Finnian, the Father of Saints.

At around this time – and thus in his mid-twenties – Columcille was ordained priest according to the annotations in the *Martyrology of Oengus*: 'Bishop Etchen is venerated in Clonard in the south of Meath, and it was to him Columcille went to have the order of bishop conferred upon him.' This sole account of his ordination at least identifies the cleric who confirmed Columcille as priest. Bishop Etchen – or Etchan – was of the Cenel Conaill, a brother of Aid, son of Ainmure, and cousin to Columcille. A complex tangle of folktale has grown up around this ordination to explain why it was that Columcille never attained the rank of bishop and remained a priest throughout his life. Yet, for whatever reason, he established a tradition of the presbyter-abbot in the Celtic Church. No abbot of Iona held episcopal rank, indeed no abbot of the Columban *familia* held such a title until Aidan became bishop of Lindisfarne in 635.

The Old Irish *Betha Coluim Cille* follows Columcille from Clonard – in company with Cainnech, Ciaran and Comgell of Bangor – to Mobi's monastery of Glasnevin near Dublin, where it offers an unusually illustrative portrait of a monastic foundation of the time, with fifty brothers living in huts of wattle and filldyke on the west bank of the Finglass river with their 'large church', most probably of similar construction, sited on the opposite bank.

The *Betha* tells of Mobi's premonition of catastrophe and how, soon afterwards, the monastic community at Glasnevin was broken up by an outbreak of a 'violent distemper'. This was the *blefed*, the bubonic plague which broke out in Egypt in 540 and two years later was claiming ten thousand victims a day in Constantinople. The *Annals of Ulster* record the first onset of 'the great mortality' in Ireland in 544, doubtlessly carried there aboard the regular traffic of merchant shipping from the Continent.

The monks of Glasnevin went their separate ways – on the advice of their abbot – to escape the pestilence. Columcille made his way north to his family's territory of Derry, beyond the reach of the pestilence, and there founded his first monastery at Daire-Calcig – 'the oak grove' – 'the place having been granted to him by his own tribe, the race of Conall Gulban, son of Niall', according to the *Annals of the Four Masters*. There is a connection, although based on little more than legend, between Columcille's foundation in Derry and the death of Mobi. The legend, faithfully recounted in the Old Irish *Life*, tells how Mobi had forbidden Columcille to found any monastery of his own without permission, and only when Columcille met with two monks bearing the deceased abbot's girdle to Derry as a token of his dying permission was his first monastery founded in that very place.

Adamnan, of course, mentions neither Clonard nor Glasnevin and it has been suggested that the Old Irish biographer added Mobi's monastery to Columcille's educational itinerary to underwrite the legendary connection between the abbot Mobi and the foundation of Daire-Calcig. The same legend may well have prompted the *Annals of Ulster* to enter 'Daire-Coluim-Cille was founded' at 546, the year after Mobi's passing. This annal entry was certainly recorded in retrospect, rather than deriving from any contemporary chronicle, because Daire-Calcig was known as 'Daire-Columcille' only from the last years of the tenth century. If we accept Adamnan's very reliable Columban chronology, then Manus O'Donnell's date of 556 would seem by far the most credible and would still leave Derry undisputed as Columcille's first monastic foundation.

'The battle of Cul-dreimne, gained over Diarmit Mac Cerbhaill, in which 3,000 fell'

ANNALS OF ULSTER

The battlefield of Culdrevny beneath Ben Bulben in Sligo.

There is no further date of any certainty in the chronology of Columcille until 561 when the battle of such momentous consequence was fought beneath Ben Bulben at Culdrevny – or *Cul-drebene*, in Adamnan's text. Between his departure from Glasnevin at some point in the mid-540s and the year of Culdrevny, the Old Irish *Life* lists the monasteries founded in the course of his 'circuit of all Ireland'. In the first lines of his second preface, Adamnan describes Columcille as 'the father and founder of monasteries'. Manus O'Donnell assures us of some three hundred Columban foundations and Jocelin of Furness, the biographer of St Kentigern, ascribes a hundred monasteries to Columcille's foundation, while the normally extravagant John Colgan is satisfied with a mere sixty-six.

Between the first foundation in Derry and the last and greatest on Iona, Columcille is claimed as the founder of – to name only the most prominent – Kells, by the fortress of the High King Diarmit mac-Cerbaill; Swords, near Dublin; Drumcliffe, near Culdrevny in Sligo; Moone in Kildare; Torach, on Tory Island off the coast of Donegal; and Durrow, the only Columban foundation apart from Iona mentioned by Bede.

Durrow – formerly known as *Dairmag*, 'the Plain of the Oaks' – was certainly the most important Columban foundation in Ireland before the Iona community transferred to Kells in the early ninth century, and has always claimed seniority to Iona. Located in the district of Ballycowan in Meath, the grant of land was bestowed on Columcille – according to the *Annals of Tighernach* – by 'Aedh, son of Brendan, King of Tebtha'. Bede dates its founding to the period before Columcille left Ireland in 563, and O'Donnell fixes it at 561. Much learned debate has ensued as to whether Durrow was established before 563 or much later in the 580s, but the Old Irish *Life* certainly dates its foundation to the 560s and names Cormac ua-Liathain as its first abbot. The identification of Cormac is important because he was certainly far from Durrow and engaged in his mission to the islands of Orkney by 580.

The most plausible resolution of a welter of dates and their manifold implications seems to be that the land for the monastery was granted to Columcille in 561 and a small monastic community established there at that time. The turbulent events after 561 would certainly have prevented any further development of the monastery, but it seems likely that a small complement of brothers remained at Durrow until it was enlarged into a major Columban foundation more than twenty years later.

There may be a curious footnote to this account of the Columban foundations in Ireland in that the place-names of the most prominent – Derry and Durrow – are both associated with the oak, long a symbol sacred to the ancient pagan tradition of the druids. The Christian Church of Columcille's time was grafted, albeit with some difficulty, on to the ancient roots of the pagan faith of the Celts.

The year 561 brings the story of Columcille to the great turning-point of his life. The surviving evidence of an ancient manuscript psalter, a reference to his excommunication by synod, and a fearsome conflict at Culdrevny has become fused with legend to produce the popular explanation of how an Irish abbot born of a noble line came out of battle to a Scottish island and there entered into history as Columba of Iona.

The traditional tale of how Columcille came to Iona tells how he took a rare and valuable copy of the psalms from St Finnian of Moville and copied it out in his own hand in the night. This first recorded breach of copyright was soon discovered and brought to trial at Tara before the High King Diarmit, who ruled for Finnian and against Columcille with the verdict of 'to every cow its calf and to every book its copy'. So affronted was Columcille that he raised his own people, the northern Ui-Neill, in arms and the matter came to bloody resolution on the battlefield of Culdrevny. The copied psalter – the *cathach* or battle-book – was wielded as the battle-standard of Columcille's clan and carried them to victory. Three thousand of the enemy were slain in the triumph of Columcille's cause and so great was his offence deemed to be that he was exiled to the Irish province on the west coast of Scotland, there to reclaim for the faith the same number of souls he had caused to perish at Culdrevny.

Virtually nothing in Adamnan supports this version of events and the Old Irish *Life* makes no mention of Culdrevny. There is, none the less, substantially more supportive material to be found for it both in the annals and in the sixteenth-century *Betha Colaim Chille* of Manus O'Donnell, despite the latter's being too encrusted with folklore and tradition to be taken on the same level of provenance as Adamnan. However, the ninth abbot of Iona was at enormous pains to offer the most saintly possible portrait of Columcille and his material was almost all derived from original sources concerned with Columcille's career after his departure from Ireland. Thus the Irish sources, though laden with legend, merit consideration when examining these important events of the early 560s.

The battle of Culdrevny is an historical fact. Adamnan refers to it in his second preface – and thus acknowledges its significance – when he dates Columcille's departure for Scotland to 'the second year after the battle of Cul-drebene'. The *Annals of Ulster* for 561 record:

The battle Cul-dreimne, gained over Diarmait Mac Cerbhaill, in which 3,000 fell. Fergus and Domnall, two sons of Mac Erca, and Ainmire, son of Setna, and Nainnid, son of Duach . . . were victors, with Aedh, son of Echa Tirmchana, King of Connaught. Through the prayers of Colum-Cille they conquered.

The *Annals of the Four Masters* provide a fuller account, which offers a clue to the most likely historical cause of the conflict:

> The battle of Cul-Dreimhne was gained against Diarmaid, son of Cearball, by Feargus and Domnall, the two sons of Muircheartach, son of Earca; by Ainmire, son of Sedna; and by Ainnidh, son of Duach; and by Aedh, son of Eochaidh Tirmchana, King of Connaught. It was in revenge for the killing of Curnan, son of Aedh, son of Eochaidh Tirmchana, while under the protection of Colum Cille, the Clanna-Neill of the North and the Connaughtmen gave this battle of Cul-Dreimhne to King Diarmaid; and also on account of the false sentence which Diarmaid passed against Colum Cille about a book of Finnen, which Colum had copied without the knowledge of Finnen, when they left it to the award of Diarmaid who pronounced the celebrated decision; 'To every cow belongs its calf', & c.

Whether or not the battle of Culdrevny was the cause of Columcille's departure from Ireland – and there might certainly have been at least some connection between the two events – it marked, even on the evidence of Adamnan, a turning-point in his life. Thus its causes and consequences are worthy of investigation here.

The story of the 'book of Finnen' is most fully told in Manus O'Donnell's *Betha Colaim Chille*. On a visit to Finnian of Moville, possibly at his monastery at Dromin in Louth, Columcille borrowed a book. This was a volume of such importance that he made a copy of it for himself. Finnian, anxious for the fate of his book, sent a young monk in search of it and so it was, in the church at dead of night, that Columcille was caught in the act of copying its final pages. This monastic spy peered through a crack in the door to find Columcille at work on his manuscript and the pages illuminated by a miraculous light shining from his fingers as he wrote. Columcille was alone in the church apart from a pet crane, who regularly kept him company, and when he became aware of the presence of a spy the crane was sent to the door to deal with the intruder. This it did by poking its beak through the crack and into the eye of the watching monk. The man fled to report his discovery and his injury to Finnian, who, after first miraculously healing the eye, took his case of breach of copyright to the High King at Tara. Diarmit – of the rival southern Ui-Neill – passed judgement against Columcille in the phrase recalled by the annalist. Fiery by temperament – as even Adamnan shows him to have been on occasion – Columcille refused to surrender his transcript and returned to his own people in the north.

There is no reason to assume that such an incident did not occur. The earliest surviving Irish manuscript – now in the library of the Royal Irish Academy in Dublin – is a psalter known as *The Cathach of Saint Columba*. It was long in the care of the O'Donnells and believed to be the very book – or part of the book – which brought down the judgement of Diarmit on Columcille. There is, of course, no means of proving whether or not the manuscript is Columcille's work. It is very probably of sufficient antiquity and the Old Irish *Life* claims that he transcribed some three hundred books in his own hand. Its text is that of the Vulgate psalter of St Jerome, written by a skilled scribe and at some speed, with occasional lapses from Jerome's text into the earlier Old Latin.

St Finnian of Moville was certainly instrumental in introducing the new Vulgate version of the Bible into Ireland, possibly through his connection with the monastery at Whithorn or possibly through his visit to Rome, where he was well received by Pope Pelagius and bestowed with gifts. Columcille was a former student in Finnian's seminary on Strangford Lough and it would have been quite likely that he might return to visit his former mentor, even after his ordination into the priesthood. If Finnian did have a copy of the Vulgate text in his possession, then Columcille would have been anxious to study it and certainly capable of transcribing such a rare and important text for his own use. The magnificently illuminated gospel Book of Durrow bears a colophon claiming it to have been written by Columcille in the space of twelve days. Such an achievement, even for the most gifted calligraphic artist, would have been clearly impossible, but it would have been possible for a skilled scribe to have copied out the Vulgate text of the gospels and psalter in that time. Unless O'Donnell's account is a total fiction, it seems likely that this was precisely what Columcille accomplished. It seems no less likely that, having refused to accept the royal judgement against him, he might have kept the gospel text for his own use and passed the psalter into the safe-keeping of his family. This explanation would certainly support the provenance of the *Cathach*, and might suggest that the exemplar from which the Book of Durrow was transcribed might have been no less than a gospel text in Columcille's own hand. The story of the crane appears only in O'Donnell and must be considered a fictional decoration, but the connection between Columcille and 'cranes' – by which medieval writers on Ireland meant the grey heron – will be explored in the context of Adamnan's first book.

All these intriguing possibilities need not for a moment suggest that the judgement on Finnian's book was the cause of the bloodshed at Culdrevny, but there is no doubt that such an incident would most certainly have soured relations between the High King Diarmit and the abbot Columcille, and thus aggravated the rivalry between the two races of the Ui-Neill at a point prior to the outbreak of hostilities.

The annalist's suggestion that the killing of Curnan, son of the king of Connaught, prompted the battle is very much more likely. The holding of a hostage from the family of a lesser monarch by the High King was a customary symbol of tribute and thrall. Similarly, it was also the custom for such a hostage to be granted the protection of a churchman. There is in Adamnan a reference to a similar situation involving Columcille and Scandlan, and the killing of a hostage whilst under such sanctuary would have been a gross violation of ecclesiastical dominion. If Aedh, king of Connaught, had been proving insubordinate to his overlord at Tara, then pressure would certainly have been exerted on his hostage son. If – as other traditional sources suggest – Curnan had killed a son of Diarmit in the course of a hurling match then it is no less likely that the High King's rage might have resulted in his execution of the hostage. These are matters of 'diplomacy by other means' carried to extremes of hostility and eminently likely to provoke military retaliation.

The historical facts of the battle beneath Ben Bulben in 561 are essentially that Diarmit's army invaded Connaught and was there confronted by an alliance of the men of the *Connachta* and the northern Ui-Neill, who might well have been drawn into the conflict in consequence of Columcille's responsibility for the slain hostage. The *Annals of the Four Masters* offers 'a quatrain of Columcille' which illuminates something of the military circumstances:

> O God, wilt thou not drive off the fog which envelops our number,
> The host which has deprived us of our livelihood, the host which proceeds
>   around the carns!
> He is the son of storm who betrays us,
> My Druid – He will not refuse me – is the Son of God, and may He side with me.

The forces of the High King encountered an enemy cloaked by fog. By the time the fog had lifted they had advanced into an ambush and three thousand of their number were slain. Only one warrior of the northern Ui-Neill fell in battle, and he only because he crossed the *airbe*, the magical line of defence cast by the druids. These references from the annals clearly suggest that Diarmit's forces were pagan, going

29

into battle protected by druid war-magic. In such an event, Columcille might well have felt fully justified in wielding his *Cathach* psalter as a Christian standard on the battlefield, and similarly calling on 'my Druid . . . the Son of God'.

These events took place almost 150 years before the ratification of the *Cain Adamnain* which exempted churchmen from warfare. There is even evidence to be found in Adamnan that Columcille carried a battle-scar, which may well have been sustained on the field of Culdrevny. There remains about Columcille – despite so many portrayals of the saintly Columba – the distinctive aspect of the warrior-saint. On several occasions Adamnan records his showing a passionate, even partisan, interest in the tides of war. When Oswald of Northumbria fought Cadwallon of Gwynedd at Heavenfield in 634 he was inspired by a vision of Columcille on the eve of battle, and in later centuries the Vikings who established themselves in the western isles adopted Columcille beside such of their own warlike saints as Olaf of Norway.

The political impact of Culdrevny was to cripple the power of Diarmit. After him the throne at Tara was to pass, not just to the northern Ui-Neill, but specifically to Columcille's own Cenel Conaill. Columcille's involvement cannot have endeared him to the High King, but there is no historical evidence to suggest he was exiled from Ireland as a consequence of the battle. It was, after all, two full years after that event when he made his departure for Scotland. None the less, the wrath of the established order was apparently brought down upon Columcille at some point in the aftermath of Culdrevny. Adamnan admits that he was excommunicated for 'a venial and pardonable' offence by a synod at Teiltiu. Precisely what the offence might have been is nowhere recorded, but excommunication was never the customary sanction of the Church against the 'venial and pardonable'. Nor can it be without significance that the synod was held at Teiltiu – or Teltown – in the heart of Diarmit's territory. It cannot have been totally unconnected with the dispute which led to Culdrevny and may even have derived from some instigation of the druid faction who certainly held great sway at Tara. There is also the real possibility that Adamnan – writing 130 years after the event – was not actually describing an excommunication as later churchmen would understand it, but some less drastic form of censure, possibly effected by pagan rather than Christian authority. Adamnan at least offers evidence that Columcille did not face judgement without friends. St Brenden of Birr, inspired by a vision of Columcille in the company of angels, spoke for him and shortly afterwards, Adamnan is anxious to assure us, the sentence was rescinded and the offence pardoned.

If Adamnan is vague – even suspiciously vague – on the 'excommunication' of Columcille, he is quite specific on the occasion and circumstances of the departure from Ireland: 'In the second year after the battle of Cul-drebene, in the forty-second year of his age, Columba sailed from Ireland to Britain, wishing to become a pilgrim for Christ.'

Nowhere in the annals is there any suggestion that Columcille was exiled from Ireland. There is some evidence that he undertook the pilgrimage as an act of penance on the advice of St Molaise of Devenish, but this is very probably a later medieval addition to the burgeoning legend at a time when voluntary pilgrimage was no longer a central tenet of the Irish Church.

Perhaps an examination of the historical imperatives suggests that factors other than conscience might have had their own bearing on the situation. There is no question but that the powerful Ui-Neill, who had crushed the High King in battle, could have given all necessary sanctuary to their abbot should he have needed such protection. It is also true that Columban foundations in Ireland, many of them situated at a distance from Derry and dangerously close to Tara, continued undisturbed by any royal wrath after the departure of their abbot Columcille.

None the less, O'Donnell records that 'the saints of Ireland muttered against Columcille' and Columcille's political situation must have come under some pressure after 561, and that situation might have been best resolved by pilgrimage from

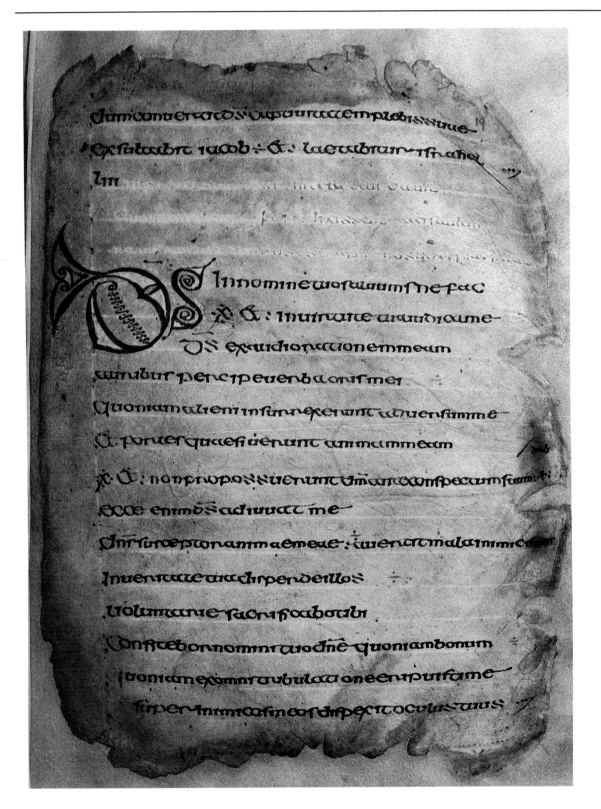

'*A book of Finnen, which Colum had copied*'

ANNALS OF THE FOUR MASTERS

Psalm 53 – *Deus in nomine* – from the Cathach psalter: f. 19.

Royal Irish Academy, Dublin: MS S.n.

Ireland. Such a 'white martyrdom' of voluntary exile to 'a desert place' was long central to the Celtic monastic tradition with its roots in the antecedent 'desert fathers' of Sinai, from whom the tenets of the ancient Irish Church may well have derived. The voyages of such saints as Columcille's contemporaries Cormac and Brenden the Navigator are vivid examples of the Celtic response to the call of 'the wave cry, the wind cry', just as Aidan's choice of Lindisfarne for his outpost of the faith in seventh-century Northumbria is in full accord with the opening exhortation of the Columban Rule: 'Be alone in a separate place near a chief city, if thy conscience is not prepared to be in common with the crowd.' It is also true that the destination chosen by Columcille for his own pilgrimage suggests a further and clearly political dimension to the prompting and purpose of his voyage.

By the mid-sixth century, the Irish settlement on the west coast of Scotland had reached a point of serious crisis. At which point in the fifth century Irish settlers first came to the highlands and islands to the west of the Spine of Britain is unclear, but the first establishment of Irish kingdoms there is recorded around the year AD 500. The settlers, it seems, were of the *Ulaid*, the men of Ulster, whose Irish homeland came under increasing pressure from the rising power of the Ui-Neill claiming ever more 'sword-land' in the north of Ireland. Twenty years before the birth of Columcille, the three sons of Erc sailed from Ireland to found their kingdoms in the north-west of the mainland of Britain, or *Alba*, as it was most anciently known. Agricola's legions had abandoned this most northerly frontier of Roman Britain, perhaps creating a territorial vacuum along the seaboard of Argyll to be filled when the sons of Erc made landfall in Islay, Kintyre and Lorne.

Of those three sons, Angus, Loern and Fergus, it was Fergus mac-Erc who claimed Kintyre and there forged the kingdom which took its name of *Dalriada* from the Irish kingdom of their father. These settlers were the *Scotti*, whose Dalriada was to unite three centuries later with the kingdoms of Pictland, giving birth to the nation of Scotland under Kenneth mac-Alpin. But even in the first decades of the sixth century, 'Scottish' Dalriada began to supersede the Irish kingdom from which it sprang. Its location was strategically placed to the north of the powerful kingdom of the Britons of Strathclyde and to the west of the land of the Picts, which lay beyond the mountains of the *Dorsum Britanniae* – the 'Spine of Britain'.

Fergus's grandson, Gabran mac-Domangart, established his fortress capital at the hillfort of Dunadd in Argyll, from where his warships commanded the sea routes to Ireland and his military presence threatened to subjugate the Pictish kingdoms to the east. As befitted the 'last men on earth, the last of the free' who had successfully resisted the all-conquering legions of Rome, the Picts' response to this relentless Irish pressure turned to military resistance in the second half of the sixth century. Between the years 555 and 557, Brude mac-Maelchon subjugated the lesser Pictish rulers to become the king who united the Picts against Dalriada. Brude was the son of Maelgwn, 'the dragon of the island' according to Gildas, a powerful warlord of the Britons of north Wales and the son of a Pictish mother. Thus it was that Brude entered into the Pictish king-lists by virtue of the revival of the ancient custom of succession through the maternal line. This custom would later provide the Picts with a number of kings of other than Pictish origins, notably Brude mac-Bile who was a Briton of Strathclyde and Talorcan who was the grandson of Aethelfrith, the Anglo-Saxon king of Northumbria.

The warriors of Brude mac-Maelchon slew Gabran on the battlefield and drove the Dalriadans back against the ramparts of their fastness of Dunadd. The *Annals of Tighernach* for the year 560 record the

death of Gabrain mac Domanguirt, Ri Albain.
Flight of the people of Alban before Bruidi mac Maelchon.

It is significant that the annalist calls Gabran *Ri Albain*, 'King of Alba', confirming his governance of all the Irish settlements in Scotland. His successor, Conall mac-Comgall, claimed only the title of 'King of Dalriada', effectively ruler of Kintyre, rather than overlord of all the settlers west of the Spine of Britain.

Thus it was that while the Ui-Neill were inflicting the defeat of Culdrevny on Diarmit, the Pictish onslaught was threatening to throw the Dalriadans back into the western sea. This precarious, even ominous, political situation may well have prompted the new king at Dunadd to look to Ireland for an ally and thus invite Columcille to Dalriada. Columcille was blood kin, not only to the Ui-Neill in Ireland, but also to the sons of Erc in Dalriada inasmuch as his father's mother was a daughter of Erc, and thus sister to Fergus of Dalriada. An invitation to a scion of the sons of Neill, a holy man born a prince of royal blood-lines, whose prayers had brought victory over the High King of Ireland at Culdrevny, might surely provide an omen of divine destiny to the embattled kingdom of Dalriada.

It is equally possible to explain Columcille's pilgrimage from Ireland as the command of conscience or the call of a king. It is just as possible to see it as a rite of passage of a man of destiny prompted by a confluence of the tides of historical circumstance. It surely throws the darkest shadow of suspicion over the traditional story of Columba driven into exile from Ireland, setting the course of his coracle to the north and coming ashore when he made landfall on a remote island from which he could no longer see his beloved Erin. Manus O'Donnell's lyric rendering of Columcille's quatrains of departure may well have inspired such an imagining:

'Saint Columba's Cave'

Columcille traditionally built the stone altar and inscribed the cross still visible on the wall in this druid's cave at Loch Caolisport when he arrived at nearby Dunadd.

33

> Derry of the Oaks, let us leave it
> With gloom and with tears, heavy-hearted;
> Anguish of heart to depart thence,
> And to go away among strangers.
>
> Great is the speed of my coracle,
> And its stern turned upon Derry;
> Woe to me that I must on the main,
> On the path to beetling-browed Alba.

Kintyre was no more than a day's sailing from Derry and Columcille would most certainly have set course for the harbour of Dunadd. His arrival on Iona must be placed at a later date than his in Dalriada, and indeed nowhere does Adamnan suggest that Columcille came directly to Iona. That suggestion can be traced to the *Annals of Ulster*, which – deriving their dating from Adamnan – record the 'voyage of Columcille to the Island of Ia, in the forty-second year of his age'. Columcille's selection of Iona can be seen to have been as much a political as a spiritual decision.

Iona – *Iou* in Adamnan, *Hii* in Bede, and *Hy, Ia* or even *I* elsewhere – had been a sacred site long before Columcille's arrival. It was certainly a holy place for the pagan druids and the three hundred 'crosses' that are said to have been found there in antiquity were probably Bronze Age megaliths, standing stones on which the Christian *chi-rho* symbol was later inscribed. At least as importantly, its territorial location – on the frontier between Dalriada and the territory of the Picts – provided Columcille's foundation there with a clear political imperative. Indeed, Bede tells us that Columcille was granted the island by the Pictish king:

> Columba came to Britain in the ninth year of the reign of Bruide, son of Maelchon, a Pictish king of great power, and converted the people to the Christian faith by his word and example; and because of this they gave him possession of the island to build a monastery.

The *Annals of Ulster* obituary of Conall mac-Comgall at 574 declares Iona to have been in the gift of the king of Dalriada:

> The death of Conall, son of Comgall, in the sixteenth year
> of his reign, who granted the island of Ia to Colum-Cille.

So do the obituaries in the *Annals of Clonmacnoise* and the *Annals of the Four Masters*, both of which identify Conall as 'he that gave the island of Ia to Colum Cille'.

Columcille's 'conversion' of the Picts – which derives from Bede, or from a misreading of Bede – does not withstand historical scrutiny. Elsewhere in his *Historia*, Bede describes Columcille as 'the first teacher of the Christian faith to the Picts who live beyond the hills to the north', which does not necessarily suggest the achievement of extensive conversion. Christian foundations in Pictland, although established from Iona in some, but certainly not all, cases, date from much later than Columcille's time. We have Adamnan's evidence that Columcille did himself venture east of the Spine of Britain and paid at least one, and probably two, visits to Brude mac-Maelchon's fortress near Inverness. He also refers to Columcille's visiting *Sci* – the Isle of Skye – which was certainly Pictish territory. The number of occasions when Adamnan describes Columcille communicating with non-Gaelic-speaking Picts through an interpreter would certainly suggest that the abbot of Iona had no command of the P-Celtic tongue. We have detailed accounts from Adamnan of Columcille's triumphs in miracle-working contests with Brude's druid Broichan, alongside clear indications of the lasting impression he made upon the Pictish king. Columcille may even have converted Brude to the Christian faith, although, if he did, Adamnan does not tell us so. Bede – probably informed by Pictish rather than Iona souces – certainly believed so. The Pictish king-lists include the unusually expansive statement that 'Bridei was baptised by Saint Columba in the eighth year of his reign', but this must be suspect, if only because the lists are derived from marginal annotations in Irish annals compiled in the fourteenth century. It is at least possible that the baptism reference was a medieval addition deriving from Bede. The inaccuracy of dating occurring in the annals might thus have rendered Bede's 'ninth year' of Brude's reign as the 'eighth year' of the king-lists. Whatever may have been the case with their king, there are certainly no records of mass baptisms of the Picts in the waters of the Ness in the time of Columcille. It seems that the wholesale Christian conversion of the populations of Pictland was a slow process, achieved by later *peregrini* of the Columban *familia*, such as Donnan on Eigg, and also by those from other Irish monastic traditions, such as Maelrub of Bangor at Applecross. There also remains the crucial impact of the mere presence of the church on Iona – the focal point of cultural interchange between Pict and Gael – which must have exerted considerable influence.

Adamnan offers numerous references to Columcille's presence 'beyond the Spine of Britain', but never does he indicate whether these refer to a series of travels into Pictland or whether they all derive from a single mission through the Great Glen to the court of King Brude on the Beauly Firth near Inverness. An overview of Columcille's various travels might suggest that he did not make journeys of any great length without a definite – often diplomatic – purpose. He would certainly have needed to travel to Brude's capital to win the Pictish king's approval for his foundation on Iona, and this diplomatic mission must certainly have been accomplished very shortly after his arrival in Scotland in 563. In the incisive introduction to his translation of Adamnan, A. O. Anderson proposes the view that Columcille made just one journey into Pictland, with the primary purpose of winning Pictish consent for the Iona monastery, and that all of Adamnan's stories set to the east of the Spine derive from this journey. It is probable that Columcille paid a second visit to Brude to negotiate a safe conduct for the voyage of St Cormac to Orkney, then an island kingdom in thrall to the all-powerful Pictish king, but it is also just possible that a guarantee of Cormac's safe passage was on the same agenda as the grant of Iona to Columcille. There is, therefore, good reason to suggest that all Adamnan's references to Columcille in Pictland may well derive from no more than two diplomatic missions, the first of them certainly undertaken in 563. Historical evidence clearly supports the dating of Columcille's diplomatic mission to the Pictish royal capital soon after his arrival in Scotland. War between the Picts and the Dalriadans had threatened the destruction of the Irish settlement after the death of Gabran in 560, and yet an enduring peace, established almost immediately on the coming of Columcille in 563, prevailed between the two nations through eight decades until the disastrous succession of Domnall Brecc.

Adamnan provides clear evidence for Columcille's travels to the west of the Spine of Britain, certainly to *Male*, the Isle of Mull, just across the Sound from Iona, and to *Artdamuirchol*, or Ardnamurchan, in the Dalriadan domain of the *Cenel Loairn*, the descendants of Fergus's brother Loern mac-Erc.

Apart from the journey – or journeys – into Pictland and visits to neighbouring islands of the Inner Hebrides, the evidence of Adamnan shows Columcille to have been resident principally on Iona and in his retreat on the still unidentified island of 'Hinba' through the first decade of his 'pilgrimage to Britain'. There is certainly little support in Adamnan for the traditional view of Columcille's evangelical journeyings across the highlands and islands. In a mould akin to that of his ancestors, he was building a power base, albeit of the scripture rather than the sword, on Iona.

By the year 574 when Conall mac-Comgall was slain, probably by a rival tribe of Irish settlers in the course of a seaborne foray in the northern reaches of Dalriada, the question of royal succession required the consent of Columcille. His choice fell upon Conall's cousin, Aidan mac-Gabran. Adamnan tells us – in a splendidly apocalyptic account – of Columcille in solitary retreat on Hinba and of three visits to him by an angel, wielding a whip and bearing a book of glass, who compelled him to elect Aidan to the succession. Why such angelic intimidation should have been necessary is not

ABOVE The entrance to the hillfort of Dunadd. Columcille would have climbed this path when he arrived at the fortress capital of Dalriada.

Port na Curaich

RIGHT The beach at 'the Bay of the Coracle' where Columcille traditionally first landed on Iona.

explained, but Aidan's claim to the throne may well have been seen as usurping the birthright of Conall's own sons. The angelic vision would have served to provide a symbol of heavenly ratification for a succession of questionable legitimacy.

However reluctantly Columcille reached his choice, it proved to be one of great historical moment, for when Aidan mac-Gabran's succession was consecrated on Iona he became king not only of Conall's Kintyre but of all the dominions of Scottish Dalriada. He was promised a great and glorious reign as long as he maintained allegiance to Iona and to Columcille's people of the Ui-Neill. History indeed records Aidan as the greatest of the kings of Dalriada, just as it records the collapse of the kingdom in the reign of his grandson, Domnall Brecc, who broke faith with Columcille's blessing when his warlike ambition turned against the Ui-Neill at the battle of Mag-Roth in 637.

The nature and circumstances of Aidan's succession bear impressive testimony to the extraordinary stature of the abbot of Iona little more than a decade after the monastery's foundation. No other Irish abbot, indeed no European churchman of less than papal rank, commanded such authority over the destiny of kings in the sixth century, and yet, in Ireland's pre-Christian antiquity, the naming of the High King fell always to the arch-druid in the pagan rite at the Stone of Destiny on the hill at Tara.

The succession of Aidan was shortly followed by what Adamnan describes as a *condictum regum* or 'conference of kings' called by Aid mac-Ainmure of the northern Ui-Neill at Druim Ceatt, 'the Ridge of Cete', in Londonderry. The *Annals of Ulster* for the year 575 record

the great convention of Druim-Ceta, at which were
Colum-Cille and Aedh son of Ainmire.

The historical causes and consequences of Druim Ceatt are complex and their complexity is aggravated by the accretion of Columban legend which surrounds the documentary evidence. The central issue was certainly the political situation of Alban Dalriada, which was represented for the first time in royal assembly on the Irish mainland by its own legitimate overlord. The negotiations were apparently conducted between Aidan of Dalriada and Aid of the northern Ui-Neill, who was himself to become High King of all Ireland more than ten years later. Columcille attended, clearly, in the role of advisor to Aidan, and his influence can have been in no degree hampered by the fact that Aid was his cousin. The result was effectively to establish for the first time the independence of Dalriada from the mainland. The men of the islands were no longer to pay tribute to the king in Ireland. Their obligation was to be solely that of military alliance, to join with them in 'hosting and expedition'. Aidan's power in his own independent kingdom was firmly established and Columcille's standing had reached a new peak of political eminence.

A further question at issue at Druim Ceatt – at least according to tradition – was the standing of the bards of Ireland. The *olave filidh*, the order of the bards, had long held the status of poet-chroniclers of kings and time-honoured guardians of tradition. Their ancient stature had fallen under an ever darker shadow, in consequence of its druidic associations, in Ireland's early Christian centuries. The response of the bards was to demand ever greater privileges for their order until, on some three historical occasions, they were threatened with expulsion from Ireland. One of these occasions was the convention of kings at Druim Ceatt, and tradition – enshrined in the bardic praise-song of the *Amra Cholum Chille* – tells us that it was Columcille who spoke in the cause of the *filidh*. Columcille's eloquent defence preserved the bards from expulsion, albeit at the price of some moderation of their privileges. In gratitude for his advocacy twelve hundred bards are said to have risen as one to sing verses in his praise. Columcille – who certainly fully appreciated the value of the ancient bardic heritage and traditionally shared some measure of their art – expressed gratitude at their tribute asking only that they sang no more of his praises until after his death.

Thus came about the traditional origin of the verses of the *Amra Cholum Chille*, which are believed to include the song sung by the bards at Druim Ceatt, and the extended eulogy which follows it to be an obituary composed by the *filidh* on the death of the saint. The *Amra* – although it may have been retouched in the ninth century – could well have originated as early as the sixth century, but there is no firm evidence in Adamnan for Columcille's defence of the bards at Druim Ceatt. None the less, it is to the preface or forespeech of the *Amra* that we owe a colourful account of Columcille's appearance at Druim Ceatt, setting foot on Irish soil for the first time since his departure from Derry twelve years earlier. Tradition tells how he had taken a vow of pilgrimage that he would never again set eye on his homeland or foot on Irish soil and thus came to Druim Ceatt with his eyes covered by a blindfold and Scottish turf tied to his feet. The poetic testimony of the *Amra* describes how Columcille

> saw not Ireland then, for a cerecloth used to be over his eyes, the reason thereof being that when passing from Ireland he promised he would never see it thenceforward, saying: 'There is a grey eye that looks back at Erin, never thenceforth shall it see Erin's men nor their women'.

Adamnan attaches other Columban anecdotes with an Irish setting to the visit to Druim Ceatt and while there is no reason to doubt his accuracy, he was working from almost exclusively Iona source material and seems far from fully informed on the chronology and geography of Columcille's Irish activities. He does, however, offer evidence that Columcille came again to Ireland ten years after Druim Ceatt, visiting his own foundation at Durrow and that of Ciaran at Clonmacnoise. The Old Irish *Life* places these travels at a much earlier date, part of his 'circuit of all Ireland' between Culdrevny and the departure for Scotland, but Adamnan specifically mentions the name of Alither as abbot of Clonmacnoise, who succeeded to that office in 585, and his evidence must be accepted as the more reliable. The Old Irish biographer, writing long after Adamnan, tells of Columcille visiting the tomb of St Martin at Tours which can be accepted as no more historical than O'Donnell's bizarre legend of Columcille flying to Rome in the course of an airborne battle with demons.

The historical background to the last years of Columcille is dominated by the weakening thrall of Brude mac-Maelchon over his widespread Pictish kingdom. Brude was killed by southern Pictish rebels in 584 and interred on Iona, but through his latter years there is increasing evidence of insurgency and piracy in the territories at the edge of his kingdom. In 580 or 581, Aidan's warfleet sailed north, certainly to the outer isles and probably as far as Orkney, to do battle with encroaching sea-raiders. He was at war again three years later against the *Maetae* Picts in the 'battle of the Miathi' fought in the region of Stirling, which brought him precipitously close to the borders of the increasingly powerful Northumbria and eventually led to his own crushing defeat at the hands of Aethelfrith of Northumbria at Degsastan in 603.

But the life of Columcille was long over when the advance of Dalriada was finally thrown back at Degsastan. The longest and probably the finest chapter of Adamnan's *Vita Columbae* is his elegiac and visionary rendering of the last days of Columcille on Iona, which must stand as an historical documentary record of the highest order.

Acceptance of Adamnan's Columban chronology places the death of Columcille in the year 597. The annalists are – once again – at variance on the year. The *Annals of Ulster* offer it as both 595 and 601, those of the *Four Masters* as 592, and the *Annals of Clonmacnoise* as 590. But all accounts are in agreement on the day and time of his passing – 'the fifth of the Ides of June' – shortly after the hour of midnight in the first moments of Whit Sunday, which fell that year on 9 June.

The first and fullest entry in the *Annals of Ulster* records:

> The repose of Colum-Cille, on the fifth of the Ides of
> June in the seventy-sixth year of his age.

The *Annals of Clonmacnoise* are somewhat more informative:

> Saint Columbkill died at Whitsuntide eve, on the fifth of the Ides of June, in the island of Hugh in the thirty-fifth year of his pilgrimage and banishment into Scotland, and in the seventy-seventh year of his age, as he was saying his prayers in the church of that isle, with his monks about him.

But the *Annals of the Four Masters* reveal the chronicles at their most poetically elegiac:

> Colum Cille, son of Feidhlimidh, apostle of Alba, head of the piety of the most part of Ireland and Alba after Patrick, died in his own church, on Sunday night precisely, the 9th day of June. Seventy-seven years was his whole age when he resigned his spirit to heaven as is said in this quatrain:

> > Three years without light
> >   was Colum in his Duibh-regles;
> > He went to the angels from his body,
> >   after seven years and seventy.

The reference to *Duibh-regles*, his 'black church' in Derry, echoes the foretelling of the 'full habitation of Columcille' found in the *Prophecy of Berchan*:

> > His grace in Hii without stain,
> > And his soul in Derry.

Neither history nor tradition could deny Columcille so modest yet consummate an epitaph.

The prophecies of Columcille

Adamnan begins his *Vita Columbae* with two prefaces, the first of them couched in terms of a formal dedication, but both of them substantially revealing beneath their hagiographical veneer.

In his first preface, Adamnan explains that he is writing in response to 'the entreaties of the brothers', thus implying that his work was intended for the Iona community. Yet he immediately goes on to offer apologies for his unpolished Latin and for the inclusion of 'obscure names . . . which belong to the poor Irish tongue'. This is certainly the first evidence that Adamnan did not intend his principal readership to be the Iona brethren, or Irish monasteries of the Columban *familia*. If his Latin text was directed at readers whose first language was not Gaelic, then he was certainly writing with Northumbria prominently in mind. Adamnan began work on these prefaces very soon after his return to Iona from his visit to Wearmouth/Jarrow of 688. The churches of St Peter at Wearmouth and St Paul at Jarrow were sumptuously appointed with the finest of ecclesiastical furnishing and decoration, but the library which inspired the scholarship of the Venerable Bede and the scriptorium which produced such magnificent volumes as the *Codex Amiatinus* must have impressed Adamnan as one of the great centres of learning in seventh-century Europe. The traditional esteem for Irish learning had been long diminished by the encroaching influence of Rome and even an erudite abbot of Iona would have stood in awe of the continental polish so evident in the Northumbrian monasteries.

Adamnan's second preface provides the kernel of 'biographical' content of his three books, yet it also reveals much of its author's own perspective and intent. This second preface begins by proposing the name of *Columba* as the Latin form of the Irish name *Columb* and with a Latin meaning of 'the dove . . . a simple and innocent bird, and so it was right that a simple and innocent man should be called by this name'.

It is of some importance that the first identification of Columcille as 'St Columba' is found in these prefaces, and it is similarly significant that Adamnan's choice of that Latin form was inextricably linked to his presentation of Columcille as 'a simple and innocent man'. Adamnan was dealing in hagiography rather than in historical biography and presenting his saint as an icon compatible with the wider context of his own times, but it must already be clear that simplicity and innocence were not the most prominent amongst the remarkable qualities of the historical Columcille. None the less, it is only fair to remember that Adamnan was working almost entirely from Iona sources, whose account of Columcille must have been based on his later benign maturity rather than the 'turbulent priest' of Culdrevny.

Adamnan's preface next records the foretelling of Columcille which he attributes to St Mauchte – or Mochta – of Louth, the fifth-century disciple of St Patrick. Adamnan's choice of this prophecy of Columcille certainly lends it a provenance beyond the other prophecies recorded by the medieval author of the Old Irish *Life*. It seems unlikely that Adamnan would have omitted the foretellings attributed to Patrick and Brigid had he known of them and it is most likely that they derived from later Irish tradition. According to the Old Irish *Life*, Patrick's prophecy of Columcille – which has already

'The fleeing and despotic glory of kings, which endureth but a moment in the world'

THE *ALTUS PROSATOR* ATTRIBUTED TO COLUMCILLE

Sunset at Dunadd.

been set out here – was made to Fergus, the son of Conall Gulban, predicting 'a man-child will be born of his race'. St Brigid's foretelling even includes the name of Columcille's mother, predicting

> The man-child of longsided Ethne,
> As a sage he is a-blossoming.
> Columcille, pure without blemish.
> It is not oversoon to perceive him.

The Old Irish *Life* also includes the prophecy of Mauchte, in content very similar to Adamnan's rendering, but with the characteristic addition of a verse quatrain.

Adamnan's second preface concludes with his crucially important summary biography of Columcille, outlining his lineage and making no reference to any event earlier than the departure 'from Ireland to Britain, wishing to become a pilgrim for Christ'. He also provides an outline of the structure of his *Vita Columbae* into three books recording in turn prophecies, miracles and visions, and an indication of his sources, namely 'earlier writings', which we can take to be principally the lost Cummene *Life*, and oral tradition 'by thorough questioning of trustworthy and knowledgeable elders'.

Adamnan curiously devotes the first chapter of his book of Columcille's 'prophecies' to 'a summary of his miracles'. Adamnan's organisational approach is generally thematic, grouping anecdotes together largely by their similarity of subject, and the explanation of the prefatory summary of miracles is certainly to be found in Adamnan's Northumbrian experience. The miracles selected for such early prominence concern Columcille's miraculous presentation to the Pictish King Brude mac-Maelchon and his posthumous visionary appearance to the Northumbrian King Oswald on the eve of the victory at Heavenfield, which secured Oswald's kingdom for its subsequent conversion to Christianity. Both of these accounts are certainly directed towards a Northumbrian readership, with at least a sideways glance at the Pictish Church in eastern Scotland. There was extensive contact between the monastery at Jarrow and the court of the Pictish King Nechtan, and an account of Columcille's miracle-working 'east of the Spine of Britain' could well be calculated to enhance his standing at Wearmouth/Jarrow. Adamnan's impressive account of Oswald's vision might be expected similarly to impress a Northumbrian readership. Oswald, who found sanctuary on Iona after the defeat of his father Aethelfrith by Edwin of Deira in 616, returned to confront the Britons of Gwynedd when they in turn had overthrown Edwin. Oswald's forces vanquished the superior numbers of their enemy on the vallum of the Roman wall near Chollerford, and established him as the overlord of a vast and powerful Christian kingdom of Northumbria.

It was certainly the first time that an English king had raised the cross as his battle-standard, and the form of that cross was surely derived from the Celtic crosses Oswald would have known on Iona. The vision of Columcille, appearing on the eve of battle with divine assurance of victory, was later described by Oswald to the abbot on Iona in the presence of Failbe, Adamnan's predecessor, and can be effectively accepted as a first-hand account. Oswald's quoted reference to Columcille's 'great stature' is of genuine value, because at the time of his arrival on Iona the founder had been dead barely thirty years. Oswald would certainly have been educated by monks who had known Columcille personally and been able to provide him with an accurate description of the saint's physical appearance.

Adamnan did not apparently feel it necessary to mention Oswald's summoning of Aidan from Iona to be the first and founding bishop of Lindisfarne in order to remind Wearmouth/Jarrow of the Columban claim to be the well-spring of Northumbria's golden age, but such was quite clearly the underlying intent of this first chapter. It is also perhaps worth observing how swiftly the 'simple and innocent man' of the prefaces is transformed into Columcille the warrior-saint and maker of kings.

Adamnan moves then into a sequence of prophecies concerning saints and holy men, almost all of whom are identifiable historical personalities. The first of these is St Finten, who arrived on Iona as a young monk shortly after the death of Columcille only to be refused admission to the community. His arrival had been prophesied and his entry into the monastery denied by Columcille, who had foretold that Finten's greater destiny lay on the Irish mainland. Born like both Columcille and Adamnan of the lineage of the Ui-Neill, Finten – who is also known as St Munna – founded the monastery of Taghmon in Wexford and merits mention in the *Lives* of a number of Irish saints.

The prophecy of the future achievement of the boy Ernene – who grew up to found monasteries at Rathnew in Wicklow and Kildreenagh in County Carlow – is confirmed in the *Annals of Tighernach*, which enter his obituary at the year 635. Perhaps of greater interest is Adamnan's account of the circumstances of the prophecy which was delivered when the young Ernene approached Columcille on his visit to Clonmacnoise. Adamnan describes the visit to Ireland as the occasion of the 'founding of the monastery known as Dairmag' – or Durrow – and mentions the presence of Alither as the abbot of Clonmacnoise. Alither succeeded to the abbacy in 585, which has prompted the suggestion discussed earlier that Durrow must have been founded after that date. On this same occasion, Columcille is quoted by Adamnan as prophesying 'the dispute . . . of the lack of uniformity in the keeping of Easter'. Adamnan offers no further details, but the paschal controversy was already rumbling on the Continent and Columcille would certainly have been aware of the wrangle centering on his contemporary, St Columbanus. This Leinsterman, remembered as the greatest of the Irish *peregrini* in Europe, had travelled to Gaul where his insistence on the Celtic tradition was already drawing down the displeasure of the Frankish church and would later involve him in a succession of disputatious exchanges with continental adherents of the Roman orthodoxy.

At this point Adamnan enters into a sequence of prophecies concerning seafaring saints, and prompts a consideration of how very prominently the perilous winds and waves of Scotland's western shore must have loomed in the lives of the Iona community. An ancient Irish quatrain provides a vivid – and very Celtic – portrait of the hardy monks of Columcille's *familia*:

> Wondrous the warriors who abode in Hi,
> Thrice fifty in the monastic rule,
> With their boats along the main sea,
> Three score men a-rowing.

Adamnan himself would have experienced many crossings of the Sound between Iona and the Ross of Mull in weather conditions which must have rendered the hide-hulled *curragh*, even of the larger sixty-foot type which it seems carried Columcille to the island, at best a perilous craft. In 691, while Adamnan was certainly on Iona and working on his *Vita Columbae*, the *Annals of Ulster* record:

> a great storm, on the 16th of the Kalends of October,
> overwhelmed some six persons of the community of Ia.

On a day of 'violent storm and waves of daunting height', Columcille prophesies a coming calm to enable St Cainnech to cross the Sound. Cainnech – or Kenneth – was one of those 'Apostles of Ireland' traditionally educated at Finnian's seminary in Clonard. A close friend of Columcille, his principal foundation was Aghaboe in Ossory, but the many Scottish churches dedicated to him confirm that he travelled extensively in the western islands of Dalriada.

A similar prophecy assures the safety of Colman mocu-Sailni 'in the seething waves of the whirlpool of Brecan'. There are some three hundred Colmans in the Irish calendar of saints, but Dr Reeves identifies this one as Colman-Eala – or Colmanus –

'The island of Iou'

'Iona – there is truly a very Ossianic and sweetly sad sound about that name,' wrote the composer Felix Mendelssohn and yet the name 'Iona' apparently derives from an error made by a medieval scribe. Adamnan uses Latin forms of the apparently Pictish *Iou*, which translates as 'Yew Island' and suggests that the island was anciently the centre of a pagan druid cult of the yew tree.

The name later appears as *Iou-a*, which at some point was transcribed in error as 'Iona', by which name the island has been known throughout modern times. Bede used the Anglo-Saxon form of *Hii*. The German monk Walafrid Strabo writes of Iona in the ninth century as *Eo*:

> Far on the Pictish coast is seen a sea-girded islet
> Floating amidst the billows:
> Eo the name that it beareth.

The simplest Gaelic form is *I* – 'the Island' – but it is also known to the Gael as *Icolmkill*, 'the island of Columcille', and, interestingly, as *Innis nan Druidhneach*, 'the island of the druids'.

All of which suggests that Iona has been regarded as a holy place throughout its history, and indeed throughout its pre-history. The pagan druids seemed always to seek out the most ancient rock of the earth's crust for their sacred sites, and the rock of Iona is older than almost any other on the planet.

The geologist E. C. Trenholme explains how 'the beginning of Iona is almost part of the beginning of the earth itself. When our planet, from a flaming mass of combustion like the sun, shrivelled into a globe with a solid crust, and the first oceans condensed in the hollows of its hot surface – thus it was that the Archaean rocks of which Iona and the Outer Hebrides consist were formed on the sea-bottom. They contain no fossils; for, so far as is known, no living creature as yet existed in the desolate waste of waters or on the primeval land.'

Long before Columcille, the legendary St Bride of the Isles provided a link between Bride, the Celtic goddess of the spring, and Brigid, the Christian saint of Kildare. Gaelic tradition tells how Bride of the Isles was a herd-maid on Iona who was miraculously transported to Bethlehem to serve as aid-woman to Mary on the eve of Christ's Nativity. If the legend of Bride marks the transition of Iona from druid antiquity to the firmer historical ground of the Columban period, the tradition of Columcille's pilgrimage claims that he sailed north from Ireland until he reached an island from which he could no longer see his homeland and there founded his monastery.

Above the bay *Port na Curaich*, where his coracle is said to have made landfall on Iona, is the cliff called *Carn Cull ri Eirinn*, the Cairn of the Back to Ireland, from which Columcille is said to have scanned the horizon to confirm that Derry was no longer in sight. That legend finds little support in historical probability. There are cairns called *Carn Cull ri Eirinn* on Oronsay and on Mull, where there is a similar *Carn Cull ri Albain*, the Cairn of the Back to Scotland. Mull – like Iona – stood on the frontier between Dalriada and Pictland and these place-names suggest an origin in the territorial claims of the Pict and the Gael which long pre-date 'the grey eye' with which Columcille looked back toward Erin.

Iona from the Ross of Mull.

who was the patron saint of Kilconnell, east of Knapdale in Argyll. The 'whirlpool of Brecan' has often been identified with the notorious Corryvreckan between the islands of Scarba and Jura, but Adamnan quite specifically locates this maritime danger zone off the coast of Antrim, where it is identified by Reeves as the channel between the island of Rathlin and Ballycastle. Its name of 'Brecan's Cauldron' derives from the tradition that Brecan, a son of Niall of the Nine Hostages, was drowned in its waters. The first identification of the Scottish Corryvreckan – or *Corebrekane* – does not occur until the late fourteenth-century chronicles of Fordun.

Another similar prophecy concerns the celebrated seagoing saint, Cormac ua-Liathain – or 'grandson of Lethan' in Adamnan's archaic Irish form. The unfortunate Cormac set sail on three occasions in search of 'a hermitage in the Ocean', each time without success. Columcille identified his misfortune as the consequence of divine displeasure over a member of his company of *peregrini* who was travelling without leave of his abbot. St Cormac was later to reselect his travelling companions and succeed in making his pilgrimage to the islands of Orkney, greatly assisted by Columcille's securing of his safe passage through the northern fringes of Pictland.

In a later chapter, a prophecy foretells the outcome of a similar quest for a 'desert hermitage in the sea' in the case of one Baitan of the Ui-Niath Taloirc, who will find his final resting place in the oakwoods of Derry, where sheep will be driven over his grave. There are a number of Baitans, or Bathans, associated with the islands of Shetland, but Reeves suggests the remote St Kilda as the probable landfall in this case.

The similarly named Baithene, who appears in many of Adamnan's stories, is very decidedly identifiable. The close companion and kinsman of Columcille who was to become his immediate successor as abbot of Iona, Baithene shares with Adamnan and Columcille the eminence of being the subject of a hagiographical *Life*, the *Vita Baithene*. He was also for a time the prior of the Columban monastery of *Magh Lunge* on 'the land of Eth', Adamnan's name for the Hebridean island of Tiree, 'the low-lying land of the barley'.

Baithene features in company with Berach – possibly the St Berach, founder of the church at Kilbarry – in Columcille's prophecy of a great whale in the sea-lane between Iona and Tiree. Berach is advised to reroute his journey to avoid the creature, but disregards the advice and suffers dramatic disruption of his voyage by 'a whale of marvellous and immense size' rising from the swelling waves with its fearsome jaws 'gaping full of teeth'. Baithene encounters the same denizen of the deep on the same course, but his calm self-possession in blessing the beast from the bows of his boat ensures his safe passage. We can only speculate on the precise nature of this creature, as several species of greater marine mammal have been recorded in the Hebrides, and were certainly both more numerous and more evident in Columcille's time than today. A time-honoured poetic sequence from the Gaelic, found in the *Carmina Gadelica*, suggests a variety of possible candidate species ranging from the marine biological to the awesomely mythical:

> Seven herrings,
>   Feast of salmon,
> Seven salmon,
>   Feast of seal;
> Seven seals,
>   Feast of little whale of the ocean;
> Seven little whales of the ocean,
>   Feast of large whale of the ocean;
> Seven large whales of the ocean,
>   Feast of the 'cionarain-cro';
> Seven 'cionarain-cro',
>   Feast of great beast of the ocean.

This miniature epic of the Hebridean seas was collected on Skye in the 1860s. It echoes a whole kaleidoscope of myth and legend, not least the world-serpent of the northern mythos, but the reference to the *cionarain-cro* appears on only one other occasion, when the same creature – which Carmichael likens to the kracken – is said to have been that which carried St Ronan, a contemporary of Adamnan, to his sea-girt hermitage on the remote island of North Rona.

Two other holy men, who came to prominence as superiors of Columban founda-tions, feature in later chapters of prophecy and are perhaps most usefully introduced here. Laisran, son of Feradach and a first cousin of Columcille, rose to a position of authority at Durrow, where his enthusiastic overworking of the labouring brothers incurred Columcille's generous displeasure. He was eventually to succeed Baithene and become the third abbot of Iona in 600.

Like Laisran, Ernan was a blood relative of Columcille. He was the brother of the saint's mother, Ethne, and one of the company of twelve whom Adamnan lists as sailing with him to Scotland. Ernan was appointed prior on Hinba, and Columcille's foreknowledge of his death is fulfilled in an especially poignant chapter which clearly derives from Iona tradition. Adamnan tells of crosses raised on Iona to mark the site of Ernan's passing and records one of these crosses still standing at his time of writ-ing, very probably in the place where the fifteenth-century Maclean's Cross stands today between the harbour on St Ronan's Bay and the abbey.

When Adamnan takes up the theme of foreknowledge and foretelling of the tides of battle, the 'warrior-saint' Columcille assumes very definite precedence over the 'simple and innocent' Columba. The chapters of prophecies 'concerning the clash of distant battles' carry a very resonant echo of the holy man born of a line of Celtic warlords to become the counsellor of warrior-kings.

Columcille's prophecy of the outcome of the 'battle of Ond-moin' – Ondemone in Coleraine – is dated to 563, 'two years since . . . the battle of Cul-drebene', when he was newly arrived at Conall's fortress capital of Dunadd in Argyll. This battle of 'Ond-moin' is recorded in the *Annals of Clonmacnoise* at 563 as

> the battle of Moin-Daire-Lothaire against the Cruithne
> by the Hy Neill of the north; in which seven kings
> of the Cruithne were slain, with Aedh Breac.

A similar entry in the *Annals of Ulster* is illustrated with splendidly evocative lines of battle-song:

> Sharp weapons stretch, men stretch,
> In the great bog of Daire-Lothair.

The conflict resulted from a disputed partition of territories in the Pictish domain of northern Ireland. The northern Ui-Neill were drawn into the battle fought not far from Coleraine town as allies of a chieftain of the Cruithne who claimed to have been wronged by his own people. Columcille's prophetic account of the victory, by which the Ui-Neill won more sword-land towards the east bank of the River Bann, must have been received with great interest by Conall of Dalriada. The victorious kings, Ainmure of the Cenel Connaill and Domnall and Forcus of the Cenel Eogain, had already fought side by side at the battle of Sligo and again on the field of Culdrevny. The brothers Domnall and Forcus had jointly succeeded Diarmit as High Kings after Culdrevny as Ainmure was to succeed them when they fell in battle in 569.

Columcille's foreknowledge of the fortunes of war is demonstrated again on the occasion of his spiritual intervention on behalf of Aidan in 'the battle of the Miathi'. Adamnan provides the primary documentary source on this elusive conflict and later historians are at variance on the specific battle to which his chapter refers. A. O. Anderson convincingly identifies 'the Miathi' with the *Maetae* Picts, whose territory could have extended from the region of Manau on the Forth up into the valley of the

Tay. It seems possible that Adamnan's 'battle of the Miathi' might refer to a sequence of conflicts, even a full-scale campaign fought by Aidan against southern Picts of the Manau in revolt against the ageing Brude mac-Maelchon. Annal entries recording *Cath Manand*, 'the battle of Man in which Aidan, Gabran's son was the conqueror', around 583 would suggest a probable date for the decisive victory in such a campaign.

A further battle-prophecy is recorded in one of the later chapters of this first book, but might be best introduced here. Adamnan dates this prophecy, accurately or otherwise, to the occasion of Columcille's return to Ireland for the convention at Druim Ceatt, the Ridge of Cete, in 575. The foretelling of the bloody battle of Cethirn emerges from a conversation between Columcille and St Comgell – or Comgall – of Bangor, himself one of Finnian of Clonard's Apostles of Ireland and of Cruithne stock. When water is brought to the two holy men engaged in conversation near the hillfort of Dun Cethirn, Columcille predicts a time when water from that same well will be defiled by human blood after a conflict between his own Ui-Neill and Comgell's Cruithne. The battle of the prophecy was to occur as he foretold over fifty years later in 629, when the *Annals of Ulster* record

> the battle of Dun-Ceithiran,
> in which Congal Caech fled,
> and Domnall, son of Aedh, was victor.

It is worth noting the provenance of Adamnan's story provided by the two monks of Cambas who were old enough to remember Columcille's prophecy and survived long enough to see it fulfilled as 'was foretold in our hearing many years ago'.

The hillfort of Cethirn to the north of Derry had long been a prize of war, passing from the Cruithne to the Ui-Neill and back again. Its name was taken from Cethern, an ally of the legendary Cuchulainn, and it passed first from his people to the sons of Neill. It was restored to the Cruithne after the battle of Ocha in 483 and won back by the Ui-Neill after their victory at Moin-Daire-Lothair – or Ondemone – in 563. The battle of Columcille's prophecy grew out of a complex chronicle of rivalry and regicide culminating in the slaughter of Suibnhe Meann, a king of the Cenel Eogain, by Congall Claen of the Cruithne, who was promised restoration of territories which had been seized by the Cenel Eogain at the battle of Mag-Roth. The conflict – recorded in the resonant Latin of the *Annals of Tighernach* as '*combustio regum in Dun Ceithern*' – brought the sanguinary chronicle of the fortress to a merciful close and its ancient ramparts were afterwards finally abandoned.

There is another chapter of Adamnan – 'concerning a city under Roman dominion destroyed by sulphurous fire' – which records a curiously atypical prophecy of events beyond the British Isles and might be suitably introduced here. It records Columcille's foreknowledge of divine retribution visited on an Italian city in the form of sulphurous fire and, as might be expected, the prophecy is confirmed when a ship from Gaul arrives in Kintyre bearing news from the Continent. Historical confirmation of these prophesied events is to be found in the writings of Notker Balbulus, the historian-monk of the monastery at St Gallen in Switzerland. Notker records Columcille's foretelling and helpfully identifies the city as '*Civitas Nova*', the *Alvum* of Ptolemy, on the north bank of the River Quieto in Istria.

These battles and cataclysms of ancient days have long passed beyond the mists of antiquity for the modern reader, but for Adamnan and his readers they might well have been as familiar as Ypres and Arnhem remain today.

The prophecies of the destinies of kings and sons of kings similarly concern individuals who have long been consigned to the obscurity of 'Dark Age history', but to the contemporaries of Adamnan many of those names were at least as well known as we might consider those of Alfred the Great and William the Conqueror. The intervening centuries have thus ironically revealed such prophecies of ancient monarchs and their heirs as an echo of lines in the liturgical verses of the *Altus*

Prosator, attributed to Columcille, pointing to 'the fleeing and despotic glory of kings, which endureth but a moment in the world'.

But those kings and sons of kings named in Columcille's prophecies can still be traced as historical personalities of greater or lesser prominence. Before the war against the Miathi, Aidan asked Columcille to prophesy which of his sons would succeed him. He was possibly concerned that his elder sons, or even himself, might fall in the coming conflict. Such a concern would seem to be borne out by the *Annals of Tighernach* recording 'the slaughter of the sons of Aidan . . . in the battle of Circhend'. *Circhend* has been proposed as the Howe of Mearns, once known as *Mag Circin* and located within the territory of the Maetae Picts, and may well represent a battlefield in Aidan's campaign against 'the Miathi'. Although the annals date the battle of Circhend to the latter 590s, their dates could well be inaccurate by as much as a decade and Adamnan must be the more reliable source, when he identifies two sons of Aidan – named by Tighernach as killed at Circhend – as slain in 'the battle of the Miathi', and a third falling in battle 'in the land of the Saxons', most probably in the defeat of Dalriada by Aethelfrith of Northumbria at Degsastan.

Columcille was called upon at Druim Ceatt to bless Domnall, the young son of Aid mac-Ainmure, king of the Ui-Neill. This he did, prophesying that Domnall would outlive his brothers to become a great king and die peacefully in his bed. Domnall did indeed outlive his brothers and survived the battlefields of Dun Cethirn and Mag-Roth to die the natural death of the prophecy. That was in itself extraordinary in the light of the fact that of the twelve kings who succeeded to their kingdoms between Columcille's prophecy and Domnall's death only two died in their beds.

The visit to Druim Ceatt of 575 was also – according to Adamnan – the occasion of a prophecy concerning Scandlan, a prince held hostage by Aid for refusing payment of tribute. Here, it seems, was another example of ecclesiastical guardianship of a hostage prince comparable with the case of Curnan which resulted in the battle of Culdrevny. Dr Reeves suggests that the case of Scandlan was central to the assembly of Druim Ceatt, although other authorities suggest that it was a totally separate incident. The 'Edinburgh manuscript' recension of the Old Irish *Life* includes a version of the same story in which Columcille effects the release of Scandlan, but Adamnan records only the foretelling that Scandlan would outlive King Aid and eventually rule as a king in his own right. The annals confirm the fulfilment of that prophecy when they enter the death of Aid in 598 and Scandlan's succession to his father's kingdom in Ossory seven years later in 605.

The prophecy of the death of 'two other kings' can be precisely dated to the year 572. Columcille foretold the deaths of Baitan and Echoid, who had jointly succeeded Ainmure to the High Kingship and were slain, according to the *Annals of Tighernach*, on the same day in 572. A ship putting in to the island of Lismore confirmed the prophecy which Columcille had made on *Artda-muirchol*, Adamnan's name for the Ardnamurchan peninsula.

The prophecy concerning Oingus Bronbachal, who had been driven out of his homeland and came to seek Columcille's blessing, assured that he would outlive his brothers to reign long and peacefully in his native land. It is similarly borne out in the *Annals of Ulster* at 648 by the obituary entry which identifies Oingus as a king of the *Cenel Cairpre*, a branch of the Ui-Neill in the north of Sligo.

The more ominous prophecy concerning Aid Slane, the eldest son of the High King Diarmit mac-Cerbaill, promised that he would lose his royal birthright 'through the sin of parricide' – in fact the murder of his nephew – and suffer an early death in consequence.

The *Annals of Tighernach* provide confirmation of the fulfilment of both prophecies, firstly at 600:

> the assassination of Suibhne, son of Colman Mor,
> by Aedh Slaine at Bridemh on the Suainu.

and later at 604 recording

> the murder of Aedh Slaine by Conall son of Suibhne
> on the brink of Lough Sewdy . . . from which it is said
>   'Conall slew Aedh Slaine,
>   Aedh Slaine slew Suibhne.'

The prophecies of kings and sons of kings conclude with a neatly pointed anecdote prophesying the long and illustrious reign of the British king, 'Roderc, son of Tothal, who reigned on the Rock of Clota'. Roderc – or *Rhydderch Hen* in the Welsh sources – was an historical figure of no less standing than Aidan mac-Gabran. His power base was the fortress capital on the Rock of Clota, or *Alcluith* in Bede, known today as Dumbarton Rock in the Clyde. He seems to have established his kingdom of Strathclyde in the aftermath of 'the blood-fray of Ardderyd', a savage internecine conflict of British warlords fought at Arthuret north of Carlisle and entered in the *Annales Cambriae* at 573. Although Geoffrey of Monmouth claimed that Roderc fought at Arthuret, the more reliable Nennius lists him among the four British kings who fought against 'the sons of Ida' and almost drove the Northumbrian Saxons into the sea at Lindisfarne around the year 590. Columcille's prophecy of Roderc's destiny could even be tentatively dated to the time of that campaign, when a king well into middle age might have sought the saint's foreknowledge on the eve of battle. The prophecy is certainly borne out by all the contemporary annals, traditional sources and medieval histories when they record Roderc's surviving to die in his bed in 601.

Adamnan follows this sequence of prophecies of wars and warlords with a series of chapters concerning less-celebrated, although often still historically identifiable, personalities, which offer their own historical evidence for several aspects of Columcille's world and time.

The theme of 'sins of the flesh' can be discerned in a number of prophecies, such as those where a sinful man's demise is foretold with the appended prophecy that he will die in the 'bed of a harlot'. In the case of the man who 'has committed fratricide in the manner of Cain, and incest with his own mother', Columcille sends word to the harbour that the Oedipal offender be prevented from disembarking on Iona 'that his feet may not tread the soil of this island.'

Columcille's foreknowledge of the adultery of the mother of his monk Colcu is supported by a quatrain in Oengus's tract *De Matribus Sanctorum Hiberniae*:

> Cuillenn the mother of Colga the chaste
> Was reared at Magh Ullen for a time
> By Faibhe, without charge of guilt:
> She went to Cashel straying.

Colcu, of the Ui-Fiachnach whose extensive lands lay in Galway and Mayo, believed his mother to be a woman of virtue until Columcille sent him home to confront her with her sins. This prophecy invites comparison with Christ's foreknowledge of the similar *peccatum* of the woman at the well in Samaria recorded in the fourth chapter of St John's gospel: 'Jesus said unto her, Thou hast well said, I have no husband: For thou hast five husbands; and he whom thou now hast is not thy husband.'

The prophesied retribution for the respective and related sins of Findchan, founding abbot of another monastery on Tiree which Adamnan identifies as *Artchain*, and the historically villainous Aid the Black – or *Aed Dubh* – might even seem to imply an allegation of homosexuality quite rare in the literature of hagiography. Findchan, Adamnan tells us, was possessed by 'an earthly love' for Aid and offered him not only sanctuary in his monastery but illicit ordination as a priest. Columcille prophesies ferocious retribution, firstly on Findchan whose hand had blessed Aid's ordination and was to wither in consequence; and secondly on Aid the Black who was to meet a violent end. Aid, son of Suibne, entered the annals when he slew the High King

Diarmit mac-Cerbaill in 565 in vengeance for the death of his father. He fled to Tiree in search of sanctuary from Findchan, but before 581 returned to Ireland, where he usurped the kingship of Ulster on the death of Baedan. Thus it was that Aid the Black came to suffer his own death – as Columcille had prophesied – in a boat on Lough Neagh at the hand of Baedan's son Fiachna. The *Annals of Ulster* for the year 588 contain the summary record of 'the death of Aedh Dubh, son of Suibnhe, in a ship.'

It is, perhaps, in the detail woven into his record of prophecies, which themselves range from the epic to the utterly mundane, that Adamnan sheds especial illumination on Columcille the man. One example is the sequence of prophecies concerning manuscripts and their making, of a book dropped into a water-jug, of a visitor who will knock over the inkhorn immediately on arrival, and the omission of a 'vowel I' from a freshly completed manuscript psalter. It seems that Columcille is always surrounded by books, inkhorn and vellum. Although Adamnan makes no reference to the *Cathach* psalter or the gospel book of Finnian, he certainly portrays a Columcille eminently capable of that controversial calligraphic accomplishment.

He offers numerous references to landmarks on Iona, all of them clearly evident to the modern visitor, which provide their own vivid impression of the ninth abbot of Iona setting down the prophecies of his predecessor in the very place where so many of those prophecies were uttered. When he wrote of Columcille's watching for the ship bringing Fechna the sage from Ireland from 'the top of a hill which overlooks this monastery', Adamnan himself was working in the shadow of the hill of Dun I. When he describes Columcille at work 'in his hut built on planks', he would have been writing in full view of Tor Abb, on which Columcille's abbot's cell was certainly sited.

Only a few hundred yards from Adamnan's abbot's cell, at the mid-point between the monastery and the monks' farmland on the fertile plain of the *machair*, is the place known as *Cuul-Eilne* or *Bol Ieithne*, 'Ethne's Fold', where the monks returning wearily from their labours were miraculously refreshed by the posthumous presence of Columcille's spirit. Adamnan's detailed account of this phenomenon, which had certainly become firmly established in the monastic tradition of the island by the time of his abbacy, includes a reference to the sound of the saint's voice singing a psalm. Adamnan makes more than one reference to the remarkable qualities of the voice of Columcille, most especially when singing the 'three fifties' of the psalter. The Old Irish *Life* offers a quatrain to support Adamnan's account:

> The sound of the voice of Columcille,
> Great its sweetness above all clerics.
> To the end of fifteen hundred paces,
> Though great the distance, it was clearly heard.

In the last pages of his book of prophecies, Adamnan tells of Columcille's foreknowledge of 'another matter slighter yet so delightful that . . . it ought not to go unnoticed'. This is the prophecy of 'the crane' – or more probably a heron – whose exhausted arrival on the island Columcille foretells and whose hospitable welcome he ensures. It is an appealing anecdote of holy man and wild creature to match the similar stories of St Cuthbert which Adamnan would certainly have heard in Northumbria. But this 'slighter matter' may well shroud a shrewd intent. Adamnan tells how the crane arrives from Ireland and is provided with rest and sustenance in no less measure than that provided for a human guest of the monastery. Refreshed and restored, the bird flies off with a favourable wind to carry it home to Derry. The symbolism of the homesick pilgrim would not have been lost on an Irish reader and neither would the bardic symbolism of the crane itself, a species which was frequently associated with Columcille in Irish tradition. It was, after all, his pet crane which injured the monk who came to spy on his transcription of Finnian's book.

To the druids, the crane was a bird of evil omen, and its traditional connection with Columcille might well have stemmed from an attempt at slander by association. Thus

Adamnan deftly converts any sinister symbolism of Columcille's crane into an anecdote to stand beside those of the eider duck of St Cuthbert and St Brigid's falcon of Kildare.

Adamnan offers several and various portraits of his saint throughout his three books, but perhaps nowhere does he offer quite so immediate and so intimate an impression of the historical Columcille as in this first book 'concerning his prophetic revelations . . .'

'A crane, very tired and weary after circling far through the air on buffeting winds'

A grey heron on Mull.

In the name of Jesus Christ
the preface begins

With the help of Christ, and wishing to comply with the entreaties of the brothers, I propose to describe the life of our blessed patron. At the outset I shall take care to advise all who may read it to put their trust in the reliability of the narrative and appraise the content rather than the words, which are likely to seem unpolished and of little worth. Let them remember that the Kingdom of God is grounded not in richness of rhetoric but in the flowering of faith; and let them not despise an account of profitable deeds performed with the help of God, because of some obscure names for persons, peoples or places which belong to the poor Irish tongue and are held in low esteem, I suppose, among the different tongues of foreign peoples.

I have considered that the reader should also be advised that I have omitted many facts concerning the man of blessed memory, deserving of record though they are, from a concern for brevity, and have included only a small sample to avoid wearying my readers. I also believe that everyone who reads this account will perhaps notice that rumour has published and spread abroad among the nations only very little of the great events of this blessed man's life, even in comparison with this short summary that I now set myself to write.

Now, after this first little preface, I shall begin, with God's help, at the beginning of the second to explain our superior's name.

In the name of Jesus Christ
the second preface

There was a man of venerable life and blessed memory, the father and founder of monasteries, who was given the same name as the prophet Jonah. For the Hebrew word *iona*, the Greek name *peristera* and the Latin term *columba* all alike have the meaning *dove*, though expressed in the different sounds of three different languages. It is thought that it was by divine providence that a name of such great significance was conferred on the man of God. For by the true testimony of the gospels it is revealed that the Holy Spirit came down upon the only begotten son of the eternal Father in the form of that bird called a dove. Usually, therefore, in sacred books a dove is understood allegorically to mean the Holy Spirit. Similarly in the gospel our Saviour instructed His disciples to have implanted in a pure heart the simplicity of the dove; for the dove is a simple and innocent bird. And so it was right that a simple and innocent man, who by his dove-like character made a dwelling within himself for the Holy Spirit, should be called by this name. An apt comment upon it is that saying in the Book of Proverbs: '*Better is a good name than many riches.*' Not only, then, was this superior of ours deservedly and by the gift of God adorned and enriched by this special name from the days of his infancy, but also, many circling years before the day of his birth, he was named as a son of promise in a miraculous prophecy, by the revelation of the Holy Spirit to a soldier of Christ. A stranger of British race, a holy man and a disciple of the holy Bishop Patrick, named Mauchte, made the following prophecy concerning our patron, as we know from the reliable tradition of our forefathers: 'In the last years of the world', he said, 'there will be born a son whose name Columba will become famous through all the provinces of the islands of the Ocean, and he will shed a bright light over the last years of the earth. The lands of our two monasteries, his and mine, will be separated by the distance of a single little hedge. The man will be most dear to God and of great merit in His sight.'

In describing the life and character of this our Columba I shall first set out before the reader's eyes his holy way of life, summarising it in the most concise possible language; and I shall also, to whet the appetites of my readers, record succinctly some of his miracles, which will be told more fully later in three separate books. Of these, the first will contain his prophetic revelations, the second the divine miracles wrought through him, and the third apparitions of angels and certain manifestations of celestial brightness above the man of God. No one must suppose that I shall write what is false or doubtful or uncertain about this memorable man; but let it be known that I shall set out an unequivocal account of what I have learned from the reliable tradition of trustworthy predecessors, derived either from what I could find in earlier writings or from what I learned by word of mouth by thorough questioning of trustworthy and knowledgeable elders, who told their story without hesitation.

Saint Columba, then, was born of noble parents, his father being Fedilmith, son of Fergus, and his mother Ethne, whose father's name is mac-Naue in Irish, which may be rendered 'ship's son'. In the second year after the battle of Cul-drebene, in the forty-second year of his age, Columba sailed from Ireland to Britain, wishing to become a pilgrim for Christ. Even from his boyhood he gave himself up to the Christian apprenticeship and the pursuit of wisdom, maintaining by God's gift both integrity of body and purity of soul, and while yet on earth he showed himself fit for the life of heaven. For he was angelic in countenance, refined in speech, holy in his works, and a man of excellent talents and weighty counsel. For thirty-four years, while living as an island soldier, he could not allow even a single hour to pass without devoting himself to prayer, reading, writing or some kind of work. By day and night without respite he was so engaged also in the unwearying labours of fast and vigil, that the burden of each specific task seemed beyond human capacity. And through all this he was beloved by all for the happiness that always shone in his holy face, and he was glad in the depths of his heart with the joy of the Holy Spirit.

Here begins the text of the first book
concerning his prophetic revelations

·✝·

A SUMMARY OF HIS MIRACLES

In accordance with my promise given above, I must briefly show at the outset of this work what proofs the venerable man gave of his powers.

By the power of prayer in the name of the Lord Jesus Christ he healed people suffering the affliction of a variety of diseases. Alone but for the help of God, he drove back from this island of ours, which has the primacy, countless hostile armies of demons visible to his bodily eyes, which were making war against him and beginning to inflict deadly diseases on his monastic community. He checked the raging frenzy of wild beasts, with the help of Christ, by slaying some and bravely repelling others. Surging waves, also, of mountainous size, which once rose up to a great storm, were quickly quelled and calmed by his prayer; and his own ship, in which he happened to be sailing, was then driven to its intended port when the sea was stilled. Returning after a visit of some days to the territory of the Picts, to confound the druids he hoisted a sail against the blasts of an adverse wind, and his boat put out and sped over the water as fast as if it had had a following wind. At other times also adverse winds were made favourable to voyagers through his prayers. In the same region mentioned above, he brought out of a river a white stone, which he blessed to give it healing power; and in defiance of nature it floated like an apple when dipped in water. This miracle from God was performed in the presence of King Brude and his household. In the same country also he revived the dead son of a layman and believer, which is a greater kind of miracle, and restored him alive and well to his father and mother. At another time, when he was staying as a young deacon in Ireland with the holy Bishop Findbarr, and they lacked the wine needed for the sacred mysteries, he turned pure water into real wine by the power of prayer. Moreover, a great light of celestial brightness was sometimes observed by some of the brothers on various separate occasions to be spread out above him, both in the darkness of the night and in the daylight. He was favoured also with sweet and delightful visitations of holy angels, shining in splendour. He often saw the souls of the righteous being borne by angels to highest heaven, through a revelation of the Holy Spirit; and he frequently watched other souls of the wicked being carried to hell by demons. On many occasions he foretold the future rewards, some happy, some sad, of numerous people still living in mortal flesh. In the terrifying clash of battle he obtained from God by the power of prayer defeat for some kings and victory for other rulers. This precious privilege was granted him by God, who honours all the saints, not only in this present life but also after his passing from the flesh, as to a triumphant and mighty champion.

Of this great honour, bestowed from heaven on the honourable man by the Almighty, I shall give one further example, which was shown to Oswald, the Saxon king, on the day before he made battle against Catlon, a most mighty king of the Britons. One day, after this King Oswald had pitched camp before battle and was asleep on his pillow in his tent, he saw Saint Columba in a vision, shining in the form of an angel and of such great stature that his head seemed to touch the clouds. The blessed man, revealing his own name to the king, stood in the midst of the camp and covered it with his gleaming raiment, apart from a small space at the extremity. And he spoke these words of encouragement, the same words that the Lord addressed to Joshua ben-Nun, before the crossing of the Jordan after the death of Moses, saying, 'Be strong and of a good courage. Behold I shall be with thee', and so on. Saint Columba, then, spoke these words to the king in a vision, and added, 'This coming night advance from your camp to battle. For on this occasion the Lord has granted to me that your enemies shall be put to flight and your rival Catlon be delivered into your hands, and that after the battle you shall return victorious and reign prosperously'.

After hearing these words the king awoke and told his vision to his assembled council; they were all encouraged by it, and the whole people promised to accept the faith after returning from battle, and to be baptised. For until that time the whole of that Saxon land was shrouded in the darkness of heathen ignorance, except for King Oswald himself and twelve men who were baptised with him when he was in exile among the Irish. To be brief, on that following night, as he had been instructed in the vision, King Oswald advanced from his camp to battle with a far smaller force against many thousands. As promised, he was granted by the Lord a fortunate and easy victory, and after slaying King Catlon he returned victorious from battle and was ordained by God thereafter to be supreme ruler over all of Britain. I, Adomnan, was given a sure account of this by my predecessor as abbot, Failbe, who declared that he had heard it from the mouth of King Oswald himself as he reported the vision to Abbot Segene.

There is another story that I should not omit to mention. It was through some Irish songs in praise of the blessed man and the commemoration of his name that certain laymen, though men of wicked life and guilty of bloodshed, were freed, on the night when they had sung the songs, from the hands of enemies surrounding the house where they sang. They escaped unharmed between the flames, the swords and the spears; and it was remarkable that a few of their number, who had declined to sing these chants in commemoration of the blessed man as if making light of them, were the only ones to perish in the enemies' attack. Of this miracle it was possible to produce not two or three witnesses as required by the law, but a hundred or more. For there is proof that this happened not at one place or time only: it has been found without any doubt to have occurred in the same way at various places and times in Ireland and Britain, with the same cause of deliverance. I have learned these facts for certain from people who knew in each separate district where the same miraculous event happened.

But to return to my theme: besides these miracles which this man of the Lord performed by God's gift while still living in mortal flesh, from the years of his youth he began also to be strong with the spirit of prophecy, to foretell the future, and to report distant happenings to his company, because though absent in body yet he was present in spirit, and able to discern events from afar. For as Paul says: '*He that is joined unto the Lord is one spirit*'. So also Saint Columba, the Lord's man, as he once admitted himself to a few of the brothers who questioned him closely about it, in certain observations aided by divine grace used to observe even the whole world as if gathered within a single ray of the sun, the compass of his mind miraculously widened to behold the revelation.

These examples of the holy man's powers have been related at this point in order that the reader may hunger for more and find in the brief summary a foretaste of a sweeter feast; a fuller account will be given below, with the Lord's help, in three books. At this point it seems to me to be appropriate to tell, even if out of sequence, of the prophecies which the blessed man spoke at different times about men of holiness and renown.

· † ·

OF SAINT FINTEN THE ABBOT,
SON OF TAILCHAN

Saint Finten, who later achieved great fame throughout all the churches of the Irish, maintained from his boyhood with God's help a purity of body and soul and gave himself to the study of divine wisdom. In the years of his youth he had this resolve in his heart, to leave Ireland and go to our holy Columba to live as a pilgrim. Burning with this desire, he went to a most prudent and venerable priest of his own people, an older man and a friend of his, called in Irish Columb Crag, to get some advice from him as from one of good sense. When he uncovered these thoughts to him he received from him this reply: 'I believe your desire to be devout and inspired by God. Who can forbid it and deny that you should sail across to the holy Columba?' At the same hour by chance there arrived two of Saint Columba's monks, who said, when asked about their journey, 'We have lately rowed from Britain, and have come today from the Oakwood of Calcig.' 'Is your holy father Columba well?' said Columb Crag. Bursting into tears they answered with great sorrow, 'Our patron is indeed well. In these last few days he has departed to Christ.' Hearing this, Finten, Columb and all their company bowed their faces to the ground and wept bitterly. Finten next questioned them, saying, 'Whom did he leave to succeed him?' 'Baithene,' they said, 'his foster-son.' Everyone exclaimed that it was right and proper, and Columb Crag said to Finten, 'What will you do, Finten, in view of this?' He replied, 'With the Lord's permission I shall sail out to Baithene, a holy and wise man, and if he accepts me I shall have him as my abbot.'

Then he kissed the aforementioned Columb, bade him farewell and prepared his voyage; and without delay he sailed across and arrived at the island of Iou. As yet his name was unknown in these parts, and so at first he was given hospitality as an unknown guest. The next day he sent a messenger to Baithene as he wished to talk with him face to face. Being a courteous man and accessible to strangers, Baithene ordered that he be brought to him. He was brought at once, and first, as was proper, knelt and prostrated himself on the ground. When bidden by the older saint he arose and sat down, and was questioned by Baithene, who was still in ignorance, about his people and province, his name and way of life, and the reason for his undertaking the labour of the voyage. He answered all these questions in turn and humbly begged to be accepted. When the older saint heard his guest's words and realised as he did so that this was the man of whom once before Saint Columba had prophesied, he said, 'I must indeed thank my God for your arrival, my son. But you must know this for sure, that you will not be our monk.' Hearing this, his guest was deeply saddened, and said, 'Perhaps I am unworthy and do not deserve to become your monk.' The elder then said, 'It was not, as you say, because you were unworthy that I said this. Although I would have preferred to keep you with me, yet I cannot dishonour the command of Saint Columba my predecessor, through whom the Holy Spirit prophesied about you. For one day in private he spoke words of prophecy to me alone, among which were these: "You must listen very carefully, Baithene, to these words of mine. Straight after my expected and deeply desired passing from this world to Christ, a brother from Ireland, who at present directs the years of his youth with good conduct and is being well instructed in the study of sacred literature, Finten by name, of the family of mocu-Moie and son of Tailchan, will come to you and humbly beg you to accept him and admit him to the community of the monks. But in God's foreknowledge it is not predestined that he should become the monk of any abbot: he was long since chosen by God to be the abbot of other monks and to lead souls to the Kingdom of Heaven. You shall not, therefore, keep this man with you in these islands of ours, in case you should seem to oppose even the will of God. Make known these words to him and send him back in peace to Ireland, that he may build a monastery in the land of the Lagin by the sea, and feeding Christ's flock there may bring countless souls to the country of heaven." ' Hearing this the younger saint burst into tears and gave thanks to Christ, saying, 'May Saint Columba's prophetic and miraculous foreknowledge be fulfilled in me.' In a few days he obeyed the words of the saints, and receiving a blessing from Baithene sailed across in peace to Ireland.

I had a sure account of this from a devout old priest and soldier of Christ named Oissene, son of Ernan, of the family of mocu-neth Corb. He was a monk of that same Saint Finten, son of Tailchan, and testified that he heard all the words recorded above from his lips.

· † ·

A PROPHECY OF SAINT COLUMBA CONCERNING ERNENE, SON OF CRASEN

At another time the blessed man was staying for several months in the midland part of Ireland, founding by God's will the monastery known in Irish as Dairmag, when he decided to visit the brothers who lived in the monastery of Cloin of Saint Ceran. Hearing of his arrival, they all left the fields around the monastery, and along with all who were found gathered there they followed their abbot Alither with all haste and went out from the rampart of the monastery as one man to meet Saint Columba, as if he were an angel of the Lord. They bowed their faces to the ground on seeing him, and he was kissed by them with great reverence; and they conducted him in honour to the church, singing hymns and praises. They constructed a wooden frame for the saint as he walked and had it carried by four men walking alongside him, so that the elder Saint Columba might not be troubled by the press of the brothers crowding round him.

At the same time a boy from the community, who was held in great disdain because of his looks and demeanour and had not yet found favour with his elders, came up from behind, concealing himself as well as he could, in order secretly to touch at least the hem of the cloak which the blessed man was wearing and, if possible, to do so without the saint's knowledge or perception. However, it did not escape the saint's notice, for although he could not watch what happened behind him with his bodily eyes, he perceived it with the eyes of the spirit. He suddenly stopped, therefore, and stretching his hand out behind him took hold of the boy's neck and pulled him forward and stood him in front of his face. All those who stood round him said, 'Send him away, send him away; why hold on to this wretched and disrespectful boy?' But the saint for his part brought forth from his pure heart these words of prophecy: 'Let him be, brothers, just let him be.' To the boy, who was trembling violently, he said, 'My son, open your mouth and put out your tongue.' Then at his bidding the boy, with a great shudder, opened his mouth and put out his tongue; and the saint, after stretching out his holy hand and carefully blessing it, spoke these words of prophecy: 'Although now this boy seems contemptible to you and quite without worth, yet let no one despise him on that account. For from this hour he not only will not displease you but will find great favour with you, and he will steadily grow from day to day in good conduct and in the virtues of the soul. Wisdom, too, and good sense will increase in him more and more from this day, and in this community of yours he will be a man of high achievement. His tongue also will be gifted with eloquence from God to teach the doctrine of salvation.'

This boy was Ernene, son of Crasen, who later won fame and great renown throughout all the churches of Ireland. He told all these prophetic words concerning himself, which I have recorded above, to Abbot Segene, while my predecessor Failbe, who was also with Segene, was listening with close attention. It was Failbe who revealed and made known to me this account that I have given.

There were many other prophecies that the saint uttered by the revelation of the Holy Spirit during these days when he was a guest in the monastery of Cloin. They concerned the dispute which arose many days later between the churches of Ireland because of the lack of uniformity in the keeping of Easter, and certain angelic visitations which were revealed to him and which were occurring at that time within the walls of the same monastery.

· † ·

OF THE ARRIVAL OF SAINT CAINNECH THE ABBOT WHICH SAINT COLUMBA PROPHETICALLY FORETOLD

At another time in the island of Iou, one day when there was a violent storm and waves of daunting height, the saint was sitting indoors and giving instructions to the brothers. 'Prepare the guest-house quickly,' he said, 'and draw water to wash the visitors' feet.' One of the brothers then said, 'Who can cross the Sound in safety, narrow though it is, on so stormy and perilous a day as this?' At this the saint declared, 'In spite of the storm the Almighty has granted a calm to a holy and elect man who will arrive among us before evening.' And, behold, after a while that same day the ship carrying Saint Cainnech for which the brothers had waited arrived according to the saint's prophecy. The saint went to meet him with the brothers and gave him a respectful and hospitable welcome. The sailors who were on board with Cainnech were questioned by the brothers about the nature of their voyage, and they replied, just as Saint Columba had earlier foretold, that by God's gift both a storm and a calm had occurred on the same sea and at the same time, but miraculously separated; and they declared that, though they had seen the storm in the distance, they had not felt it.

Codex Durmachensis

Of the three great gospel books of the 'insular' school, it is the Book of Durrow which offers the most impressive evidence of Columban association. That evidence is to be found in its colophon, the dedicatory 'signature' paragraph to which the palaeographer first looks for evidence of the origin and provenance of a manuscript.

> I pray you, blessed Patrick, holy priest, that whoever holds this little book in his hand may be mindful of Columba the writer. I wrote this gospel during the space of twelve days.

The calligraphy, design and, above all, the magnificent illumination of this earliest of the three great gospel books is clearly more than the accomplishment of twelve days. Thus the colophon cannot apply to the book in which it is inscribed and must refer instead to the exemplar from which it was copied. The text of the Book of Durrow is, with only occasional lapses, that of the Vulgate of St Jerome, the same gospel text which Columcille traditionally transcribed from the 'book of Finnen', which presents the dramatic possibility that the Book of Durrow is a splendidly decorated transcription of a gospel book in Columcille's hand. To investigate that possibility, it is necessary to trace the *Codex Durmachensis* back through its ascertainable history into the speculative realm of its origin.

It has been in the care of the library of Trinity College, Dublin, since the seventeenth century. It was brought to Trinity College from the monastery at Durrow where it had been housed since at least the end of the eleventh century. Yet virtually all expert opinion confirms that it was written in the scriptorium on Lindisfarne. The eminent palaeographer E. A. Lowe describes its 'expert calligraphic majuscule' as 'written in Northumbria by a hand trained in the Irish manner, and copied from an exemplar in the hand of St Columba'. Any hypothesis, however learned, as to how a Lindisfarne gospel book became 'the Book of Durrow' can only be speculative and I would offer the following scenario.

It is quite possible that Columcille might have transcribed the Vulgate of St Finnian in the form of a small personal gospel within the space of twelve days. Such a manuscript would have been prized as an eminent relic on Iona, and when Aidan came to Northumbria in 635 his mission to so powerful a kingdom would have been of quite sufficient importance for him to bring the gospel of Columcille with him as a fitting token of that standing. The official date of the Book of Durrow is 675, but there is no reason why that quite notional date should not be brought forward by at least a decade, which would still leave us with a seventh-century manuscript of a sixth-century text, but would place the making of the book in the years immediately before the Council of Whitby. There is evidence in the portrait on folio 12^v (see page 71) of a man – the symbol of Matthew – in a robe vividly reminiscent of the vision of Ethne and wearing the Celtic tonsure. Such a portrait cannot be a product of a post-Whitby scriptorium in Northumbria. But when Bishop Colman left Lindisfarne in 664 with his company of Irish and English adherents of the Celtic orthodoxy, he carried the relics of his monastery back to Iona. Amongst them he would surely have included any Columban manuscripts and illuminated transcriptions thereof. Thus when the Viking onslaught of the ninth century placed island communities at hazard, the book would have been carried on to the Irish mainland to find sanctuary in the Columban church at Dairmag to become the Book of Durrow.

'Christi Autem' – the *chi-rho-iota* monogram: f. 23^r

The Book of Durrow, Trinity College Library, Dublin: MS A.4.5

nuit iacob iacob autem genuit io
seph uirum mariae de qua na
tus est ihs qui uocatur xpi ~

OMNES ERGO GENERATIONES ab ra
cham usque ad dauid generationes
xiiii et a dauid usque ad trans mig
rationem babilonis generation
es xiiii et a trans migratione babi
lonis usque ad xpm generationes
xiiii

XPi AUTEM generatio sic erat
cum esset et despon
sata mater eius mariae io
seph ante quam conuenirent in
uentaes in utero habens de spu
sco ~

IOSEPh autem uir eius cum esset
iustus et nollet eam traducere
uoluit occulte dimittere eam

·✝·

OF THE PERIL TO THE BISHOP SAINT COLMAN MOCU-SAILNI IN THE SEA NEAR THE ISLAND CALLED RECHRU

Another day, similarly, when Saint Columba was staying in his mother church, he suddenly cried out with a smile, 'Colman, son of Beogna, has set sail to visit us but is in great danger now in the seething waves of the whirlpool of Brecan. He sits on the prow with both hands raised towards heaven, and blesses the raging and fearsome sea. However, the Lord terrifies him not that the ship in which he sits may capsize and be overwhelmed by the waves, but rather that he may be roused to more fervent prayer and reach us with God's favour after passing through the danger.'

·✝·

OF CORMAC

At another time also Saint Columba prophesied as follows concerning Cormac, grandson of Lethan, a holy man, who on no less than three occasions toiled in search of a desert hermitage in the Ocean, but without finding one. 'Once again today,' he said, 'Cormac sets sail in search of a desert hermitage, from the district called Eirros-domno which lies across the River Mod. But not even on this occasion will he find what he seeks, and for no other fault of his but that he has wrongly taken with him as companion on the voyage a monk of a devout abbot, who departed without the abbot's permission.'

·✝·

A PROPHECY OF THE BLESSED MAN CONCERNING THE CLASH OF DISTANT BATTLES

After two years had passed, according to our information, since the battle of Cul-drebene, at the time when the blessed man first set sail from Ireland to become a pilgrim, one day, at the same hour as the battle of Ond-moin, as it is called in Irish, was fought in Ireland, the same man of God while living in Britain gave a full account in the presence of King Conall, son of Comgell, both of the fighting of the battle and of those kings to whom the Lord gave victory over their enemies. The names of the kings were Ainmure, son of Setne, and two sons of mac-Erce, Domnall and Forcus. The saint also prophesied in similar fashion of how the king of the Cruithni, who was called Echoid Laib, was defeated but escaped sitting in a chariot.

·†·

OF THE BATTLE OF THE MIATHI

At another time, when many years had passed since the battle mentioned above, the holy man was on the island of Iou when he said suddenly to his attendant Diormit, 'Ring the bell.' Summoned by its sound, the brothers ran quickly to the church, led by their holy superior himself. Kneeling down there he said to them, 'Let us now pray earnestly to the Lord for this people and for King Aidan. For at this hour they go into battle.' After a little while he left the oratory and, looking into the sky, said, 'Now the barbarians are put to flight; and to Aidan has been granted victory indeed, but an unhappy victory.' Moreover, the blessed man told prophetically of the number of those killed from Aidan's army, three hundred and three men.

·†·

A PROPHECY OF SAINT COLUMBA CONCERNING THE SONS OF KING AIDAN

At another time before the above-mentioned battle the saint asked King Aidan about the succession to the throne. When he replied that he did not know which of his three sons, Artuir, Echoid Find, or Domingart, would be king, the saint then spoke as follows: 'None of these three will be king, for they will fall in battle, slain by their enemies. But now, if you have others who are younger, let them come to me, and the one whom the Lord has chosen from them to be king will at once rush upon my lap.' When they were called, Echoid Buide, in accordance with the saint's word, came and rested on his lap. At once the saint blessed and kissed him; and he said to his father, 'This is the one who will survive and reign as king after you, and his sons will reign after him.' All these things came to pass afterwards in their own time, in complete fulfilment of his words. For Artuir and Echoid Find not long after were slain in the battle of the Miathi mentioned above. Domingart was routed in battle and killed in the land of the Saxons. And Echoid Buide succeeded to the throne after his father.

·†·

OF DOMNALL, SON OF AID

Domnall, son of Aid, while yet a boy, was brought to Saint Columba by his foster-parents on the Ridge of Cete. He looked at the boy and asked, 'Whose son is this that you have brought?' They replied, 'This is Domnall, son of Aid; he has been brought to you that he may return enriched by your blessing.' The saint blessed him, and at once said, 'He will outlive all his brothers, and become a most famous king. And he will never be delivered into the hands of his enemies, but will die a peaceful death in old age, on his own bed and in his own home, amid a throng of close friends.' All these things were truly fulfilled in accordance with the blessed man's prophecy concerning him.

Carpet-page: f. 3ᵛ.

The Book of Durrow, Trinity College Library, Dublin: MS A.4.5.

·†·

OF SCANDLAN, SON OF COLMAN

At the same time and place the saint went to visit Scandlan, son of Colman, who was held in prison by King Aid; and, after blessing him, he said to comfort him, 'My son, do not be downcast, but rather be glad and take heart. For King Aid by whom you are imprisoned will leave the world before you, and after some period of exile you will reign as king among your people for thirty years. You will be driven out from the kingdom a second time, and live some days in exile, after which you will be recalled by the people and reign for three short seasons.'

All of this was completely fulfilled according to the saint's prophecy. For after thirty years he was expelled from the kingdom and lived for a period of time in exile; but later he was recalled by the people and reigned, not for three years, as he thought, but for three months, and immediately afterwards he died.

·†·

A PROPHECY OF THE BLESSED MAN CONCERNING TWO OTHER KINGS, BAITAN, SON OF MAC-ERCE, AND ECHOID, SON OF DOMNALL, WHO WERE CALLED THE GRANDSONS OF MUIREDACH

At another time while travelling through a rough and rocky district named Artda-muirchol, he heard his companions, Laisran, son of Feradach, and Diormit, his attendant, conversing on the way about the two kings mentioned above. He addressed these words to them: 'My little children, why do you talk of these men in this idle fashion? For both these kings about whom you are now conversing were lately beheaded by their enemies and have perished. And this very day some sailors will arrive from Ireland who will give you the same account of these kings.' On the same day voyagers arriving from Ireland, at the place called Muirbolc of Paradise, reported to his two above-named companions, now sailing with the saint in the same ship, that the venerable man's prophecy concerning the slaying of these kings had been fulfilled.

·†·

A PROPHECY OF THE HOLY MAN CONCERNING OINGUS, SON OF AID COMMAN

This man was driven out of his country with two brothers and came in exile to the saint, who was on pilgrimage in Britain. Blessing him, he brought forth from his holy breast these words of prophecy concerning him: 'This young man will survive the death of all his brothers and will reign for a long time in his native land, and his enemies will fall before him. But he himself will never be delivered into his enemies' hands, but will die a peaceful death in old age among his friends.' All these things were completely fulfilled according to the saint's word. This was Oingus whose surname was Bronbachal.

·†·

A PROPHECY OF THE BLESSED MAN CONCERNING KING DIORMIT'S SON, WHO WAS NAMED AID SLANE IN THE IRISH TONGUE

At another time when the blessed man was staying for some days in Ireland, he prophesied as follows when visited by Aid, mentioned above: 'You must take care, my son, not to lose, through the sin of parricide, the prerogative of sovereignty over the whole kingdom of Ireland predestined to you by God. For if ever you commit that sin, you will enjoy not the whole of your father's kingdom but some part of it, among your own race and for only a short time.' These words of the saint were thus fulfilled in accordance with his prophecy. For after Suibne, son of Colman, was treacherously killed by him, it is said that he governed a part of the kingdom that was conceded to him for no more than four years and three months.

·†·

A PROPHECY OF THE BLESSED MAN CONCERNING KING RODERC, SON OF TOTHAL, WHO REIGNED ON THE ROCK OF CLOTA

At another time this man, as he was a friend of the saint, sent Lugbe mocu-Min to him on a secret mission, wishing to know whether or not he was to be slain by his enemies. Now when Lugbe was questioned by the saint concerning the king and his kingdom and people, he answered as if in pity, 'Why do you ask of that unhappy man, who has no means of knowing at what hour he may be killed by his enemies?' The saint then declared, 'He will never be delivered into the hands of his enemies, but will die in his own home on his own feather pillow.' This prophecy of the saint concerning King Roderc was completely fulfilled; for according to his word he died a peaceful death in his own home.

·†·

A PROPHECY OF THE SAINT CONCERNING TWO BOYS, ONE OF WHOM, ACCORDING TO THE SAINT'S WORD, DIED AT THE END OF A WEEK

At another time two laymen came to the saint while he was living on the island of Iou. One of them, named Meldan, asked the saint concerning his son, who was present, as to what would become of him. The saint spoke to him as follows: 'Is not today the Sabbath day? Your son will die on Friday at the end of the week; and on the eighth day, that is the Sabbath, he will be brought here and buried.' Then the other layman also, named Glasderc, asked a similar question concerning his son, whom he had there with him, and he received from the saint this reply: 'Your son Ernan will see his own grandsons, and will be buried in old age on this island.' All these things were completely fulfilled in their time in accordance with the saint's word concerning the two boys.

·✝·

A PROPHECY OF THE SAINT CONCERNING COLCU, SON OF AID DRAIGNICHE, OF THE RACE OF FECHRE, AND CONCERNING A SECRET SIN OF HIS MOTHER

At another time the saint asked Colcu, mentioned above, who was living with him on the island of Iou, whether his mother was a devout woman or not. He said in reply, 'I know my mother to be of good character and good reputation.' The saint then spoke prophetically as follows: 'Soon, God willing, set out for Ireland, and question your mother closely about a great sin of hers that she keeps secret and is unwilling to confess to anyone.' On hearing this, he obediently left for Ireland. His mother when earnestly questioned by him at first denied it but then confessed her sin; and she was cleansed by doing penance in accordance with the saint's judgement, and was greatly astonished at what had been revealed to the saint concerning her.

Colcu returned to the saint, and while spending some days with him he questioned him about the end of his own life, and received from the saint this reply: 'In your own land, which you love, you will be for many years head of a church. And if by chance you see your butler one day making merry at a meal with friends and swinging the wine-jug round by its neck, you must know that soon after you will die.' And to be brief, this prophecy of the blessed man was fulfilled in all respects, just as it was spoken concerning Colcu.

·✝·

OF LAISRAN THE GARDENER, A HOLY MAN

One day the blessed man ordered one of his monks, named Trenan, of the family mocu-Runtir, to depart for Ireland as his emissary. In obedience to the man of God's command, he quickly prepared to sail; and he complained in the saint's presence that he lacked one of the crew. In reply to him the saint brought forth these words from his holy breast: 'I cannot at present find the sailor who you say has not yet appeared. Go in peace. You will have fair and following winds all the way till you reach Ireland. And you will see a man who will run from afar to meet you, who will be the first of all to hold on to the prow of your ship in Ireland. He will be a companion on your journey in Ireland for some days, and when you return to us from there he will accompany you. He is a man chosen by God, and in this monastery of mine he will live a good life for the remainder of his time on earth.'

To be brief, Trenan received the saint's blessing and sailed over all the sea with full sails. And behold, as the ship approached the harbour Laisran mocu-Moie ran faster than the rest to meet it, and held on to the prow. The sailors recognised that he was the very man of whom the saint had prophesied.

$\cdot \dagger \cdot$

HOW THE SAINT SPOKE WITH FOREKNOWLEDGE CONCERNING A GREAT WHALE

One day when the venerable man was staying on the island of Iou, a brother named Berach, who was proposing to sail to the island of Eth, came to the saint in the morning and asked to be blessed by him. The saint looked at him and said, 'My son, take special care today not to try to cross the open sea in a straight course to the land of Eth, but instead make your voyage around the smaller islands, in case you should be terrified by an enormous monster and hardly be able to escape from there.' He departed after receiving the saint's blessing, boarded his ship, and sailed across as if making light of the saint's word. Then, while passing over the wide expanse of the sea of Eth, he and the sailors on board looked and behold, a whale of marvellous and immense size rose up like a mountain and opened its jaws, gaping full of teeth, as it swam on the surface. Then they let down the sail in great terror and rowed back, and were hardly able to escape from the surging waves created by the beast's movements. And they recalled and marvelled at the saint's prophetic word.

On the morning of the same day also the saint told Baithene, who was about to sail to the aforementioned island, about the same whale, saying, 'Last night at midnight a great whale rose up from the depths of the sea, and it will emerge on to the surface today between the islands of Iou and Eth.' Baithene said in reply to him, 'That beast and I are under God's power.' 'Go in peace,' said the saint, 'your faith in Christ will defend you from this peril.' Baithene then received a blessing from the saint and sailed from the harbour, and after crossing a large stretch of the ocean he and his companions saw the whale. While they were all terrified, he alone was without fear, and he raised both his hands and blessed the sea and the whale; and at the same moment the great beast plunged beneath the waves and nowhere afterwards appeared to them.

$\cdot \dagger \cdot$

A PROPHECY OF THE SAINT CONCERNING ONE BAITAN, WHO SAILED WITH THE OTHERS IN SEARCH OF A DESERT PLACE IN THE SEA

At another time a certain Baitan, of the race of nia-Taloirc, asked to be blessed by the saint before going to search with others for a desert hermitage in the sea. Bidding him farewell, the saint uttered this word of prophecy concerning him: 'This man, who is going to search for a desert hermitage in the ocean, will not lie at rest in a desert place, but will be buried in that place where a woman will drive sheep across his grave.'

The same Baitan travelled far over the windy seas without finding a desert before returning to his own country and remaining there many years as head of a small church, which in Irish is called Lathreg-inden. After some time he died and was buried in the

St Matthew symbol page: f. 21ᵛ.

The Book of Durrow, Trinity College Library, Dublin: MS A.4.5.

Oakwood of Calcig; and it happened during these days that owing to an enemy attack the neighbouring people with their women and children took refuge in the church there. So it came about that one day a woman was observed driving her sheep over the grave of this man, soon after his burial. And one of those who had seen it, a holy priest, said, 'Now Saint Columba's prophecy, delivered many years ago, has been fulfilled.' It was this priest that I have mentioned who gave me this account of Baitan, and his name was Mailodran, a soldier of Christ, of the family mocu-Curin.

· † ·

A PROPHECY OF THE HOLY MAN CONCERNING NEMAN, A PRETENDED PENITENT

At another time the saint came to the island of Hinba; and on the same day he gave orders that even the penitents should be allowed some indulgence in respect of their food. Now there was among the penitents there one Neman, son of Cather, who when bidden by the saint refused to accept the concession offered to him. The saint addressed him with these words: 'Neman, you do not accept the indulgence in diet which Baithene and I have granted. The time will come when in the company of thieves in a wood you will eat the flesh of a stolen mare.' And this same man afterwards returned into the world and was found, according to the saint's word, in woodland with thieves eating flesh of that kind taken from a wooden griddle.

· † ·

OF AN UNFORTUNATE MAN WHO SLEPT WITH HIS OWN MOTHER

At another time the saint woke up the brothers at dead of night, and when they were assembled in the church he said to them, 'Let us now pray earnestly to the Lord. For at this hour a sin unheard of in this world has been committed, for which the punishment ordained is greatly to be feared.' The next day he told a few of them who asked him about this sin, saying, 'After a few months that unfortunate wretch, accompanied in all ignorance by Lugaid, will arrive at the island of Iou.'

So one day after some months had passed, the saint spoke to Diormit with these instructions: 'Get up quickly. See, Lugaid is approaching. Tell him to send to Male the unhappy man whom he has with him in the ship, so that his feet may not tread the soil of this island.' In obedience to the saint's command he went to the sea and repeated to Lugaid on his arrival all the saint's words about the unfortunate man. On hearing them, the wretch swore never to take food with others unless he could first see Saint Columba and speak to him. Diormit went back and reported his words to the saint, whereupon the saint made for the harbour. When Baithene, citing the authority of holy scripture, proposed that the unhappy man's repentance be accepted, the saint then said, 'Baithene, this man has committed fratricide in the manner of Cain, and incest with his own mother.'

Then the wretched man knelt upon the shore and promised to comply with the terms of penance in accordance with the saint's judgement. The saint said to him, 'If for twelve years you do penance among the Britons, with tears of lamentation, and do not return to Ireland as long as you live, perhaps God may pardon your sin.' With these words, the saint turned to his company and said, 'This man is a son of perdition. He will not fulfil the penance which he promised but will soon return to Ireland, and there in a short time he will perish, slain by his enemies.' All these things happened just as the saint prophesied. For the wretched man returned to Ireland about that time, and fell into the hands of his enemies in the district named Le and was murdered. He was of the race of Turtre.

OF THE VOWEL I

One day Baithene came to the saint and said, 'I need one of the brothers to go over with me and correct the psalter that I have copied.' On hearing this the saint spoke as follows: 'Why do you give us this trouble for no reason? For in this psalter of yours of which you speak not one letter will be found to be added nor any to be missing, except the vowel *I* which alone is missing.' And just so, when the entire psalter was read through, what the saint had foretold was found to be true.

OF A BOOK WHICH FELL INTO A WATER-JAR AS THE SAINT HAD FORETOLD

One day similarly, while he was sitting by the hearth in the monastery, he saw Lugbe, of the family mocu-Min, some distance away reading a book. Suddenly he said to him, 'Take care, my son, take care. I believe that the book you are reading is going to fall into a jar full of water.' And this presently happened. For after a little while that young man stood up to carry out some duty in the monastery, forgetful of the blessed man's word, and the book which he carelessly put under his arm fell into a pitcher full of water.

OF AN INKHORN FOOLISHLY UPSET

On another day also there was a shout across the Sound of the island of Iou. The saint heard the shouting while sitting in his hut built on planks, and said, 'The man who is shouting across the Sound is a man of no fine perception; for today he will upset my inkhorn and spill the ink.' Hearing this, his attendant Diormit stood and waited a little while before the door for the tiresome guest to arrive, so as to protect the inkhorn. But he soon withdrew from there on other business; and after his withdrawal the troublesome guest appeared, and in his eagerness to kiss the saint upset the inkhorn with the hem of his cloak and spilled the ink.

Carpet-page: f. 192^v.

The Book of Durrow, Trinity College Library, Dublin: MS A.4.5.

OF THE ARRIVAL OF A GUEST WHICH THE SAINT HAD FORETOLD

At another time similarly, on a Tuesday, the saint spoke to the brothers as follows: 'Tomorrow, being Wednesday, we propose to fast. However, a troublesome guest will appear and our customary fast will be broken.' This happened just as it had been revealed beforehand to the saint. For on the Wednesday of that week in the morning there was another stranger, Aidan by name, son of Fergno, shouting across the Sound; he was a most devout man, and is said to have been for twelve years attendant to Brenden mocu-Alti. His arrival broke that day's fast, according to the saint's word.

· † ·

OF A MAN IN DISTRESS WHO SHOUTED ACROSS THE AFOREMENTIONED SOUND

One day also the saint heard someone shouting across the Sound, and spoke in this fashion: 'That man who is shouting is greatly to be pitied, coming to us to seek what will heal the flesh. It were better for him to show true repentance for his sins today, for at the end of this week he will die.' Those who were present reported this saying to the unhappy man on his arrival, but he made light of it and quickly departed after receiving what he had asked for; and in accordance with the saint's prophetic word he died before the end of that week.

· † ·

A PROPHECY OF THE SAINT CONCERNING A CITY, UNDER ROMAN DOMINION, DESTROYED BY SULPHUROUS FIRE WHICH FELL FROM HEAVEN

At another time similarly Lugbe, of the family mocu-Min, whom I have mentioned before, came to the saint one day after the threshing of the corn, but was unable to look upon his face, which was strangely flushed; and he quickly made away in great alarm. The saint called him back by clapping his hands lightly. On his return he was at once asked by the saint why he had made away so fast, and gave this answer: 'I ran away because I was extremely frightened.' After a little pause he became more confident and was bold enough to question the saint, saying, 'Has some fearful vision been revealed to you in this hour?' The saint gave him this reply: 'So dreadful a retribution has just now been taken in a distant part of the world.' 'What kind of vengeance,' said the young man, 'and in what region?' The saint then spoke as follows: 'A sulphurous flame has poured forth from the sky in this hour over a city under Roman dominion within the bounds of Italy, and about three thousand men, apart from mothers and children, have perished. And before the present year ends Gallic sailors will arrive from the provinces of Gaul and report these same things to you.'

After some months these words were proved to have been truly spoken. For when Lugbe together with the saint went to the capital of the kingdom, he questioned the captain and sailors of a ship that arrived, and heard all these prophecies of the memorable man, concerning the city and its citizens, confirmed by them.

· † ·

A Vision of the Blessed Man concerning Laisran, son of Feradach

One very cold day in winter the saint wept, troubled by a great sorrow. His attendant Diormit asked him the cause of his sadness and received this reply from him: 'It is not without good reason, my little son, that I grieve at this hour, when I see my monks, already wearied with heavy toil, being burdened by Laisran in the construction of a large building. It gives me great displeasure.' Wonderful to tell, at the same moment Laisran, who was living in the monastery of the Oakwood Plain, felt a mysterious prompting and the kindling of an inward fire, and ordered the monks to stop their work and some food to be prepared to refresh them; and he told them not only to be at leisure on that day, but also to rest during any other days of severe weather. When the saint heard in his spirit these words of comfort spoken to the brothers by Laisran, he stopped weeping and became wonderfully happy, and while on the island of Iou he told the whole story to the brothers who were there at the time; and he blessed Laisran, the monks' comforter.

· † ·

How Fechna, a sage, came as a penitent to Saint Columba, as foretold by him

At another time the saint was sitting on the top of a hill which overlooks this monastery of ours at a distance, when he turned to his attendant Diormit and said, 'There is a ship from Ireland bringing a sage who fell into wrongdoing but will soon be here in tearful repentance. I wonder why it approaches so slowly.' After no long space of time his attendant, looking out towards the south, saw the sail of a ship approaching the harbour. When he pointed out its approach to the saint he quickly stood up, saying, 'Let us go to meet the stranger whose sincere repentance Christ accepts.'

Now when Fechna left the ship he ran to meet the saint as he came to the harbour. With tears of grief he knelt at his feet and cried most bitterly; and he confessed his sins before all those who were there. The saint, no less tearful, then said to him, 'Stand up, my son, and take heart. Your sins that you have committed are forgiven. For as it is written: *"A humble and contrite heart God doth not despise"*.' He stood up and was gladly received by the saint, and some days later was sent off to Baithene, who at that time lived as prior in the Plain of Long; and he went in peace.

·✝·

A PROPHECY OF THE HOLY MAN CONCERNING CAILTAN, HIS MONK

At another time he sent two monks to another monk of his named Cailtan, who was then prior in a monastery beside the lake of the River Aub, which is called even today after his brother Diun; and the saint sent these words by those messengers: 'Go quickly and make haste to Cailtan, and tell him to come to me without any delay.' In obedience to the saint's word they went out and came to the monastery of Diun, where they informed Cailtan of the nature of their mission. At the same hour without any delay he followed the saint's emissaries and accompanied them on their way, and came quickly to him on the island of Iou. Seeing him, the saint spoke as follows and addressed him with these words: 'Cailtan, you have done well to obey and make haste to me; rest for a while. I sent my invitation to you, loving you as a friend, that you may finish your life's course here with me in true obedience. For before the end of this week you will pass in peace to the Lord.' Hearing this, he gave thanks to God, kissed the saint tearfully, and after receiving his blessing went to the guest-house. And the following night he became ill and, according to the saint's word, departed to Christ the Lord that same week.

·✝·

THE SAINT'S PROPHETIC FORESIGHT CONCERNING TWO BROTHERS WHO WERE PILGRIMS

One Lord's day there was a shout across the Sound which I have often mentioned. Hearing the shout, the saint said to the brothers who were with him, 'Go quickly, and bring to us with all speed the pilgrims, who come from a distant land.' They obeyed at once, crossed the Sound and brought the guests. The saint kissed them and then asked the reason for their journey. They said in reply, 'We have come to be pilgrims with you this year.' The saint gave them this reply, 'You will not be able to be pilgrims with me, as you say, for the space of a year, unless you first take the monastic vow.' Those who were present were most surprised that this should be said to guests who had arrived that same hour. The older brother replied to the saint's words, 'Though we have had no such intention until this hour, yet we shall follow your counsel, divinely inspired as we believe it to be.'

To be brief, at the same moment they entered the oratory with the saint and knelt and devoutly took the monastic vow. The saint then turned to the brothers, and said, 'These two strangers, offering themselves as a living sacrifice to God, and fulfilling in a short time a long period of service as Christ's soldiers, will soon this same month pass in peace to Christ the Lord.' Hearing this, both brothers gave thanks to God and were taken to the guest-house. After an interval of seven days the older brother began to be ill, and at the completion of the same week he departed to the Lord. Similarly the other also, after seven more days, became ill, and at the end of the same week passed happily to the Lord. And so in accordance with the saint's true prophecy both ended this present life within the limit of that same month.

· † ·

A PROPHECY OF THE HOLY MAN CONCERNING A CERTAIN ARTBRANAN

While staying for some days on the island of Sci, the blessed man struck with his staff a little plot of ground in a place near the sea, saying to his companions, 'Wonderful to tell, my little sons, on this little plot of ground today an aged heathen, who has preserved a natural goodness throughout all his life, will be baptised, and will die and be buried.' And behold, after an interval of about one hour a boat arrived at that harbour, bringing on its prow a decrepit old man, the leader of the cohort of Geona. Two young men lifted him from the ship, and set him down before the blessed man's eyes. He at once received the word of God from the saint through an interpreter, and believed and was baptised by him. And after the service of baptism was completed, he at once died in the same place, as the saint had prophesied, and his companions buried him there, constructing a cairn of stones. This can be seen on the sea-coast even today. The river at that place in which he had received baptism is called after him to the present day, and is known to the local people as the '*dobur* of Artbranan'.

· † ·

OF A BOAT MOVED IN THE NIGHT BY THE ORDER OF THE SAINT

At another time when journeying across the Spine of Britain, the saint discovered a hamlet among deserted fields and made his lodging there by the bank of a stream which flows into a lake. The same night, when his companions were just tasting their first sleep, he woke them up, saying, 'Quickly, quickly now, go out and bring here at once our boat which you put in a house across the stream, and put it in a hut closer at hand.' They at once obeyed and did as he ordered them. When they were at rest again, the saint after a while quietly tapped Diormit and said, 'Stand outside the house now and see what is happening in that hamlet where you first put your boat.' In obedience to the saint's command he went out of the house and looked back, and saw the whole village being consumed by ravaging flames; and he returned to the saint and reported what was happening there. The saint then told the brothers about a vengeful persecutor, who had set fire to those houses that same night.

·†·

OF GALLAN, SON OF FACHTNE, WHO WAS IN THE PROVINCE OF COLCU, SON OF CELLACH

One day similarly when the saint was sitting in his hut, he prophesied to this Colcu, who was next to him reading: 'At this moment demons are dragging away to hell one of the principal men of your province, an avaricious person.' Now when Colcu heard this he wrote down the day and the hour on his writing tablet, and on returning to his country a few months later he discovered by questioning the people of that locality that Gallan, son of Fachtne, had died at the same moment as the blessed man had told him he had been dragged away by demons.

·†·

A PROPHECY OF THE BLESSED MAN CONCERNING FINDCHAN, A PRIEST, THE FOUNDER OF THE MONASTERY, CALLED IN IRISH ARTCHAIN, IN THE LAND OF ETH

At another time the priest Findchan, mentioned above, a soldier of Christ, took with him from Ireland to Britain Aid, surnamed the Black, a man of royal birth and by race a Cruithnian, who wore the clerical habit and proposed to stay for some years with Findchan in his monastery as a pilgrim. This Aid the Black had been a most bloodthirsty man and had murdered many people; he had even killed Diormit, son of Cerball, who by God's will had been ordained king of all Ireland. After this Aid, then, had spent some time in pilgrimage, the bishop was summoned and he was improperly ordained priest in the monastery of the aforementioned Findchan. The bishop, however, did not dare to lay his hand upon his head unless Findchan, who had an earthly love for Aid, first put his own right hand on his head as confirmation. When the nature of this ordination was afterwards reported to the holy man, he was vexed, and thereupon pronounced this dreadful judgement on Findchan and the ordained Aid: 'That right hand, which Findchan, in violation of divine law and the law of the Church, placed upon the head of a son of perdition, will soon rot, and after great agonies of pain will go before him into the earth to be buried. He himself will survive after his hand is buried, and will live for many years. Aid, who was undeservedly ordained, will return like a dog to his vomit. He will again become a bloody murderer, and finally, pierced by a spear, will fall from wood into water and sink to his death. Such an end has long been due to him, who slew the king of all Ireland.'

The blessed man's prophecy was fulfilled concerning them both. For the priest Findchan's right hand rotted in his lifetime and went before him into the earth, buried on the island called Ommon. He himself in accordance with Saint Columba's word lived for many years afterwards. Aid the Black, a priest in name only, reverted to his former crimes, was treacherously transfixed by a spear, and fell from the prow of a boat into the water of a lake, where he perished.

How monks wearied on their way received comfort from the saint's spirit

Among these memorable revelations of the spirit of prophecy it seems to the purpose to record also in my little book the spiritual comfort which was once felt by the monks of Saint Columba when his spirit met them on their journey.

For on one occasion, when the brothers were returning in the evening to the monastery after the work of harvesting, and came to the place called in Irish Cuul-Eilne – a place said to be midway between the little western plain of the island of Iou and our monastery – each of them privately felt a strange and unfamiliar sensation, but they did not venture to tell each other. And they experienced this for several days in the same place and at the same hour of the evening. Now during these days their tasks were assigned to them by Saint Baithene, and one day he spoke to them as follows: 'Now, brothers, you must confess one by one if you experience an unfamiliar and wondrous feeling at this place midway between the harvest and the monastery.' An elder among them then said, 'In accordance with your command I shall tell you what was revealed to me here. During the past few days, and even now, I have been sensing a perfume of wonderful fragrance, as if all the flowers in the world were gathered together in one place, also a kind of fiery glow, not painful but of a pleasurable sort; and, moreover, a strange and incomparable delight floods my heart, which at once brings wonderful comfort to me and so gladdens me that I forget all sorrow and all weariness. Furthermore, the burden that, heavy though it is, I carry on my back, is made so light – I know not how – from this place until we reach the monastery, that I do not feel myself burdened.'

In short, all those reapers declared of themselves one by one that they had felt exactly as one of them had openly described. And they all knelt together and asked Saint Baithene in their ignorance to be sure to tell them the cause and origin of this marvellous comfort, which he also felt like the rest. He then gave this reply to them: 'You know', he said, 'our father Columba's concern for us, and how distressed he is that we come late to him, being mindful of our labours. It is because he does not come in the body to meet us that his spirit comes to meet our approaching steps; and in this way he comforts us and makes us glad.' On hearing these words, they knelt down in heartfelt joy and, stretching out their hands towards heaven, they worshipped Christ in the holy and blessed man.

Nor ought I to omit to mention what has been confidently related to me by people who knew concerning the blessed man's voice when singing the psalms. The venerable man's voice, when he was chanting in church with the brothers, was raised up in matchless style so that it could be heard sometimes four stades, or five hundred paces, away, and sometimes at eight stades, or a thousand paces. Wonderful to tell, to the ears of those who stood with him in the church his voice was no louder than the normal volume of a human voice. Yet at the same time those who stood more than a thousand paces distant could hear the same voice so clearly that they could distinguish even the separate syllables in the verses he was singing. For his voice sounded alike in the ears of those who heard it, whether near or far away. It is established that this miraculous property of the blessed man's voice was not always manifested, but only on rare occasions; but that this could not have happened at all without the grace of God's Spirit.

I must also not fail to mention that instance of his matchless power of voice that is said to have occurred near the fortress of King Brude. While the saint himself with a few brothers was singing the evening praises to God as usual outside the king's fortress, some druids came close to them and did all they could to prevent the sound of God's praise from their lips being heard among the peoples of the heathen. When he perceived this, the saint began to chant the forty-fourth psalm; and so marvellously was his voice raised up in the air at that moment, like a fearful clap of thunder, that both the king and the people were terrified with an insupportable dread.

· † ·

OF A WEALTHY MAN CALLED LUGUID THE LAME

At another time, while staying for some days in Ireland, the saint saw a cleric sitting in a chariot and cheerfully travelling over the Plain of Brega. First, he asked who he was, and received this reply from the man's friends concerning him: 'This is Luguid the Lame, a wealthy man and honoured among the people.' The saint then said in reply, 'This is not how I see him: this poor, unhappy man on the day when he dies will have in his keeping, within a single cashel, three stray animals belonging to his neighbours; and he will order one cow, chosen from the strays, to be killed for him. When its meat is cooked he will order part of it to be given him as he lies on the bed with a harlot; and from this portion he will take a morsel and at once be choked and die there.' All these things, according to reliable tradition, were fulfilled in accordance with the saint's prophetic word.

· † ·

A PROPHECY OF THE SAINT CONCERNING NEMAN, SON OF GRUTHRECH

When the saint was reproaching this man for his wicked deeds, he made light of it and mocked the saint. The blessed man said in reply to him, 'In the name of the Lord, Neman, I shall speak some words of truth concerning you. Your enemies will find you lying in bed with a harlot, and you will be slain there; and demons will drag away your soul to the place of torments.' This same Neman, some years later, was found in the same bed as a harlot in the province of Cainle, and, according to the saint's prophecy, perished, beheaded by his enemies.

A PROPHECY OF THE HOLY MAN CONCERNING
A PRIEST

At another time, when the saint was staying in the province of Ireland mentioned a little earlier, he came by chance on a Lord's day to a neighbouring monastery called in Irish Trioit. The same day he heard a priest consecrating the sacred elements of the Eucharist, whom the brothers who lived there had chosen to perform the solemn rites of the Mass because they considered him especially devout; and suddenly he uttered these awesome words from his lips: 'Clean and unclean can now be seen commingled together; for the clean rites of the sacred offering are administered by an unclean man, who all this time conceals in his conscience a great sin.' When they heard this, those who were there trembled and were dumbfounded. The man of whom these words were spoken was compelled to confess his wickedness before them all. And Christ's fellow soldiers, who stood around the saint in the church and heard him reveal the secrets of the heart, glorified the divine knowledge that was in him with great wonder.

· ✝ ·

A PROPHECY OF THE HOLY MAN CONCERNING
ERC MOCU-DRUIDI, A THIEF, WHO LIVED ON
THE ISLAND OF COLOSSUS

At another time while the saint was living on the island of Iou he summoned to him two men from among the brothers, whose names were Lugbe and Silnan, and gave them these orders: 'Cross the Sound now to the island of Male and look for Erc, a thief, in the plains near the sea. Last night he came alone and in secret from the island of Colossus, and he is trying to hide by day under his boat, covered with hay, among the sand-hills, in order to sail across by night to the little island where the seals that belong to us breed; then, greedy robber that he is, he intends to kill some of them by stealth and fill his boat, before returning to his home.'

Hearing this, they obeyed and set out; and they found the thief hidden in the place foretold by the saint, and brought him to the saint as he had ordered them. Seeing him, the saint said to him, 'Why do you break God's command and keep stealing the property of others? When you have need, come to us and ask, and you will receive what you need.' And saying this he ordered wethers to be killed and given in place of the seals to the wretched thief, so that he should not go back to his home empty-handed.

Some time later the saint foresaw in the spirit that the thief's death was imminent, and sent to Baithene, at that time living as prior in the Plain of Long, with orders for him to send to the thief a fat beast and six pecks of grain as last offerings. They were sent across by Baithene as the saint had urged, but the poor thief was found that day overtaken by sudden death; and the gifts that had been sent over were consumed at his funeral.

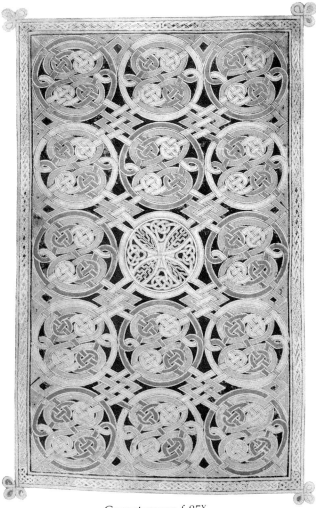

Carpet-page: f.85ᵛ.
The Book of Durrow, Trinity College Library, Dublin: MS A.4.5.

· † ·

A PROPHECY OF THE HOLY MAN CONCERNING CRONAN, A BARD

At another time, when the saint was sitting with the brothers one day by the lake of Ce, near the mouth of a river whose name means 'cow', a certain Irish bard came to them. When he had left after some conversation, the brothers said to the saint, 'When the bard, Cronan, went away from us, why did you not make the customary request for a song of his own composition to be sung to a melody?' The saint said to them, 'Why do you for your part now utter such idle words? How could I have requested a song of joy from that unhappy man, who has now been slain by his enemies and come swiftly to his life's end?' After the saint had said this, behold, a man shouted from across the river, saying, 'That bard who came back in safety from you just now has been killed this very hour on his way by enemies.' Then all who were present wondered greatly and looked at each other in amazement.

·✝·

A PROPHECY OF THE HOLY MAN CONCERNING TWO CHIEFTAINS, WHO BOTH DIED BY MUTUALLY INFLICTED WOUNDS

At another time similarly, when the saint was living on the island of Iou, suddenly while reading he appeared shocked and gave a groan of utter dejection. Seeing this, Lugbe mocu-Blai, who was with him, proceeded to ask him the reason for his sudden grief. The saint in great sorrow gave him this reply: 'Two men of royal birth have just perished in Ireland, pierced by mutually inflicted wounds, not far from the monastery called Cell-rois in the province of the Maugdorni. And on the eighth day, after the end of this week, someone coming from Ireland will shout across the Sound and will announce that this happened as I have described. But this, my little son, you must tell no one as long as I live.'

So on the eighth day there was a shout from across the Sound. Then the saint called the aforementioned Lugbe to him, and said quietly to him, 'The man who is now shouting from across the Sound is that aged traveller of whom I spoke to you before. Go and bring him to us.' He was quickly fetched, and among the news he brought was this: 'Two men of noble birth in the territory of the Maugdorni, Colman the Hound, son of Ailen, and Ronan, son of Aid the son of Colcu, of the race of the Airthir, have died of mutually inflicted wounds, near the boundaries of the territory where the monastery Cell-rois can be seen.'

After the man's story was told, Lugbe, Christ's soldier, proceeded to question the saint privately, saying, 'I pray you, tell me about such prophetic revelations as these, whether they appear to you through sight or hearing, or in some way unknown to man.' The saint replied, 'You are enquiring now about a most subtle matter, and I shall be quite unable to tell you even the smallest part of it, unless first you kneel, and in the name of the Most High God promise me strictly never to divulge this most secret mystery to anyone during all the days of my life.' On hearing this he knelt at once and, bowing his face to the ground, promised everything in full according to the saint's command. As soon as his promise was completed, the saint spoke to him as follows as he arose: 'There are some, though very few, to whom it has been granted by God's grace to observe clearly and most distinctly, on certain occasions, by the miraculous widening of their minds' compass, the whole orb of the whole earth, together with the surrounding ocean and sky, at one and the same moment as if under a single ray of the sun.'

Although the saint appears to tell this miracle concerning others of the elect, in avoidance of vainglory, yet no one who has read Paul the Apostle, a vessel of election, telling of such visions revealed to him, should doubt that he referred, albeit obliquely, to himself. For Paul did not write '*I know that I*' but '*I know a man caught up to the third heaven*'; and although he appears to say this of another, no one doubts that, while preserving his humility, he tells this of his own person. This precedent was followed by our Columba in the account, recorded above, of his spiritual visions; and the afore-mentioned man, whom the saint dearly loved, was able to draw it from him only after earnest entreaties, as he testified himself in the presence of other saints after Saint Columba's death. It was from them that I learned for certain these facts concerning the saint which I have told above.

· † ·

OF CRONAN, THE BISHOP

At another time a stranger came to the saint from the province of the Mumin, who humbly disguised himself as far as he could so that no one knew that he was a bishop. This, however, could not remain hidden from the saint. For the next Lord's day, when bidden by the saint according to custom to consecrate the body of Christ, he summoned the saint's assistance so that, as two priests together, they might break the Lord's bread. The saint, therefore, approached the altar and suddenly, looking into his face, addressed him as follows: 'Christ bless you, brother. Break this bread alone, according to the episcopal rite. We know now that you are a bishop: why till now did you try to disguise yourself, so that the reverence due to you was not paid by us?' On hearing the saint's words, the humble pilgrim was greatly astonished and worshipped Christ in the saint; and those who were present were filled with wonder and glorified God.

· † ·

A PROPHECY OF THE HOLY MAN CONCERNING ERNAN, THE PRIEST

At another time similarly the venerable man sent Ernan the priest, his aged uncle, to be prior of the monastery which he had founded on the island of Hinba some years before. On his departure the saint kissed and blessed him, and uttered this prophecy concerning him: 'This friend of mine who now takes his leave I do not expect to see again alive in this world.'

So the same Ernan, not many days after, was afflicted with a sickness, and carried back at his wish to the saint. At his arrival the saint was overjoyed, and set out to go to the harbour to meet him. Ernan himself, with halting steps, but on his own feet and with great resolution, tried to go from the harbour to meet the saint. But when the distance between them was about twenty-four paces, overtaken by sudden death, he fell to the ground and breathed his last before the saint could see his face while he yet lived, so that the saint's words should in no way be rendered vain. For this reason a cross was set up in that place in front of the door of the barn; and another cross, similarly set up where the saint stood when Ernan died, is standing even today.

Carpet-page: f. 125^v.

The Book of Durrow, Trinity College Library, Dublin: MS A.4.5.

· † ·

A PROPHECY OF THE HOLY MAN CONCERNING THE FAMILY OF A CERTAIN LAYMAN

At another time also, when the saint was a guest at a place called in Irish Coire-salchain, among those who came to him one evening was a certain layman; and when the saint saw him approaching he said, 'Where do you live?' He replied, 'I live in the district which borders the shores of the lake of Crog-reth.' 'The province that you mention,' said the saint, 'is now being laid waste by barbarian marauders.' On hearing this, the poor layman began to weep for his wife and children. Seeing his great sorrow, the saint said to comfort him, 'Go, my child, go! All your family have escaped by fleeing to the mountain, but the invaders have driven away with them all your cattle, and among their plunder also the savage robbers have seized all the furniture from your home.' After hearing this the layman returned to his own country, and found that everything had been fulfilled just as it had been foretold by the saint.

A PROPHECY OF THE HOLY MAN CONCERNING A LAYMAN NAMED GORE, SON OF AIDAN

At another time similarly a layman, who was the most valiant of all men at that time among the people of the corcu-Reti, enquired of the holy man by what death he would be overtaken. The saint said to him, 'You will die neither in battle nor at sea. A companion on your journey of whom you have no suspicion will be the cause of your death.' 'Perhaps', said Gore, 'one of the friends in my company is plotting to murder me; or my wife intends to kill me by sorcery out of love for a younger man.' The saint said, 'That is not what will happen.' 'Why', said Gore, 'do you refuse to tell me now who shall slay me?' The saint said, 'My purpose in refusing to speak more plainly now, concerning the companion that is to harm you, is that you may not be too saddened by the constant remembrance of what you have learned, before the day comes when you will test the truth of it.'

Not to waste words, after some years had passed the aforementioned Gore chanced one day to be sitting beneath a boat, shaving the bark off a spear-shaft with his own knife. Then, on hearing some men nearby fighting each other, he rose quickly to stop them fighting; and in his sudden haste he dropped the knife carelessly on the ground, and was badly injured when his knee struck it. It was through such a companion as this that the cause of his death came about; and in astonishment he at once realised that it was in fulfilment of the holy man's prophecy. And after some months he succumbed to this wound and died.

· † ·

THE HOLY MAN'S FOREKNOWLEDGE AND PROPHECY CONCERNING ANOTHER MATTER, SLIGHTER YET SO DELIGHTFUL THAT I BELIEVE IT OUGHT NOT TO GO UNNOTICED

At another time, when the saint was living on the island of Iou, he summoned one of the brothers and spoke to him as follows: 'On the third day after this which now dawns, you must keep watch on the west of this island, sitting above the seashore. For after the ninth hour of the day a guest will arrive from the north of Ireland, a crane, very tired and weary after circling far through the air on buffeting winds; and, its strength almost spent, it will fall on the shore before you and rest. You shall take care to lift it up gently and take it to a nearby house where it will be given hospitality, and for three days and nights you shall nurse it carefully and feed it. After that, when three days have passed and it is refreshed, it will not wish to make a longer pilgrimage with us, but will return to that sweet district of Ireland from where it came, its strength fully restored. My reason for giving you special charge of this bird is that it comes from the district of our fathers.'

The brother obeyed, and on the third day after the ninth hour, as he had been bidden, he waited for the arrival of the foreknown guest; and when it arrived he lifted it from the shore where it fell, carried its weak body to a lodging, and fed it in its hunger. When he returned to the monastery in the evening, the saint did not question him but gave this account to him: 'God bless you, my son, for your kind attention to our guest, the pilgrim. It will not linger in pilgrimage, but after three days will go back to its own country.' Just as the saint foretold, so the event proved. For after staying for three days as a guest, in the sight of the host who had nursed it, it first flew from the ground and soared aloft, and then, after marking the way for a short time in the air, it crossed the ocean on a straight line of flight and returned to Ireland in calm weather.

· † ·

THE BLESSED MAN'S FOREKNOWLEDGE OF A BATTLE FOUGHT MANY YEARS LATER IN THE FORT OF CETHIRN, AND OF A WELL NEAR THE TERRITORY OF THE FORT

At another time, after the conference on the Ridge of Cete between King Aid, son of Ainmurech, and King Aidan, son of Gabran, when the blessed man was returning to the plains by the sea, he and Abbot Comgell sat down one fine summer day not far from the fort mentioned above. Then water was brought in a bronze jug from a nearby well for the saints to wash their hands. After taking it, Saint Columba spoke thus to Abbot Comgell as he sat beside him: 'As for that well, Comgell, from which this water has been drawn and brought to us, the day will come when it will be unfit for human use.' 'How', said Comgell, 'will the water from that well be defiled?' Then Saint Columba said, 'Because it will be filled with human blood. For my friends by kinship and your kinsfolk after the flesh, that is the race of Niall and the Cruithnian peoples, will go to war and join battle in this nearby fort of Cethirn. As a result, one of my poor kinsmen will be slain in that same well, among the other dead, and the well will be filled with his blood.'

This true prophecy of his was fulfilled in its own time after many years. In that battle, as many people know, Domnall, son of Aid, was raised up in victory; and in that well, according to the holy man's prophecy, one of his kindred was killed. Another soldier of Christ, named Finan, who lived the life of an anchorite blamelessly for many years near the monastery of the Oakwood Plain, was present when that battle was joined and gave me, Adomnan, some report of it, and he testified that he had seen a dismembered corpse in the aforementioned well. He said that he had returned the same day after the battle was fought to the monastery of Saint Comgell, called in Irish Cambas, because he had come from there earlier, and had found there two old monks of Saint Comgell, to whom he told something of the battle he had witnessed and of the well defiled with human blood. They had at once replied, 'A true prophet was Columba, for all that you tell us was accomplished today, concerning the battle and the well, he foretold in our hearing many years ago, when sitting with Saint Comgell by the fort of Cethirn.'

·✝·

OF THE DISTINCTION BETWEEN DIFFERENT GIFTS REVEALED TO THE HOLY MAN BY THE GRACE OF GOD

About the same time, Conall, bishop of Cul-rathin, collected gifts almost beyond count from the people of the Plain of Eilne, and prepared to entertain the blessed man as he was returning, accompanied by a large crowd, after the conference of the aforementioned kings. So when the holy man arrived, the many gifts of the people were laid out in the courtyard of the monastery and presented to him for his blessing. As he blessed them he looked at them, and pointed out in particular the gift of a wealthy man: 'God's mercy', he said, 'attends the man whose gift this is, in return for his mercies to the poor and his generosity.'

Similarly he picked out another of the many gifts, saying, 'This is the gift of a sage, but an avaricious man, and I cannot taste of it unless first he sincerely repents of his sin of avarice.' These words were quickly spread abroad among the crowd, and when he heard them the guilty man, Columb, son of Aid, ran up, knelt before the saint and repented, promising thereafter to renounce avarice and to practise liberality, with amendment of life. Bidden to rise by the saint, he was cured from that hour of the vice of the miser. For he was a sage, as had been revealed to the saint in his gift.

Now when that generous and wealthy man, named Brenden, whose gift was mentioned a little earlier, also heard the words spoken about him by the saint, he knelt at the saint's feet and prayed that the saint might utter a prayer for him to the Lord. First, he was reproached by him for certain of his sins and repented, promising thereafter to amend his life. And thus both of them were corrected and cured of their particular faults.

By like knowledge at another time, also, the saint recognised the gift of an avaricious man named Diormit, among many gifts which had been collected on his arrival at the Great Cell of Deathrib.

Let it suffice to have recorded in the text of this first book these few instances as a small sample of the blessed man's gift of prophecy. I said 'these few' because there is no doubt that those instances of the venerable man's foreknowledge which were hidden within as holy mysteries, and could not come to men's awareness, were far more numerous than those that came to light, like little drops dripping through cracks in a cask full of new wine in full ferment. For holy and apostolic men in general, to avoid vainglory, make all haste to hide those inner secrets that are privately revealed to them by God. But God, whether they will or no, makes some of them known and by various means brings them into view, wishing thereby to glorify the saints who glorify Him, the Lord Himself, to whom be glory for ever and ever.

Here an end is put to this first book.

The Miracles of Columcille

When Adamnan took the miracles of Columcille as the subject of his second book he seemed to recognise, even as soon as setting down the title, that miracles and foreknowledge are not always easily separated. None the less, while these pages 'concerning his miracles' might reveal rather less solid historical material than is to be found in the first book, they do tell us much of Adamnan's vision of Columcille and also provide the fullest account of Columcille in the land of the Picts.

Adamnan always judiciously selected the subject of the first chapter of each of his three books, and it is no accident that the miracle which opens this second one is that of the transmutation of water into wine. He tells how 'by some mischance no wine could be found for the sacrificial rite' on a festal day in the monastery of 'Saint Find-barr the bishop'. Columcille, not yet ordained priest and still in deacon's orders, blessed water from the well which was miraculously 'changed into the more precious form of wine'.

The miracle of 'water into wine' occurs in very many other hagiographies. Closely similar miracles were ascribed to many other saints – notably David, Gildas, Cuthbert and Finnian of Clonard – while Brigid is said to have transformed water into beer. But the inspiration for the prominence which Adamnan accords this first miracle of Col-umcille is clearly that of Christ's own first miracle, the transformation of water into wine for the wedding feast at Cana in Galilee recorded in the second chapter of the gospel of St John.

Other miracles of Columcille bear a like similarity to those of the gospels. Although Adamnan records rather fewer miracles of healing than many other hagiographers, he does tell of Columcille's ministrations to several patients, including his personal attendant Diormit and a monk by the name of Finten, of his curing the nose-bleed of Lugne mocu-Min and mending the broken hip of Maugin the virgin. Yet the clearest echo of Christ's miracles of healing is found in his account of Columcille's curing 'the disorders of various sick people . . . when he went to the conference of kings at the Ridge of Cete' by his blessing and the touch of his hand, even by contact with the hem of his robe. The mass healing at Druim Ceatt is certainly reminiscent of St Mark's account of Christ's similar miracle in Galilee:

> And, at even, when the sun did set, they brought unto him all that were diseased, and them that were possessed with devils. . . . And he healed many that were sick of divers diseases, and cast out many devils.

Adamnan's story of 'a boy raised from the dead in the land of the Picts' bears similar comparison to Christ's raising of Lazarus in the gospel of John and of the daughter of Jairus in the gospels of both Luke and Matthew, especially when the awed response of the Pictish druids is compared to the response of the Pharisees. Columcille's miraculous command over wind and wave offers numerous examples of miracles to be compared with Christ's stilling of the tempest in the fifth chapter of Mark: 'And he arose, and rebuked the wind, and said unto the sea, Peace, be still. And the wind ceased, and there was a great calm.'

'The appointed girth of the great deep, Borne up by the hand of God Almighty'

THE *ALTUS PROSATOR* ATTRIBUTED TO COLUMCILLE

The Spouting Cave, Iona.

If all of this seems to suggest that Adamnan was setting down nothing less than a 'gospel of Columcille', that possibility will be given more extensive consideration in my afterword. There does remain another, more specifically historical point of interest in the first miracle of water into wine, throwing light on Columcille's education. Adamnan sets the miracle in the monastery of 'Saint Findbarr the bishop' where the teenage Columcille was under deacon's orders. Finnian of Moville, unlike his namesake of Clonard, was elsewhere entitled 'Bishop' and we can thus take Adamnan as setting this miracle in the monastery of St Finnian at Moville. The Old Irish *Life* certainly supports that reading of Adamnan, when it records how

> to learn wisdom he went to the arch-presbyter, even to the bishop Finnen of Moville. At a certain time wine and bread were lacking unto Finnen at the Mass. But Colum Cille blest the water, and it was turned into wine and put into the chalice of the offering.

Having confirmed Columcille's education under Finnian of Moville, Adamnan goes on also to confirm the saint's later period of study with the bard Gemman in Leinster. He tells how a young girl fleeing from a persecutor seeks sanctuary behind the clerical robes of Columcille and his tutor. The pursuer will brook no impediment and slays the girl even as she claims the sanctuary of the holy men, suffering in consequence the swift and fatal retribution of Columcille. Adamnan's story is once again supported by a closely similar account in the Old Irish *Life* which succinctly concludes: 'Colomb Cille set a word of banning upon him and he perished forthwith.'

There is, intriguingly, one miracle story recorded by both Adamnan and the Old Irish biographer and yet located quite differently in each version. Adamnan tells of Columcille's miraculous foretelling fulfilled when 'corn sown after midsummer . . . brought forth a ripe harvest at the beginning of August'. Adamnan sets the miracle on Iona, and indeed there are records of crops sown on the island as late as July, though more often in June, and harvested in early September. The Old Irish *Life* sets precisely the same miracle in Derry at the time of the building of Columcille's first monastery, many years before his settlement on Iona.

Adamnan's sequence of miracles concerning manuscripts written in the saint's hand emphasises once again the theme of Columcille the calligrapher, which recurs throughout the Columban literature, from the story of the 'book of Finnian', through the tradition of the *Cathach*, to Adamnan's account of Columcille's transcribing a psalm in the afternoon immediately before his passing. These miraculous accounts of Columban manuscripts accidentally falling into water and rediscovered immaculately preserved – even whilst other accompanying pages in a less exalted hand are ruined – have numerous echoes in other hagiographies. There are similar stories of St Ciaran's copy of the gospels which fell into a lake and emerged unharmed, of St Cronan's gospel manuscript which fell into Loch Cre and lay there undamaged for forty days, and of a book of St Finnian unscathed by his leaving it out in the pouring rain. In the last quarter of the ninth century, the great gospel book of Lindisfarne miraculously survived a similar experience. When the Lindisfarne monks set sail for Ireland to escape the renewed Viking onslaught – according to Simeon's twelfth-century *History of the Church of Durham* – 'the ship heeled over on one side, and the copy of the gospels, adorned with gold figures, fell overboard, and sank to the bottom of the sea'. The monks had abandoned the voyage and returned to dry land when a miraculous vision directed them to the shore near Whithorn, where

> the sea had receded much further back than usual, and going out three miles or more they discovered the volume of the holy gospels, which had lost none of the external brilliancy of its gems and gold, nor any of the internal beauty of its illuminations, and the fairness of its leaves, but appeared just as if it had never come into any contact whatever with the water.

'Because mention was made just above of the element of water,' writes Adamnan, 'we ought not to pass over in silence some other miracles concerning the same substance.' So saying, he goes on to chronicle Columcille's striking water out of rock at Ardnamurchan and purifying a poisoned well in Pictland with his blessing. The element of water, essential to the sustenance of life, has enjoyed a sacred significance since the earliest times. The Old Testament tells of the sons of Abraham laying claim to tracts of land by naming the wells which supplied their fertility. The pagan Celts named wells after their tribal gods, and those who settled in the valley of the Boyne ascribed magical powers to that river. As with so many ancient pagan traditions, the magical associations of water and wells became incorporated into the new traditions of Christianity, and most especially in those of the Celtic Church. Holy wells are often found in the vicinity of the oldest churches, and the Chalice Well at Glastonbury – so long associated with the cult of the first-century St Joseph of Arimathea – bears the most ancient testimony to the Christian tradition of the sacred well.

The striking of water from rock at the command of a holy man can be traced back, through all the hagiographies of Christian saints, at least as far as the Old Testament book of Exodus. Adamnan would certainly have heard stories of St Cuthbert on his visits to Northumbria, amongst them his striking of water from rock when he established his island hermitage on Inner Farne, which might have recalled for him Columcille's similar miracle at Ardnamurchan where a spring has long borne the dedication of 'St Columba's Well'.

Through countless centuries, the poisoning of the water supply to a settlement was considered to be a fearsome weapon of the forces of evil, and certainly served human aggressors as the most ancient form of chemical and biological warfare. There is an echo of this in the prophecy of the battle of Dun Cethirn – in Adamnan's first book – when Columcille foretells the poisoning of a well by the corpses from that coming conflict. Similarly, on a journey east of the Spine, Columcille comes upon a well whose waters have been poisoned by a pagan malediction and are subsequently purified by his blessing, thus providing another victory over the druids in the wonder-working contests which dominate Adamnan's chronicle of Columcille in Pictland.

After the series of miracles concerning water and wells, Adamnan returns to the theme of Columcille's power over the greater waters of the ocean, telling the clearly gospel-related story of Columcille's calming the stormy waters during one of his own voyages, followed by two miracles concerning St Cainnech of Aghaboe – 'Ached-bou meaning the Plain of the Cow' – in Ossory. In the first of these, Columcille is preserved from peril at sea by the prayers of Cainnech, who hurries from the refectory to pray in the church of his monastery at the urgent prompting of his sudden fore-knowledge of the saint's hazardous predicament.

The second miracle concerns Cainnech's staff, presumably a handsomely decorated crosier, left behind on Iona when he set sail for Ireland. Columcille retrieves the staff and miraculously transports it to 'the land of Oidech' – the Mull of Oa at the southern tip of Islay – where Cainnech's ship will put in on the voyage back to Ireland and he will be able to reclaim his loss. An abbot's crosier was of great symbolic, even talismanic, importance. At Druim Ceatt, Columcille traditionally passed his pastoral staff, or *Bachill Mor*, to the hostage Scandlan as a token of his protection.

St Cainnech was an immediate contemporary of Columcille and is frequently mentioned by Adamnan. He was born the son of a bard in Derry around 525 and would certainly have met Columcille at Glasnevin. When the monastic community there was broken up by the plague in 544, Cainnech journeyed to Llancarvan in Wales before returning to Ireland to found his churches at Aghaboe and at Drumahose in Derry. He is known as St Kenneth in Scotland, where dedications to him can be traced in numerous place-names, amongst them Cambuskenneth, Kilchenich on Tiree, Kilchainie on South Uist, and Inchkenneth off Mull. On Adamnan's evidence alone, Cainnech was a frequent visitor to Iona, but was also given to spending periods of time as a hermit and traditionally associated with wild creatures, notably the mice who nibbled his shoes and the birds whom he admonished for interrupting his prayers with their song.

Another miracle story of seagoing saints tells how Baithene intended to sail to Tiree on the same day as Colman Ela, the son of Columcille's sister, was journeying south to Ireland. To ensure that both enjoy fair winds for their voyages, Columcille advises Baithene to set sail at dawn and Colman to follow him at the third hour, about nine in the morning. Adamnan attributes the consequent favourably disposed winds to Columcille's miraculous guidance, but it might not be disrespectful to point out that an offshore wind at dawn is often succeeded by a returning wind when the morning sun grows warmer on the western coastline. Such meteorological wisdom would not have been lost on so experienced an islander as the abbot of Iona. Indeed there is a verse in the *Amra Cholum Cille* which tells how

> Storms and seasons he perceived,
> He used to understand when calm and storm would come.
> He was skilful in the course of the sea.

Adamnan's miracle stories concerning Columcille's casting out of demonic and evil powers from milk reflect manifold and enduring superstitions from the Gaelic folklore of both Scotland and Ireland. The widespread presence of demons lurking in cow's milk must derive from ancient pagan origins and the cross-shaped bar which fastened the lid on to the traditional milk-pail cannot possibly be without its own later symbolic significance.

There is a significant symbolism also to be found in Adamnan's accounts of the miraculous provision of fish for Columcille on two occasions, once on 'the River Sale', certainly the tributary of Loch Sheil, and again in 'the Lake of Ce', Lough Key in Roscommon. The fish is the oldest image in Christian iconography. Its use as a symbol of Christ can be traced back to the first century AD and derives from the letters of the Greek word for fish – ΙΧΘΥΣ – which correspond to the initial letters of 'Jesus Christ, Son of God, Saviour' – Ἰησοῦς Χριστὸς Θεοῦ Ὑιὸς Σωτήρ. This symbolism held for the whole of the Christian world of Adamnan's time and certainly for the iconography of the Celtic church, where the *chi-rho* monogram, always chosen for especially elaborate decoration in the illuminated gospel books, developed into the characteristic form of the Celtic cross. The symbol of a fish, carved by the first Christians on the walls of the catacombs of Rome, is also to be found carved beside the Celtic cross on the tombstone of Oidican at Fuerty, perhaps coincidentally, in Roscommon.

The miracles by which Columcille bestowed improved fortunes on those who found favour and retribution on those who did not are interesting in the emphasis which Adamnan places on cattle as a measure of wealth and prosperity. Nesan the Crooked provides the saint with hospitality in Lochaber, as does the poor layman called Colman, and both are rewarded with an increase in the number of their cattle from 5 to 105. Cattle were certainly the measure of wealth in Columcille's time when trade was by barter and such ritual payments as marital dowries were bestowed in cattle, but it is not without significance that while Adamnan was writing of these matters the controversial remission of the *boruma* was arising in Ireland. The High King Finnachta Fledach of the southern Ui-Neill proposed to absolve the men of Leinster from their traditional cattle-tribute to Adamnan's – and Columcille's – people of the northern Ui-Neill. Such a concern must have been prominent in Adamnan's mind at that time and would very shortly take him back to Ireland to confront Finnachta at Tara in 692. These chapters relating Columcille's divinely inspired favour directly to the prosperity of cattle herds may well have some bearing on Adamnan's immediate political anxiety regarding the threatened impoverishment of the clan of Columcille.

The significance of cattle might prompt consideration of Columcille's traditional distrust of the female gender, which stems from the legend that cows were prohibited from Iona by the abbot's own decree:

> For where there is a cow there will be a woman,
> And where there is a woman there will be mischief.

There is certainly no overwhelming evidence in Adamnan to claim Columcille as an ardent feminist by the standards of the modern orthodoxy, but there are some insights into his attitudes to women to be found in this second book. He offers his prayers to ease the labour pains of his kinswoman in his mother's homeland of Leinster, and he exerts all his miraculous powers to compel the druid Broichan to liberate an Irish slave-girl he holds captive. Adamnan certainly offers no evidence of Columcille as a confirmed misogynist and, indeed, his many references to a herd of cows on Iona even call the authenticity of the couplet attributed to Columcille into the gravest question.

There is also the story of the saint's assistance to Lugne Tudicla, whose appearance was so unappealing that his wife was unable to bring herself to share the conjugal relations of the marriage bed. In a rare hagiographical example of marriage-guidance counselling, Columcille resolves the disharmony through prayer and fasting. Adamnan also refers to the reluctant wife's pleading with the saint to send her to 'a monastery for women' rather than compel her to fulfill her marital obligations. This remark provides clear evidence of the existence of some form of nunnery in the Columban *familia*. Just off the Ross of Mull in the Sound of Iona there is a small island with the Gaelic name of Eilean nam Ban, the 'Island of the Women', which suggests that it was the site of a women's foundation associated with the monastery on Iona, possibly as early as Columcille's own time. There were certainly nunneries in Northumbria – notably St Ebba's at Coldingham and St Hild's at Whitby – which were administered under a form of the Columban monastic rule from the early seventh century, and there is no evidence that women were excluded from the monastic *familia* of Columcille. Indeed, the saint's mother, Ethne, traditionally followed her son to Scotland and is there said to have established 'a monastery for women' on the island of Hinba.

Adamnan's accounts of miraculous vengeance visited on malefactors again casts Columcille in the role of the warrior-saint. He confronts the pirate Ioan, who has plundered the crofter Colman, striding after him into the surf calling down divine retribution. A storm cloud appears in a clear sky and unleashes its fury to sink the pirate's vessel.

Adamnan specifically locates this incident on the shore at Ardnamurchan and thus usefully enables identification of the island of 'Colossus'. This island has been claimed on occasions as Colonsay, but it is clear from Adamnan's topography that it is, in fact, the island of Coll. Ioan's boat is sunk in the sound between 'Male and Colossus' – Mull and Coll – both of which can be seen from the Ardnamurchan peninsula, while Colonsay lies away to the south, hidden from view by the hills of Mull.

Columcille's encounter with another pirate, Lam Dess, results in the only attempt on the saint's life recorded by Adamnan. Columcille 'excommunicates' a company of pirates and one of their number, this Lam Dess, sails to Hinba to assassinate him. The monk Findlugan dons Columcille's cowl to confuse the attack, and when the assassin throws a spear at his intended victim the cowl miraculously deflects the weapon. Adamnan's story hinges on the difference between the white cowl of an abbot and that of unbleached wool worn by his monks. From a distance, a white cowl would indicate an abbot and thus offer a deceptive target to the attacker. The miraculous properties of the cowl – or *cochall* from the Latin *cucullus* – of Columcille have entered into folklore. The saint's cowl given to King Aid provided him with a garment which 'served as a most secure and impenetrable coat of armour'. Irish tradition tells how

Aid went to war against Leinster to avenge the killing of his son and left the *cochall* behind him. As soon as he realised his forgetfulness, he knew he was doomed to suffer his own death at the hands of the Leinstermen.

Although Lam Dess escaped from Hinba after his foiled assassination attempt, he did not escape the saint's retribution. One year later to the day, he was himself slain by the spear of an adversary in the course of an affray on 'the island whose name means ''Long'' ', probably Luing in the Firth of Lorne or the Treshnish island of Lunga. Both Ioan and Lam Dess apparently belonged to the same piratical clan of 'the sons of Conall, son of Domnall', a renegade branch of the founding dynasty of Dunadd which had broken away to live as outlaws along the coast of Argyll.

'Let this be a sufficient account of the terrible punishments inflicted on his adversaries,' writes Adamnan. 'We shall now relate a few miracles concerning wild beasts . . .' and he passes on to a sequence of miraculous anecdotes which range from the symbolic to the quite extraordinary. The first of them might surely be read as more symbolic than historical, when Columcille confronts a wild boar on Skye and commands its demise by the power of 'his holy hand'. Wild boar were certainly to be found in Britain in Columcille's time, but they are not commonly recorded in the islands. One possible explanation of the story – to which Adamnan grants some prominence – may well lie in the symbol of the boar as the totem of the Pictish warrior. On one of the occasions when the Picts besieged and conquered the fortress of Dunadd they inscribed a boar on the supposed 'coronation stone' of the Dalriadan kings. The Isle of Skye lay just beyond the frontier of the territory of Dalriada and just within the boundary of Pictland, which would explain why Adamnan selects it as the site of Columcille's symbolic boar-slaying. He immediately passes on to a chronicle of miracles performed 'east of the Spine of Britain' in the heartland of the Picts, perhaps further indicating the symbolism rather than the historicity of this first 'miracle concerning wild beasts'.

It was to the east of the Spine, on the River Ness, that Columcille faced the most celebrated 'wild beast' of all, the creature which is still universally known – and still sought out by scientists and sightseers – as the Loch Ness Monster. Adamnan tells how Columcille and his company of monks come to the bank of the river where a Pict who has been savaged by the 'water beast' is about to be interred. Columcille despatches the ever-obedient Lugne mocu-Min to swim over the river to bring back a boat from the far bank, thus prompting the monster, 'whose hunger had not been satisfied earlier', to rise from the depths to claim another victim. Lugne is preserved from peril only when Columcille commands the monster to 'Go back with all speed'. Adamnan's account remains the first documentary report of the Loch Ness Monster, but it can be shown to bear comparison with very similar monsters in Irish tradition where demoniacal serpents have lurked in rivers since remote antiquity. Such stories can be found in the lives of St Mochua of Balla and St Colman of Dromore, while in Londonderry there is a stretch of riverside known as *Lig-na-Peiste* on account of the water serpent which traditionally makes its home there. All of which might suggest that Adamnan was adapting Irish legend to enhance the miraculous powers of Columcille and unwittingly creating one of Scotland's most eminent and enduring tourist attractions.

There is more zoological substance in Adamnan's brief chapter on Columcille's banishment of poisonous snakes from Iona. It is a matter of scientific record that there are no snakes found on the island, although the adder, known locally as *nathair*, has been recorded just across the Sound on the Ross of Mull. St Patrick has long been accredited with the banning of snakes from the Irish mainland, and Bede's eulogy on the virtues of Ireland assures us that 'no snake can live there'. However, Bede makes no connection with Patrick and the first-century Latin topography of Solinus records Ireland as devoid of venomous snakes more than three hundred years before Patrick's arrival.

97

'The royal fortress of King Brude'
The ramparts of the hillfort at Craig Phadrig near Inverness.

This second book includes most of Adamnan's material on Columcille in Pictland and raises the question of precisely how many journeys he might have made to the court of Brude mac-Maelchon, king of the Picts. The location of King Brude's capital was certainly in the region of Moray near Inverness, the part of Scotland where the most numerous concentrations of early Pictish symbol stones have been found. Here stands the ancient hillfort of Craig Phadrig, overlooking the Beauly Firth, which offers the most probable location of the royal fortress of Brude mac-Maelchon. In the sixth century it must have offered a formidable bulwark against any enemy and the ascent to its ramparts for a company of monks from the rival kingdom of Dalriada would certainly have amounted to 'the first laborious journey' of which Adamnan writes.

While he is never specifically chronological in his references to Columcille's travels in Pictland, we can certainly associate the great majority of the miracles performed amongst the Picts – and the sighting of the 'water beast' of Ness – with Columcille's first mission to the court of Brude. This was certainly the occasion of Columcille's miraculous opening of the door of Brude's fortress, which had not unreasonably been bolted against the emissaries of a hostile kingdom, and also of Columcille's sequence of wonder-working contests with Broichan, the fearsome arch-druid of the Pictish kingdom. This 'first laborious journey' was that undertaken to establish a diplomatic mission into Pictland, to ensure peace between the Picts and Dalriada, and to obtain Brude's guarantees for the monastic foundation on Iona.

Adamnan tells also of Columcille's gaining from Brude a safe conduct for St Cormac's mission to the 'Orcades', the northern islands of Orkney, and records how this was granted by the king in the presence of his hostage Orcadian chieftain. The tone of this encounter does appear very different from that of Adamnan's earlier anecdotes from Pictland. On this occasion no hostile druid stands by seething with anti-Christian rage and there is every appearance of an amicable diplomatic exchange between king and saint. Historical dating of Cormac's voyage to Orkney is at best speculative, but it can be reasonably placed in the last quarter of the sixth century. That chronology would put it more than a decade after Columcille's first mission to Pictland within a year of his arrival in Scotland, if not in 563 then in the spring of 564. Adamnan's specific reference to a 'first journey' clearly implies a second visit to King Brude, probably accomplished in the years after the succession of Aidan mac-Gabran as king at Dunadd in 574. In his third book, Adamnan does tell of Columcille's conversion of a dying Pict to the faith in Glen Urquhart. He states that Columcille was 'journeying beyond the Spine of Britain beside the lake of the River Nes' and describes him as 'the aged saint'. Although any man over the age of forty could be considered *senex* or 'aged' in Columcille's time, it is rare for Adamnan to apply that adjective to Columcille. Thus we can be certain that this 'journeying' was undertaken in the later years, certainly many years after the first journey to Pictland in the early 560s. Having established this second journey beyond the Spine, it becomes at least possible to suggest it as the occasion of the negotiations of Cormac's safe conduct to Orkney. Thus a date around 580 might correspond both with the dating of Cormac's voyage and with the description of Columcille as 'the aged saint'.

There is an interesting reference in the Latin *Life* of St Comgell of Bangor which names him with Cainnech of Aghaboe as 'the companions' mentioned – but not named – by Adamnan as accompanying Columcille at the door of Brude's fortress. This account, which has been incorporated as historical fact into many later biographies of Columcille, also refers to the journey's being made from Hinba to Pictland, which might suggest that the mission was undertaken prior to the foundation on Iona. There is a further historical likelihood to support Columcille's choice of such companions in that both men were of Cruithne, or Irish Pict, descent with command of a P-Celtic tongue closely similar to that spoken in Brude's kingdom. They would certainly have been invaluable companions in seeking to establish understanding between Columcille and Brude.

It is a point of decisive significance in the dating of this first journey that hostilities between Pictland and Dalriada ceased precisely from the date of Columcille's arrival in Argyll in 563. No reason for that peace is evident other than his successful diplomatic mission to King Brude, which must thus have been accomplished soon after his arrival in Scotland. On the grounds of these interpretations of Adamnan's evidence, I would suggest that Columcille certainly made two journeys to Brude, the first of them to his fortress capital at Craig Phadrig in 563 or 564, and the second, possibly but not necessarily to Craig Phadrig, at some point between 574 and 580.

Whilst still to the east of the Spine, it is interesting to consider A. O. Anderson's intriguing, and remarkably convincing, theory about the identity of the druid Broichan. Broichan features prominently as the evil genius dogging Columcille's footsteps at the court of King Brude. Columcille engages and roundly defeats him in a series of exchanges which set the miraculous powers of the saint against the ancient magic of the shaman, a sequence strikingly reminiscent of similar contests in which Patrick triumphed over the druids of Ireland. Columcille demands of Broichan that he liberate an Irish slave-girl from his thrall and, when he refuses, the saint's awesome powers bring him to the point of death. Only when Broichan finally relents does Columcille bless a white pebble as the healing talisman which restores him to health. There is another interesting sidelight in the frequent occurrence of magic stones with curative powers in the folklore of the Western Isles, and in the pebble blessed to heal ills which is recorded among the miracles of St Martin of Tours.

Adamnan tells us that *Broichanus magus* – 'Broichan the wizard' – was the foster-father of Brude mac-Maelchon, just as the Pictish priest Cruithnecan had been to Columcille. *Broichanus* seems to be a Latinisation of the north British name *Broichan*, which would take the Irish form of *Froichan* or *Fraechan*, and it was a druid named Fraechan who cast the *airbe* of defence around Diarmit mac-Cerbaill's army at the battle of Culdrevny. He is entered in the *Annals of Ulster* as 'Fraechan, son of Ternan', and in those of Tighernach as 'Fraechan, son of Teniusan', corresponding to the Irish tradition of a fearsome wizard named Froichan contemporary with Columcille. Anderson suggests that there cannot have been two separate wizards named Froichan/Broichan, both bitterly hostile to the saint, in one case battle-magus to the High King Diarmit and in the other foster-father to King Brude of the Picts. His conclusion thus emerges that Broichan and Froichan were the same man, and the historical circumstances would certainly support him. Brude was the son of Maelgwn, king of Gwynedd and overlord of Man and Anglesey where druidism flourished, not least in its contacts with the Cruithne of eastern Ireland. Such a network of contact may well have taken Froichan from Tara, after the defeat of Diarmit at Culdrevny, to the court of his foster-son Brude, arriving there in time to confront once again the warrior-saint of Culdrevny. Adamnan implies his own supportive evidence when he acknowledges that Columcille and Broichan spoke without an interpreter. If Columcille had no command of a P-Celtic tongue, then it follows that Broichan must have had the Q-Celtic of the Gael, and the druid Froichan would most certainly have spoken just such a tongue.

The historical evidence for the seafaring St Cormac, of the lineage of the third-century Munster chieftain Eochaid Liathain, is substantially less of an enigma. Cormac Ua-Liathain was one of the Twelve Apostles of Ireland traditionally schooled at Clonard and certainly enjoyed a long-standing friendship with Columcille. According to the Old Irish *Life*, he was the first abbot of Durrow immediately after its foundation in the early 560s: 'Colomb blessed Durrow, and left therein as warden one of his household, even Cormac descendant of Liathan.' His feast day is entered in the calendars at 21 June, where he is recorded as 'abbot of Dearmagh' yet is nowhere accredited with his own monastic foundation. From Adamnan we have the clearest evidence for Cormac's voyaging – in the tradition of Brenden the sailor-monk of Clonfert and in accordance with the first tenet of the Columban Rule – to the northern isles of the 'Orcades', as the Orkney archipelago was known to Pliny and Adamnan, while the Irish name was 'Islands of the Orcs'. Orkney was, according to both Adamnan and modern archaeologists, a domain of Pictland and its earliest Christian settlements certainly date from an early mission of conversion, if not by monks of the Columban *familia*, then by those of St Ninian of Whithorn. Indeed, when the northmen claimed Orkney as their *jarldom* before the end of the ninth century, they recorded the islands as the home of the *peti* and the *papae* – the Picts and the priests. Precisely when Cormac sailed to Orkney is unclear. It was certainly after 563, because Columcille was in Scotland at the time, and before 584, because Brude was alive to provide his safe conduct, and most opinion would accept a date between 575 and 580. The Orkney-born poet Edwin Muir tells of a local tradition that the ruined chapel on the Brough of Deerness was the site of Cormac's first foundation on Orkney and its location on those exposed eastern cliffs is certainly characteristic of the monastic tenets of the hardy Celtic fathers.

The concluding chapter of Adamnan's second book sets out to chronicle a posthumous example of the saint's miraculous powers, but its historical value is most important for Adamnan himself. He tells of his own two journeys to Northumbria, thus providing the evidence for the writing of his *Vita Columbae* after 688.

During both of his visits 'the land of the Saxons' was rife with the 'yellow plague' – called *buide chonnaill* by the Irish and *vad velen* in England – that had ravaged not only Britain and Ireland but 'twice in our times laid waste the greater part of the world'. In the year 664, the *buide chonnaill* reached Ireland in its rage across Europe and the *Annals of Ulster* record

> Darkness on the Kalends of May, at the ninth hour;
> and in the same summer the sky seemed to be on fire.
> A pestilence reached Ireland on the Kalends of August.

The following year, the annalist chronicles

> a great mortality.
> Diarmit, son of Aedh Slane . . . and bishops and abbots,
> and other persons innumerable, died.

Adamnan reassures us that 'two peoples, the Picts and the Irish in Britain', were spared the pestilence which had devastated seventh-century Europe from 'the city of Rome to the islands of the Ocean'.

Having already offered an account, as does the Old Irish *Life*, of the blessing of Columcille providing protection and relief from plague, Adamnan's conclusion is quite unequivocal:

> We give frequent thanks to God, who protects us from attacks of plagues both in these islands of ours, through our venerable patron's prayers on our behalf, and in the land of the Saxons. To whom else can this grace granted by God be attributed, but to Saint Columba?

The implications of this conclusion to Adamnan's second book would certainly not have been lost on any monastic readership of his time, and especially not in those monasteries at Wearmouth and Jarrow 'in the land of the Saxons'.

'The Spine of Britain'

OVERLEAF The Pass of Brander, Argyll.

Now begins the second book concerning his miracles,
which are often accompanied by prophetic foreknowledge

· † ·

OF WINE THAT WAS MADE FROM WATER

At another time, when the venerable man was living in Ireland with Saint Findbarr the bishop, and acquiring knowledge of sacred scripture while still a young man, one feast day by some mischance no wine could be found for the sacrificial rite. Hearing the altar servers complaining to each other of the lack of it, he took a pitcher and went to the well, so that as deacon he might draw water from the well for the sacred office of the Eucharist; for at that time he was himself serving in the order of deacon. So the blessed man pronounced a faithful blessing over the element of water that he had drawn from the spring, invoking the name of the Lord Jesus Christ, who transmuted water in Cana of Galilee; and by His operation in this miracle also, a baser substance, that of water, was changed into the more precious form of wine through the hands of the memorable man.

The holy man then returned from the well, entered the church and put down beside the altar the pitcher containing this liquid, saying to the servers, 'Here you have wine which the Lord Jesus has sent for the celebration of His mysteries.' When they discovered this, the holy bishop and the servers gave great thanks to God. But the holy young man ascribed it not to himself but to Saint Findbarr the bishop. This, then, was the first proof of miraculous power that Christ the Lord made manifest through His disciple, the same that He had wrought through Himself in Cana of Galilee as the beginning of His miraculous signs.

Let this miracle of God manifested through our Columba illumine like a lamp the opening of this book, that we may now pass on to the other miracles shown through his powers.

· † ·

OF THE BITTER FRUIT OF A TREE CHANGED INTO SWEETNESS BY THE SAINT'S BLESSING

There was a most fruitful apple tree near the monastery of the Plain of the Oak, on its southern side, whose fruit the local people complained was excessively bitter. One day in autumn the saint went up to it, and seeing its branches laden to no purpose with fruit that gave more hurt than pleasure to those who tasted it, he raised his holy hand, blessed the tree, and said, 'In the name of Almighty God, bitter tree, may all your bitterness depart from you, and may your apples, most bitter hitherto, become now most sweet.' Wonderful to tell, more swiftly than words and at that same instant all the apples on that tree lost their bitterness, and according to the saint's word became wonderfully sweet.

· † ·

OF CORN SOWN AFTER MIDSUMMER AND REAPED AT THE BEGINNING OF AUGUST, THROUGH THE PRAYER OF THE SAINT WHILE HE WAS LIVING ON THE ISLAND OF IOU

At another time the saint sent his monks to fetch bundles of wattle from a layman's field to build a guest-house. They filled a freight-ship with that supply of wattle, and when they returned and came to the saint said that the layman was deeply distressed at the loss of it. The saint at once gave them these instructions, 'In that case, to avoid giving offence to that man, let us take him twice three pecks of barley, and let him sow it now in ploughed land.' In accordance with the saint's command, this grain was sent to the layman, whose name was Findchan, and delivered to him with that instruction. He received it gratefully, but said, 'What good will corn sown after midsummer do against the nature of this soil?' His wife, on the other hand, said, 'Do according to the saint's bidding. The Lord will grant him whatever he asks of Him.' Moreover, those who were sent gave this further message: 'Saint Columba, who sent us to you with this gift, charged us with this instruction regarding your corn, "Let that man trust in God's omnipotence. His corn, though sown when fifteen days of June are passed, will be reaped at the beginning of August."' In obedience the layman ploughed and sowed; and the crop which, against all hope, he sowed at the time aforesaid he gathered fully ripe, to the astonishment of all his neighbours, at the start of August, in accordance with the saint's word. The name of that place is Delcros.

· † ·

OF A PESTIFEROUS CLOUD AND THE HEALING OF VERY MANY SUFFERERS

At another time also when the saint was living on the island of Iou, he was sitting on the hill whose name means 'Great Fortress' when he saw in the north a thick raincloud that had risen from the sea on a fine day. Seeing it as it rose, the saint said to one of his monks, called Silnan, son of Nemaid mocu-Sogin, who was sitting beside him, 'This cloud will bring great harm to men and beasts. It will pass over quickly today, and upon a large area of Ireland, that is from the stream called Ailbine as far as Ath-cliath, it will drop in the evening a pestiferous rain, which will cause severe and festering ulcers to develop on human bodies and the udders of cattle. Men and cattle afflicted with them will sicken even unto death in the throes of that venomous disease. But we must pity them and, by God's mercy, bring help to them in their sufferings. You therefore, Silnan, go down from the hill now with me and prepare to sail tomorrow, if we yet live and God be willing, after taking bread from me that has been blessed with the invocation of God's name. When it is dipped in water, men and beasts sprinkled with the water will quickly recover their health.'

Not to waste words, on the next day, after quickly making the necessary preparations, Silnan took the bread that had been blessed from the saint's hand, and sailed off in peace. At the time of his departure, the saint gave him this further word of comfort: 'Be of good courage, my son; you will have fair and following winds by day and night until you reach that district that is called Ard-ceannachte, so that you may quickly come to the help of those who are sick there with the healing bread.'

To be brief, Silnan obeyed the saint's word and, after a fair and speedy voyage, came with the Lord's help to the aforementioned place, where he found the people of that district, of whom the saint had prophesied, ravaged by the pestiferous rain falling on them from the cloud, which had sped rapidly on before him. And first of all, six men who were found in the same house near the sea, in desperate straits and on the point of death, were sprinkled by Silnan with the holy water and made a timely recovery that same day. The news of this sudden cure spread swiftly through the whole of that district ravaged by the grievous pestilence and drew all the sick people to Saint Columba's emissary; and he, in accordance with the saint's command, sprinkled men and beasts with the water in which the blessed bread had been dipped. And at once restored to full health, the men who were saved with their cattle praised Christ in Saint Columba, with great thankfulness.

Now in the story recorded above these two things, I believe, are clearly conjoined: the gift of prophecy concerning the cloud and the miraculous power in the healing of the sick. As to the complete truth of this account, in every particular, the aforesaid Silnan, soldier of Christ and Saint Columba's minister, testified before Abbot Segene and the other elders.

· † ·

OF MAUGIN, A HOLY VIRGIN, DAUGHTER OF DAIMEN, WHO LIVED IN CLOCHER OF THE SONS OF DAIMEN

At another time, when the saint was staying on the island of Iou, at the first hour of the day he called to him a brother called Lugaid, surnamed in Irish Lathir, and addressed him as follows: 'Prepare at once to sail swiftly to Ireland, as there is an urgent need for me to send you as my minister to Clocher of the sons of Daimen. For during the past night by some mischance Maugin, a holy virgin and daughter of Daimen, stumbled when returning home from the oratory after the office, and her hip was broken quite through. She keeps calling out and repeating my name, in the hope of receiving comfort from the Lord through me.'

In short, Lugaid obeyed and at once set out, and as he did so the saint gave him a little box of pine-wood with a blessing, saying: 'When you arrive to visit Maugin, let the blessing contained in this little box be dipped in a vessel of water, and let the water thus blessed be poured over her hip; and at once, upon the invocation of God's name, the hip-bone will be joined and knit together, and the holy virgin will be restored to full health.' And the saint added this: 'See, in your presence I write on the lid of this box the number twenty-three, which is the number of years that the holy virgin will live in the present life after this healing.'

All these things were completely fulfilled as they had been foretold by the saint. For as soon as Lugaid came to the holy virgin, and her hip was washed with the blessed water as the saint had instructed, the bone knit together without delay, and it was completely healed. And she rejoiced with great thankfulness over the arrival of Saint Columba's minister, and, according to the saint's prophecy, she lived for twenty-three years after her healing, continuing in good works.

· † ·

OF THE CURES OF VARIOUS DISEASES, PERFORMED AT THE RIDGE OF CETE

The man of memorable life, as we have been informed on reliable authority, healed the disorders of various sick people, by invoking the name of Christ, during the days when he went to the conference of kings and stayed for a short time at the Ridge of Cete. For either by the stretching out of his holy hand, or by sprinkling with water blessed by him, or by touching even the hem of his cloak, or by taking something blessed by him, such as salt or bread, and dipping it in water, many sick people who had faith were restored to health.

· † ·

OF ROCK-SALT, BLESSED BY THE SAINT, WHICH FIRE COULD NOT CONSUME

At another time similarly Colcu, son of Cellach, asked the saint for a piece of rock-salt blessed by him and received it for the relief of the sister who had nursed him, and who was suffering from a very severe attack of ophthalmia. This same sister and nurse accepted that blessed gift from her brother's hand, and hung it on the wall above her bed; and after some days by a mischance it happened that the village, including that woman's cottage, was ravaged by fire and utterly destroyed. Strange to say, a small part of that wall remained standing and undamaged after the whole house around it was burned down, so that the blessed man's gift, which hung on it, should not perish; and the fire did not venture to touch the two stakes on which the blessed rock-salt was hanging.

· † ·

OF A PAGE OF A BOOK WRITTEN BY THE SAINT'S HAND, WHICH COULD NOT BE DAMAGED BY WATER

There is another miracle that I consider should not be omitted, which was once performed through the opposite element. Many circling years had run by after the blessed man's passing to the Lord, when a certain young man, falling from his horse, was drowned in the river called in Irish Boend, and remained beneath the water for twenty days. And just as when he fell he had books under his arm packed in a leather satchel, so also after the said number of days he was found holding the satchel with the books between his arm and his side. After his body was carried back to dry land, and the satchel opened, among other books whose pages were not only damaged but even rotten there was found a page, written by Saint Columba's holy fingers, which was dry and in no way damaged, as if it had been kept in a book-chest.

· † ·

OF ANOTHER MIRACLE PERFORMED IN SIMILAR CIRCUMSTANCES

At another time a book of hymns for the week, written in Saint Columba's hand, dropped from the shoulders of a boy who fell from a bridge, and with the leather satchel that contained it sank in a river in the province of the Lagin. This book, which remained in the water from the Lord's nativity until the completion of the Easter season, was afterwards found on the river bank by some women who were walking there; and it was carried to one Iogenan, a priest of Pictish race, to whom it formerly belonged, in the same satchel, which was now not only sodden but even rotten. When this same Iogenan opened the satchel, he found his book undamaged, and as clean and dry as if it had remained all the time in a book-chest and had never fallen into the water.

We have learned for certain also, on good authority, of other similar miracles concerning books written in Saint Columba's hand, which occurred in various places; books, that is to say, which when sunk in water were able to remain completely undamaged. But concerning the above-named Iogenan's book we have received a wholly unequivocal account from truthful and blameless men of reliable testimony, who observed the same book, after so many days of submersion, to be perfectly white and clear.

These two miracles, though performed in matters of small moment and shown through opposite elements, namely fire and water, bear witness to the honour of the blessed man and to the extent and nature of his merit in the sight of God.

· † ·

OF WATER DRAWN FROM HARD ROCK BY THE SAINT'S PRAYERS

And because mention was made just above of the element of water, we ought not to pass over in silence some other miracles involving the same substance, which the Lord performed through the saint at different times and places.

On one occasion, during the time the saint spent in pilgrimage, an infant was presented to him for baptism by its parents when he was on a journey. And because water could not be found in the neighbourhood, the saint turned aside to a rock close by, and prayed for a while on his knees; and rising up from his prayer he blessed the face of that rock. Presently there gushed out from it an abundant stream of water, in which he at once baptised the little infant. He also uttered these words of prophecy concerning him after the baptism:

'This little boy will live to a very great age. In the years of his youth he will give due obedience to the desires of the flesh, and afterwards, serving as a soldier of Christ until his death, he will depart to the Lord in a good old age.'

All these things befell that man in accordance with the saint's prophecy. This was Ligu Cen-calad, whose parents were from Artda-muirchol, where even today a well, potent by the name of Saint Columba, can be seen.

· † ·

OF THE MALIGN WATER OF ANOTHER WELL, WHICH THE HOLY MAN BLESSED IN THE LAND OF THE PICTS

At another time, when the blessed man was staying for some days in the province of the Picts, he heard that the fame of another well was widespread among the heathen population, and that the devil darkened their understanding so that the foolish people worshipped it as a god. For those who drank from this well, or purposely washed their hands or feet in it, were allowed by God to be struck by devilish art, so that they returned either leprous or half-blind, or crippled or afflicted with infirmities of some other sort. Led astray by all this, the heathen paid divine honour to the well. After learning of this, the saint one day fearlessly approached the well; and the druids, whom he often drove from him confounded and vanquished, were overjoyed to see it, supposing that he would suffer similar ills from contact with that noxious water. He, however, raising his holy hand and invoking the name of Christ, first washed his hands and feet; and next, together with his companions, drank of the same water which he had blessed. And from that day the demons withdrew from that well; and not only was it not allowed to harm anyone, but after the saint's blessing and washing in it many infirmities among the people were even cured by the same well.

· † ·

OF THE BLESSED MAN'S PERIL AT SEA, AND THE SUDDEN CALMING OF A STORM AT HIS PRAYER

At another time the holy man began to be in peril at sea; for all the hull of the ship was violently shaken and fiercely buffeted by great, swelling waves, while a mighty storm of winds was raging on every side. The sailors then said by chance to the saint, as he joined them in trying to bail out the bilge-water, 'What you are doing now is no great help to us in our danger; you should rather pray for us, as we perish.' Hearing this, he ceased the empty labour of pouring bitter water into the green sea, and began to pour out to the Lord a sweet and fervent prayer. Wonderful to tell, at the same moment when the saint, standing in the prow with hands outstretched to heaven, prayed to the Almighty, the stormy winds and raging sea, more swiftly than words, subsided and became still, and a perfect calm at once ensued. Those who were in the ship were astounded, and in great wonder gave thanks and glorified God in the holy and memorable man.

109

Codex Lindisfarnensis

If the colophon of the Book of Durrow offers a feast for palaeographic speculation, that of the Book of Lindisfarne – or the Lindisfarne Gospels as it has become more familiarly known – offers an unrivalled source of provenance:

> Eadfrid, bishop of the church of Lindisfarne, originally wrote this book for God and for Saint Cuthbert and jointly for all the saints whose relics are in the island.
>
> And Ethelwald, bishop of the islanders of Lindisfarne, impressed it on the outside and covered it as well he knew how to do.
>
> And Billfrid, the anchorite, forged the ornaments which are on the outside and adorned it with gold and gems and gilded silver.

The colophon was added to the manuscript by Aldred, provost of the Lindisfarne monks at Chester-le-Street, where the community took refuge between their departure from the island in 875 and their eventual settlement at Durham in the last years of the tenth century. Aldred adds his own name to the colophon as the author of the Anglo-Saxon gloss on the Latin text and his inscription can be dated to around 970. Eadfrith succeeded to the bishopric of Lindisfarne in 698, followed by Ethelwald in 721. The manuscript can thus be dated to the first years of the eighth century and Aldred's colophon to more than 250 years later, yet clearly deriving from the reliable tradition of the community.

The Book of Lindisfarne itself offers confirmation of the origin of the Book of Durrow in the same scriptorium. Such a masterwork of manuscript art cannot spring unheralded on to vellum and the Celtic artistry of the scribe of the *Codex Durmachensis* was clearly the model for his successor at work on the *Codex Lindisfarnensis*.

It is in the divergent texts of the two books that the clearest reflection of a hundred years of liturgical history is revealed. The Durrow text is certainly a seventh-century transcription of a sixth-century text – the almost-pure Vulgate of the Hieronymian gospels – while the Lindisfarne text corresponds even in its errors with that of the *Codex Amiatinus* of the Jarrow scriptorium, indicating that the scribes of Aidan's foundation were firmly under the influence of Rome before the year 720.

In *From Durrow to Kells*, George Henderson observes how important is the Book of Lindisfarne's dedication to St Cuthbert, rather than to the church of Lindisfarne, or to Peter, the saint to whom that church is dedicated. The zoomorphic interlacing on the magnificent decorated pages underlines that dedication in its abundance of discernible bird-forms so evocative of the wildlife of the Farne Islands and the Lindisfarne shore. In her monograph on *The Lindisfarne Gospels*, Janet Backhouse admits that 'it is hard not to see in them some reflection of the cormorant family, seated in characteristic attitude on the rocks with necks and beaks proudly extended and with the sun striking the gleaming iridescence of their feathers'. Those seabirds were Cuthbert's companions through all his years as a hermit on Inner Farne and his affection for the wild creatures of the islands is central to his legend and tradition. Neither can it be accidental that Eadfrith, the scribe of the manuscript, succeeded to the bishopric in the year of the translation of Cuthbert's uncorrupt remains, and is himself the dedicatee of Bede's prose *Vita Sancti Cuthberti*.

'Christi Autem' – the *chi-rho-iota* monogram: f. 29^r.

The Lindisfarne Gospels, the British Library: Cotton MS Nero D iv.

onginneð   godspell   æfð   matheus

ILICIPIT euangeli   um secundum mattheu::

cyster

ħ II
ħ III
ħ II
tu II

untedlice
ruæt par
enipter enau
ne ro

roð lice

cynn pæccenne t enaureru   ruæt ður   pær   mið ðy

RATIOXILERATUM

pær   bi poedded t beboden t bereurtnud t betaht   togemanne
                                                                     nalleſ to hab
                                                                     banne. ſ̄ſ̄

EXSHOXBOLKATA

moder   hur   abrahan
                                                                     ðe aldonmon
                                                                     pær in ðem
                                                                     tid in hienu
                                                                     ralem ƿone
                                                                     bircob. he be
                                                                     beod maƿia
                                                                     iorephe to
                                                                     gemenne ŋ
                                                                     tob ðgeong,
                                                                     annet mið
                                                                     claenmreſ,

MATER EIUS MARIGUIOSEBH

OF ANOTHER SIMILAR PERIL TO HIM AT SEA

At another time also, when a most wild and perilous storm was raging, and his companions cried out to the saint to pray to the Lord for them, he gave them this reply: 'Today it is not for me to pray for you in the peril that threatens you, but for the holy man, Abbot Cainnech.' I have a marvellous tale to tell. At that same hour Saint Cainnech, who was living in his own monastery, called in the Irish Ached-bou, meaning Plain of the Cow, heard the aforesaid words of Saint Columba with the inner ear of his heart, by a revelation of the Holy Spirit. It was after the ninth hour, but although it chanced that he had begun to break the holy bread in the refectory, he swiftly abandoned the table, and with one shoe on his foot and the other left behind in his great haste he went hurriedly to the church, with these words, 'It is not for us to be dining at a time like this, when Saint Columba's ship is in peril at sea. For at this moment he keeps calling on the name of Cainnech here, to pray to Christ for him and his companions in their peril.' After speaking these words he entered the oratory and prayed for a while on his knees. And the Lord heard his prayer, the storm at once ceased, and the sea became very calm. Then Saint Columba, seeing in the spirit Saint Cainnech's haste in going to the church, though he lived far away, brought forth these remarkable words from his pure heart: 'Now I know, Cainnech, that God has heard your prayer. Your running swiftly to the church with a single shoe is a great help to us now.' In such a miracle as this, then, it is our belief that the prayers of both saints worked together.

· † ·

OF SAINT CAINNECH'S STAFF, FORGOTTEN AT THE HARBOUR

At another time, when the same Cainnech mentioned above was setting out from the harbour of the island of Iou to sail to Ireland, he forgot to carry his staff with him. This staff of his, after his departure, was found on the shore and handed over to Saint Columba; and he, after returning home, carried it into the oratory and remained alone there for a long time in prayer.

Then, as Cainnech was approaching the island of Oidech, he was suddenly conscious of his forgetfulness, and deeply shocked. But after a little while, leaving the ship and kneeling on the ground in prayer, he found the staff, that he had forgotten at the harbour of the island of Iou and left behind him, lying on the turf of the land of Oidech in front of him. And, greatly surprised at its being transported by divine power, he gave thanks to God.

·†·

Of the holy priests, Baithene and Colman, son of Beogna, who on the same day asked, through the blessed man's prayer, for a favourable wind to be granted them by God, though they were sailing in different directions

At another time also, the holy men named above came to the saint and asked him, at the same time and in one accord, to obtain by prayer from the Lord that a favourable wind should be given them the next day, when they were to set out in different directions. The saint gave them this reply: 'Early tomorrow, when Baithene sails out from the harbour of the island of Iou, he will have a following wind until he reaches the harbour of the Plain of Long.' And this the Lord granted, in accordance with the saint's word. For on that day Baithene crossed the whole of that broad sea with full sails to the land of Eth.

But at the third hour of the same day the venerable man summoned the priest Colman, and said, 'Baithene has now arrived successfully at his intended harbour. Make ready to sail today. Soon the Lord will change the wind to the north.' And at the same hour, after the blessed man had spoken these words, the south wind obediently changed to a northern breeze. And in this way on the same day the two holy men, parting from each other in peace, sailed with full sails and following winds; Baithene in the morning to the land of Eth, and Colman in the afternoon setting out for Ireland.

This miracle was wrought by the gift of the Lord through the power of the illustrious man's prayers, because, as it is written, '*All things are possible to him that believeth.*' After the departure of Saint Colman on that day, Saint Columba uttered this prophecy concerning him, 'The holy man Colman, whom we have blessed on his departure, will never in this world see my face again.' And this was afterwards fulfilled, for in the same year Saint Columba departed to the Lord.

·†·

Of the driving out of a demon that lurked in a milk-vessel

At another time, a certain young man, named Colman, of the race of Briun, suddenly stopped upon reaching the door of the little hut in which the blessed man was writing. He was returning after the milking of the cows, carrying on his back a vessel full of fresh milk, and asked the saint to give this burden the usual blessing. Then the saint, as he faced him some distance away, raised his hand and described in the air the sign of salvation, and invoking God's name, he blessed the vessel. It at once shook violently, and the bolt that held the lid was forced out through its two holes and shot far away, while the lid fell to the ground. The greater part of the milk was spilled on the earth. The youth put down the vessel on its bottom, with the little milk that was left, on the ground, and knelt in

supplication. The saint said to him, 'Rise, Colman. Today you have been careless in your work. For there was a demon lurking in the bottom of the empty vessel, and before pouring in the milk you failed to drive it out by forming the sign of the Lord's cross on it. It was the power of this sign just now that he was unable to endure, and that made him tremble as the whole vessel shook, and take swiftly to flight, spilling the milk. So bring the vessel closer to me here, that I may bless it.' After this was done, the half-empty vessel which the saint had blessed was found to have been filled again by God at that same moment; and the little that had remained before in the bottom of the vessel had at once increased, under the blessing of his holy hand, till it reached the brim.

OF A VESSEL WHICH A SORCERER NAMED SILNAN HAD FILLED WITH MILK TAKEN FROM A BULL

This is said to have happened in the home of a rich layman called Foirtgern, who lived on Mount Cainle. When the saint was a guest there, he determined the just settlement of a dispute between two rustics, whose arrival he had foreseen. One of them, who was a sorcerer, at the saint's bidding used diabolic art to take milk from a bull that was nearby. The saint gave this command not to confirm those sorceries – God forbid – but to confound them before the people. So the blessed man asked that the vessel be given him at once, full, as it seemed, of such milk; and he blessed it with this judgement: 'It will presently be proved that this is not the true milk it is thought to be but blood robbed of its colour by the artifice of demons to deceive mankind.' And at once that milky colour changed into its proper nature, that is into blood. The bull also, which for the space of one hour had been close to death, hideously shrunk and emaciated, was sprinkled with water blessed by the saint and was cured wonderfully quickly.

OF LUGNE MOCU-MIN

One day a young man of good disposition named Lugne, who afterwards, when an old man, was prior of a monastery on the island of Elen, came to the saint and complained about a severe bleeding from the nostrils which he had suffered frequently over several months. Calling him closer, the saint pressed both his nostrils together with two fingers of his right hand, and blessed him. And from that hour when he was blessed no drop of blood ever fell from his nose until his life's end.

Carpet-page from the gospel of Matthew: f. 26ᵛ.
The Lindisfarne Gospels, the British Library: Cotton MS Nero D iv.

·✝·

OF FISHES SPECIALLY PROVIDED FOR THE BLESSED MAN BY GOD

At another time, when some busy fishermen, companions of the memorable man, had caught five fishes in their net in the River Sale, where fish are plentiful, the saint said to them, 'Once again cast your net into the river, and you will immediately find a great fish which the Lord has provided for me.' They obeyed the saint's word, and hauled in with their net a salmon of marvellous size, provided for them by God.

At another time also, when the saint was staying for some days beside the Lake of Ce, his companions wished to go fishing, but he kept them back, saying, 'Today and tomorrow no fish will be found in the river: I will send you on the third day, and you will find caught in the net two great river salmon.' So after two days they cast their net, and found in the river, which is called Bo, those two fish of extraordinary size, and drew them to land.

In the catches of fish here recorded there is revealed miraculous power in conjunction with prophetic foreknowledge. And the saint and his companions gave great thanks to God for them.

·✝·

OF NESAN THE CROOKED, WHO LIVED IN THE DISTRICT BORDERING ON THE LAKE OF APORS

This Nesan, when he was very poor, was once glad to welcome the holy man as his guest. After he had entertained him for one night with the hospitality that his means would afford, the saint enquired of him how many cows he owned. He said, 'Five.' The saint then said, 'Bring them to me, that I may bless them.' When they were brought, the saint raised his holy hand and blessed them, saying, 'From this day your little herd of five cows will increase to the number of one hundred and five.' And because this Nesan was a layman with wife and children, the blessed man added these further words of blessing: 'Your seed will be blessed in your sons and grandsons.' All of this was completely fulfilled, according to the saint's word, in every particular.

But concerning a most avaricious man of wealth named Vigenus, who had despised Saint Columba and did not welcome him as a guest, he pronounced a contrary prophetic judgement, speaking as follows: 'The wealth of that avaricious man, who has spurned Christ in the strangers that visit him, will from this day gradually be diminished, and will be reduced to nothing; he himself will be a beggar, and his son will run about from house to house with a half-empty bag; and he will be struck with an axe by one of his enemies and will die, in the trench of a threshing-floor.' All of these things were completely fulfilled concerning each of them, according to the holy man's prophecy.

·✝·

OF COLMAN, ANOTHER LAYMAN, WHOSE CATTLE WERE VERY FEW WHEN THE SAINT BLESSED THEM, BUT AFTER HIS BLESSING THEY INCREASED TO A HUNDRED

At another time, also, the blessed man had been well treated one night as the guest of the aforesaid Colman, who at the time was a poor layman; and early in the morning the saint questioned his host about the quantity and nature of his property, as has been recorded above in the case of Nesan. On being questioned, he said, 'I have only five small cows; but if you bless them, they will increase to more.' At the saint's bidding he at once brought them; and blessing the five little cows of this Colman in just the same way as described above in the case of Nesan, he said, 'You will have, by God's gift, a hundred and five cows, and on your sons and grandsons there will be an abundant blessing.'

All these things were completely fulfilled, according to the blessed man's prophecy, in his fields, cattle and offspring. And strange to tell, when the number of one hundred and five cows, predetermined by the saint for both the aforesaid men, had been reached, it could in no way be increased; for those beasts that were surplus to the number predetermined were carried away by various mischances and disappeared, apart from any that could be used for the private needs of the family or for the work of charity.

In this story, then, as in the others, miraculous power and the gift of prophecy are plainly revealed in conjunction. For in the large increase of the cattle can be seen the power of blessing and of prayer, and in the determination of the number, prophetic foreknowledge.

·✝·

OF THE DEATH OF SOME MALEFACTORS WHO HAD DESPISED THE SAINT

The venerable man had a great love for the above-mentioned Colman, whom he raised from poverty to wealth by the power of his blessing, because he performed many kind services for him. Now there was at that time a certain malefactor and persecutor of the righteous, named Ioan, son of Conall, son of Domnall, sprung from the royal family of Gabran. The man persecuted the aforesaid Colman, the friend of Saint Columba, and not once but twice had attacked and plundered his house, carrying off everything he found in it. It was therefore not undeserved, after he had plundered the same house for the third time, and was returning with his companions, laden with booty, to his ship, that it befell this wicked man to meet at close quarters the blessed man whom he had despised, supposing him to be far off. When the saint reproached him for his evil deeds, and begged and urged him to put down the booty, he remained hard-hearted and obstinate and scorned the saint, and boarding his ship with the booty he derided and mocked the blessed man. The saint followed him to the sea, and entering the glassy waters of the ocean up to his knees, and raising both hands to heaven, he prayed earnestly to Christ, who glorifies His chosen ones as they glorify Him.

That harbour in which after the persecutor's departure he stood and prayed for a while to the Lord is at a place called in Irish Aithchambas Artmuirchol. After finishing his prayer, the saint next returned to dry land and sat on the higher ground with his companions. And in that hour he spoke the most terrible words to them, saying, 'This miserable wretch, who has despised Christ in His servants, will never return to the harbour from which he set sail before your eyes, nor will he with his wicked accomplices reach any other lands to which he plies; instead, a sudden death shall overtake him. Today, as you will soon see, a cloud rising in the north will unleash a violent storm which will sink him with his companions, and not even one of them will survive to tell the story.'

It was a perfectly calm day, yet only a few moments later, behold, a cloud arose from the sea, as the saint had said, accompanied by a thundering wind, and finding the robber with his booty between the islands of Male and Colossus, it stirred up a sudden storm and sank him in the midst of the sea. And, in accordance with the saint's word, of those who were on board not even one escaped. It was strange that all the sea round about remained calm, while an isolated storm such as this sank the robbers and flung them down to hell, a wretched fate indeed, but one deserved.

· † ·

OF ONE FERADACH, CARRIED OFF BY SUDDEN DEATH

At another time also the holy man entrusted a Pictish exile of noble family, named Tarain, to the protection of a certain Feradach, a rich man who lived on the island of Ile; and he requested particularly that he might live in his retinue for some months as one of his friends. After receiving him with this charge from the holy man's hand, a few days later Feradach dealt treacherously with him and had him murdered by a cruel order. When the monstrous crime had been reported to the saint by travellers, he made this reply: 'That unhappy wretch has lied not to me, but to God, and his name shall be struck from the book of life. We speak these words now in midsummer, but in the autumn, before he can taste the flesh of swine fattened on the fruit of trees, he will be overtaken by sudden death and dragged off to hell.'

When this prophecy of the holy man was reported to the miserable wretch, he scoffed at the saint in contempt. And after some days of autumn had passed, a sow fattened on the kernels of nuts was slaughtered by his order, before any of his other pigs were slaughtered; and he gave instructions that it should be quickly drawn and a part hastily roasted for him on a spit, wishing impatiently to have a foretaste of it so as to confound the blessed man's prophecy. When this had been roasted, he asked for a tiny morsel to be given him as a foretaste, and stretched out his hand to take it; but before he could put it to his mouth he expired, and fell dead on his back. And those who saw it and those who heard were filled with fear and wonder, and gave honour and glory to Christ in His holy prophet.

·†·

OF ANOTHER IMPIOUS MAN, A PERSECUTOR OF CHURCHES, WHOSE NAME MEANS 'RIGHT HAND'

At another time, when the blessed man was living on the island of Hinba and had begun to excommunicate some persecutors of churches, namely the sons of Conall, son of Domnall, among whom was Ioan of whom we spoke above, one malefactor who belonged to their company, prompted by the devil, rushed in with a spear to kill the saint. To prevent this, one of the brothers, called Findlugan, put on the holy man's cowl and interposed, ready to die for him. But miraculously, even such a garment of the blessed man as this served as a most secure and impenetrable coat of armour, and could not be pierced by a strong thrust from the sharpest spear, strong though the assailant was, but remained undamaged. Such was the protection that kept its wearer untouched and unharmed. But that villain, who was called Right Hand, withdrew, supposing that he had transfixed the holy man with his spear.

Exactly a year from that day, when the saint was living on the island of Iou, he said, 'This day is exactly one year from the day when Lam Dess tried with all his might to slay Findlugan in my stead; but I believe that he himself is being slain at this very hour.' In accordance with the saint's revelation, this happened at the same moment on the island whose name means 'Long', where in the course of a fight between two groups of men Lam Dess alone was killed, transfixed with a javelin, said to have been thrown in Saint Columba's name, by Cronan, son of Baitan; and after his death, the men stopped fighting.

·†·

OF ONE MORE PERSECUTOR OF THE INNOCENT

When the blessed man was still a young deacon, and living in the province of the Lagin, studying divine wisdom, it happened one day that a certain cruel man, a ruthless persecutor of the innocent, was pursuing a young girl who fled before him over a level plain. By chance she saw Gemman, the old teacher of the aforesaid young deacon, reading on the plain, and she ran straight to him for protection as fast as she could. Alarmed at the sudden threat, he called Columba, who was reading some distance away, that both together they might do all in their power to protect the girl from her pursuer. He presently appeared, and showing them no respect killed the girl with his spear as she hid beneath their robes; and leaving her lying dead at their feet, he turned away and began to depart.

Then the old man, stricken with grief, turned to Columba and said, 'For how long, holy young Columba, will God, the just judge, allow this crime, and this insult to us, to go unavenged?' Then the saint pronounced this sentence upon that author of the crime: 'In the same hour in which the soul of the girl slain by him ascends to heaven, may the soul of the slayer himself descend to hell.' And, more swiftly than words, as he said it, like Ananias before Peter, so too that murderer of the innocent fell dead before the eyes of the young

119

saint at that very spot. The news of this sudden and terrible vengeance was at once spread abroad through many provinces of Ireland, and the holy deacon won great renown by it.

Let this be a sufficient account of the terrible punishments inflicted on his adversaries. We shall now relate a few miracles concerning wild beasts.

At another time, when the blessed man was staying for some days on the island of Sci, he went alone to pray some distance apart from the brothers and entered a thick wood, where he was confronted by a boar of marvellous size which hunting dogs were pursuing. Seeing it at some distance, the saint stopped and looked at it. Then, invoking the name of God, he raised his holy hand and with a fervent prayer said to it, 'You shall approach no further; at the place you have now reached, die.' As these words of the saint rang out in the wood, not only was it unable to approach further, but the fearsome beast fell at once before his face, slain by the power of his word.

· † ·

OF THE DRIVING AWAY OF A WATER BEAST, BY THE POWER OF THE BLESSED MAN'S PRAYER

At another time also, when the blessed man was staying for some days in the province of the Picts, he had to cross the River Nes. When he reached its bank, he saw some of the local people burying an unfortunate man who, as the burial party themselves said, had been seized while swimming a little earlier by a beast that lived in the water, and bitten very severely. Some men went to help, though too late, in a wooden boat, and putting out hooks they caught hold of his poor body. The blessed man, however, on hearing of this, gave orders that one of his companions should swim out and bring back to him a boat that stood on the other bank. When he heard this order from the holy and memorable man, Lugne mocu-Min obeyed without delay, and taking off his clothes except his tunic plunged into the water. But the monster, whose hunger had not been satisfied earlier, was lurking in the depths of the river, keen for more prey. Feeling the water disturbed by his swimming, it suddenly swam to the surface, and with a mighty roar from its gaping mouth it sped towards the man as he swam in midstream. Then, as all who were there, both the barbarians and even the brothers, were stricken with great fear, the blessed man raised his hand at the sight and described the saving sign of the cross in the empty air; and invoking the name of God he gave the savage beast this command: 'You shall not advance further, nor touch the man. Go back with all speed.' Then the beast, hearing these words of the saint, fled back terrified at full speed, as if dragged away by ropes, although it had previously approached so close to Lugne as he swam, that between the man and the beast there was no more than one pole's length. The brothers then, seeing that the beast had retreated, and that their fellow soldier Lugne had returned to them in the boat untouched and unharmed, were filled with wonder and glorified God in the blessed man. Moreover, the heathen barbarians who were there at the time were impelled by the great power of this miracle, which they had seen with their own eyes, to magnify the God of the Christians.

·✝·

Of the saint's blessing of the soil of this island, in order that snakes might never thereafter poison anyone on it

One day during that summer in which he passed to the Lord, the saint rode in a wagon to visit the brothers who were busy building a cashel on the little plain in the west of the island of Iou. After speaking some words of comfort to them, the saint stood on higher ground and prophesied as follows: 'From this day, my little children, I know that you will never again be able to see my face upon this plain.' Seeing their great sorrow at hearing these words, he tried to console them as best he could, and raising both his holy hands he blessed all this island of ours, saying, 'From this moment no snake shall be able to poison men or cattle on the soil of this island, as long as the inhabitants of this settlement observe the commandments of Christ.'

·✝·

Of the saint's blessing of a dagger with the sign of the Lord's cross

At another time a brother named Mo-lua, of the race of Briun, came to the saint as he was writing, and said to him, 'I pray you, bless this blade that I have in my hand.' Holding out his holy hand with the pen a little way and making the sign of the cross, he blessed it with his face turned towards the book from which he was copying. After the aforesaid brother withdrew with the blade that had been blessed, the saint asked, 'What was the blade that I blessed for the brother?' Diormit, his faithful attendant, said, 'It was a dagger that you blessed, for slaughtering bulls or cows.' But he said in reply, 'I trust in my Lord that the blade which I blessed will harm neither men nor cattle.'

These words of the saint were fully confirmed that very hour. For the same brother went outside the rampart of the monastery intending to slaughter a cow, but although he struck three strong blows in his attempt he was unable even to pierce its hide. When they learned of this, skilled monks melted down the metal of that dagger in a hot fire and used the liquid to coat all the tools in the monastery; and afterwards these were unable to wound any flesh, through the abiding power of that blessing by the saint.

'The island of Hinba'

The significance of Hinba is greater than that of any other island of the Columban dominion apart from Iona. Yet, for all the frequency of Adamnan's references to it, he provides no certain topographical identity for the island on which Columcille was visited by the Holy Spirit, celebrated Mass for the saints of Ireland and received angelic ordinance over the succession of Aidan mac-Gabran.

The presence of ancient monastic ruins on *Eilean na Naoimh*, the southernmost of the Garvellach isles, has prompted no less an authority than Skene to support the tradition that this tiny island, long believed to be the burial place of Columcille's mother, was 'Hinba'. The evidence of Adamnan would suggest otherwise. The Hinba he describes was large and fertile enough to accommodate a substantial monastic establishment, over which Columcille's uncle presided as prior. The only place-name on Hinba to which he refers is *Muirbolc-mar*, which translates from the Gaelic as 'the great sea-bag' and could not describe any natural feature of the seagirt rock of Eilean na Naoimh.

The principal claim of the Garvellach to be Hinba is the cluster of ruined monastic cells which cling to its cliffs. W. J. Watson, in his study of *The Celtic Place-Names of Scotland*, identifies those ruins as 'beyond reasonable doubt' the remains of Brenden mocu-Alti's monastery of Ailech, which was certainly founded before 563 and probably between 524 and 558. The *Life* of Brenden tells how 'Brendan of Clonfert came to a certain island of Britain called Auerech, and there he founded a church, proposing to remain there to the end.'

The name *Ailech*, by which it was certainly known in Columcille's time, derives from the Gaelic word *ail* meaning 'a rock', and accurately describes the island as 'a rocky place'. Skene proposed that Columcille restored Brenden's monastery as his foundation of Hinba, but while the Garvellach might have appealed to a man such as Brenden the Navigator – indeed the neighbouring Garvellach is known as *Cuil Bhrrianainn*, or 'Brenden's Retreat' – it would have been at least untypical of the self-supporting monastic sites of the Columban *familia*.

Watson offers a very convincing alternative in the island known by the Norse name of *Jura*. Here is an island with a 'great sea-bag', sited on the sea-lane to Ireland and close by the fortress of Dunadd, which would certainly have provided an ideal location for Columcille's first foundation in Scotland. Watson offers further evidence in the name of 'Hinba', which suggests a Latin form of the Old Irish *inbe* meaning 'an incision'. Thus *Hinbina insula*, 'the Island of the Incision', would describe Jura's sea inlet of Loch Tarbert as well as it would describe the cleft between the Paps of Jura so clearly visible from Iona. Watson also records a local name for Jura of *t-Eilean Ban*, 'the Blessed Isle', and of a cave on its shore called *Uaimh mhuinn tir Idhe*, 'the Cave of the Folk of Hy', to which might be added the resting place of Columcille's uncle Ernan, the prior of Hinba, which is to be found in the graveyard of Inverlussa on Jura.

Watson offers a most impressive case for Jura as the location of Hinba, even to the satisfaction of the Ancient Monuments Commission whose inventory of Iona includes the almost officially convinced entry of 'Hinba (Jura?)'. To which I can only add a quotation from the first tenet of the Columban Rule: 'Be alone in a separate place near a chief city. . . .'

Jura from Kintyre.

· † ·

OF THE HEALING OF DIORMIT WHEN HE WAS SICK

At another time Diormit, the saint's faithful attendant, was sick unto death. The saint went to visit him in his extremity, and invoking the name of Christ as he stood by the sick man's bed and prayed for him, he said, 'Hear my prayer, my Lord, I beseech thee, and take not away the soul of my faithful servant from the habitation of this flesh as long as I live.' And when he had said this he became silent for a while. After that, he spoke these words from his holy lips: 'Not only will this servant of mine not die on this occasion, but he will even live for many years after my death.' This prayer of the saint was heard, for immediately after the saint's request found favour, Diormit recovered his full health. He also lived on for many years after the saint's passing to the Lord.

· † ·

OF THE HEALING OF FINTEN, SON OF AID, WHEN AT THE POINT OF DEATH

At another time also, when the saint was travelling across the Spine of Britain, one of his companions, a young man named Finten, was afflicted with a sudden sickness and brought to the point of death; and in their grief his fellow soldiers begged the saint to pray for him. In compassion for them he at once held out his holy hands towards heaven in earnest prayer, blessed the sick man, and said, 'This youth for whom you plead will live a long life, and will survive after the death of all of us who are here present, to die in a good old age.'

This prophecy of the blessed man was completely fulfilled in every particular. For the same young man, who afterwards was the founder of the monastery called Cailli aufinde, ended this present life in a good old age.

· † ·

OF A BOY WHOM THE VENERABLE MAN RAISED FROM THE DEAD IN THE NAME OF CHRIST THE LORD

At the time when Saint Columba was staying for some days in the province of the Picts, a certain layman with his whole household heard the word of life through an interpreter as the saint preached, and believed; and believing, he was baptised, the husband with his wife, children and servants. And after the interval of but a few days, one of the sons of the father of the house was seized by a severe sickness and brought to the very boundary that separates death from life. When the druids saw him dying, they began to mock the parents with loud reproaches, and to exalt their own gods as the more powerful, while disparaging the God of the Christians as the weaker.

When the blessed man was told of all this, roused with zeal for God he went with his companions to the house of his layman friend, where the parents were carrying out the sad obsequies for their child, who had just died. Seeing their great sorrow, the saint spoke words of comfort and encouragement to them, that they might have no doubt of God's omnipotence. And he next questioned them, saying, 'In what resting place is the dead boy's body lying?' The bereaved father then took the saint beneath the sad roof, and he entered the place of mourning alone, leaving the attendant throng outside. At once he knelt, and with tears streaming down his face prayed to Christ the Lord; and then rising from his knees he turned his eyes to the one that was dead, saying, 'In the name of the Lord Jesus Christ, rise up again, and stand on your feet.' With these noble words of the saint, the soul returned to the body, and he that was dead came back to life and opened his eyes; and the apostolic man held out his hand and lifted him up, and holding him steady on his feet led him out of the house, and returned him alive again to his parents. Then a shout rose up from the people, lamentation was turned into joy, and the God of the Christians was glorified.

In this miracle of the raising of the dead, let our Columba be accredited with the same power as the prophets Elijah and Elisha, and have a like share of honour with the apostles Peter, Paul and John; and among them both, the companies of the prophets and of the apostles, may this prophetic and apostolic man receive a place of honour for all eternity in the land of heaven, with Christ who reigns with the Father in the unity of the Holy Spirit for ever and ever.

· † ·

OF BROICHAN THE DRUID, PUNISHED WITH SICKNESS FOR KEEPING A WOMAN SLAVE, BUT CURED IN RETURN FOR HER RELEASE

About the same time, the venerable man asked the druid Broichan, who had an Irish woman as his slave, to pity her humanity and release her. When Broichan resisted most stubbornly and continued to keep her, the saint addressed him as follows: 'Know this, Broichan, know this: if you refuse to release this foreign captive for me before I return from this province, you will at once die.' He said this in the presence of King Brude, and then left the royal house and came to the River Nes. And picking up a white stone from this river, he said to his companions, 'Mark this white stone: through this the Lord will bring about many cures of the sick among this heathen people.' And after speaking these words he at once added, 'Now has Broichan suffered a mighty blow; for an angel sent from heaven has struck him grievously, shattered into many fragments the glass cup from which he was drinking, and left him gasping for breath and close to death. Here let us wait a little while for two messengers from the king, sent to us in haste to ask our immediate help for the dying Broichan. In his terrible plight, Broichan is now ready to release the slave-girl.'

While the saint was still speaking these words, behold, as he had foretold, two horse-men arrived sent by the king; and they described everything that had befallen Broichan in

the king's fortress, just as the saint had prophesied, regarding the breaking of the cup, the seizure of the druid, and his readiness to release the slave-girl. And they added this: 'The king and his household have sent us to you to ask your help for his foster-father Broichan, who is close to death.'

On hearing these words of the emissaries, the saint sent two of his company to the king with the stone blessed by him, saying, 'If Broichan first promises to free the slave-girl, then let this little stone be dipped in water and so let him drink of it, and at once he will recover his health. But if he refuses and opposes the slave-girl's release, he will immediately die.'

The two messengers, in obedience to the word of the saint, came to the king's court and reported to the king the venerable man's words. When these were made known to the king and his foster-father Broichan, they were most alarmed. And in the same hour the slave-girl was freed and entrusted to the holy man's emissaries, and the stone was dipped in water; and in miraculous defiance of nature it floated on the water like an apple or a nut, and the holy man's blessing could not be submerged. Broichan, after he had drunk of the floating stone, at once returned from the brink of death and recovered full health of body.

This miraculous stone was afterwards preserved among the king's treasures and brought about by the Lord's mercy the cure of many sicknesses among the people, after it was dipped in water and floated in the same manner. Strange to tell, when it was sought by those sick people whose life had reached its close, the same stone could not be found. For example, a search was made for it on the day of King Brude's death, but it could not be found in the place where it had previously been kept.

· † ·

OF THE BLESSED MAN'S OPPOSITION TO BROICHAN THE DRUID, AND OF AN ADVERSE WIND

One day after the events related above, Broichan said to the holy man, 'Tell me, Columba, when do you propose to set sail?' The saint said, 'We propose to start our voyage in two days' time, if God wills and we yet live.' But Broichan replied, 'You will not be able, for I have the power to create an adverse wind against you and to raise up a dark pall of mist.' The saint said, 'God's omnipotence rules over all things, and in His name and by His guidance all our movements are directed.' To be brief, the saint, accompanied by a large crowd, came to the long lake of the River Nes on that day, just as he had intended; while the druids began to rejoice as they saw a great mist and a storm raised up, with an adverse wind.

It is not surprising that happenings of this kind can sometimes, when God permits, be brought about by the art of demons, so that even the winds and waves are roused to fury. For in just the same way, when the holy Bishop Germanus was once sailing from a bay of Gaul to Britain for the salvation of souls, legions of demons confronted him far out at sea and stirred up menacing storms, hiding the sky and the daylight with a dark pall of mist. But at the prayer of Saint Germanus, and more swiftly than words, all became calm and still, and the mist was dispersed.

Carpet-page from the gospel of Mark: f. 94ᵛ.

The Lindisfarne Gospels, the British Library: Cotton MS Nero D iv.

Our Columba, therefore, seeing the elements being roused to fury against him, invoked Christ the Lord; and boarding the boat, more resolute than the hesitant crew, he ordered the sail to be hoist against the wind. At this, with the whole crowd looking on, the ship sailed against the adverse wind with astonishing speed. And after a short time the adverse winds, to the amazement of everyone, were turned round so as to prosper the voyage. And thus for the whole of that day a gentle and favourable breeze continued to blow, and the blessed man's boat was driven on to its intended harbour.

Let the reader, therefore, reflect on the greatness and character of this venerable man, in whom Almighty God, by the working of these miraculous powers recorded here, made manifest His glorious name before a heathen people.

· † ·

OF THE SUDDEN OPENING, OF ITS OWN ACCORD, OF THE GATE OF THE ROYAL FORTRESS

At another time, on the occasion of the saint's first laborious journey to King Brude, it happened by chance that this king, puffed up with the pride of kingship, haughtily refused to open the gates of his fortress when the blessed man first arrived. When the man of God learned this, he approached the doors of the gate with his companions, and first formed the sign of the Lord's cross on them, and then knocked and placed his hand against them; and at once the bars were forced back and the gate opened of its own accord with all speed. As soon as it opened, the saint at once entered with his companions. On learning of this, the king with his council, in great alarm, left the house and went respectfully to meet the blessed man, whom he addressed with words of peace in a most friendly manner. And from that day onwards, this monarch, as long as he lived, treated the holy and venerable man with the great honour that was due to him.

· † ·

OF THE SIMILAR UNLOCKING OF THE CHURCH OF THE LAND OF TWO STREAMS

At another time similarly, while spending some days in Ireland the blessed man went to visit, at their invitation, the brothers who lived in the monastery of the Land of Two Streams. But it happened by some chance that when he approached the church the keys of the oratory could not be found. When the saint heard the others complaining that the keys had still not been found and the doors were locked, he approached the entrance himself, and said, 'The Lord has power to open His house for His servants even without keys.' Then, with these words the bolts were suddenly forced back, the door opened of its own accord, and to the astonishment of everyone the saint entered the church at their head. And he was received hospitably by the brothers and treated by everyone with honour and reverence.

Of a layman who was a beggar, for whom the saint made a stake and blessed it for the killing of wild beasts

At another time there came to the saint a certain layman, a very poor man, who lived in the region that borders on the shores of the Lake of Apors. As this wretched man lacked the means to feed his wife and children, the blessed man took pity on him and at his request gave him such alms as he could afford, saying, 'Poor, unhappy man, fetch a branch from the neighbouring forest, and bring it to me quickly.' The poor man obeyed, and brought the wood according to the saint's bidding; and the saint took it and made a sharp stake of it. He sharpened it with his own hand and, blessing it and giving it to that destitute man, he said, 'Take good care of this stake; it will have no power, I believe, to harm either men or cattle, but only wild beasts and fish. And as long as you keep this special stake, your house will always have venison in plenty for your table.' On hearing this, the wretched beggar returned home in great delight, and fixed the stake in a remote part of the district, which was frequented by wild beasts of the forest. And when the next night had passed, he went early in the morning to visit the stake again, and found that a stag of marvellous size had fallen and been impaled upon it.

In short, no day could pass, as we are told, without his finding that a stag or a hind or some other beast had fallen upon the stake which he had fixed there. Moreover, when his whole house was filled with the flesh of wild animals, he sold to his neighbours what was left over after his own house was provided with all that hospitality required. However, the malice of the devil found out this wretched man, as it did Adam, through his wife, who gave her husband this imprudent and foolish advice: 'Take the stake up from the ground. For if men or cattle perish on it, you yourself and I, with our children, will either be put to death or led into slavery.' To this her husband said, 'This will not be, for when he blessed the stake the holy man told me that it will never harm men or cattle.'

After saying this, the beggar yielded to his wife and went and took up the stake from the ground; and, as if he loved it, he put it inside his house by the wall. Soon after, his house dog ran into it and was killed. After it died, his wife again said, 'One of your children will run into the stake and be killed.' On hearing her words, her husband removed the stake from the wall and carried it back to the forest, fixing it among the densest thickets, where he supposed that no living creature could stumble on it; but returning the following day he found that a she-goat had fallen upon it and perished. Removing it from there also, he fixed it in the river whose name means 'Black Goddess', hiding it under the water near the bank. When he came to visit it again the next day, he found impaled and held fast upon it, a salmon of marvellous size, which he lifted from the river and was scarcely able to carry home by himself. At the same time, he carried back the stake with him from the water, and fixed it higher up outside on his roof; but a raven dropped down from its swift flight and was transfixed and perished on it. At this, the unhappy man, led astray by the advice of his foolish wife, lifted the stake down from the roof, took an axe, and chopped it into small pieces and threw them on a fire. And afterwards, inasmuch as an important relief of his poverty had been lost, he took to begging again as his due. For that relief of his penury depended on the stake mentioned often above, which, if he had kept it, could have served instead of traps, nets and every method of hunting and fishing, once it had received the blessed man's benediction. After it was lost, the wretched layman, who for a time had been enriched by it, together with his whole family, mourned for it thereafter, though too late, for all the remaining days of his life.

· † ·

OF A MILK-SKIN WHICH THE EBB-TIDE CARRIED AWAY, AND WHICH APPEARED AGAIN IN ITS FORMER PLACE WITH THE FLOOD-TIDE

At another time, the blessed man's minister named Lugaid, surnamed Laitir, who was intending to do his bidding and sail to Ireland, searched among the tackle on the saint's ship for a milk-skin, and after finding it put it in the sea to soak, with a pile of large stones over it. When he came to the saint and told him what he had done with the skin, the saint smiled and said, 'The skin which you say you have put beneath the waves will not, I believe, accompany you to Ireland on this occasion.' 'Why', he said, 'shall I not be able to have it with me to accompany me on the ship?' The saint said, 'Tomorrow you will know the reason, as the event will prove.'

And so early the next day Lugaid went to pull the skin out from the sea; but the ebb-tide had carried it off in the night. Unable to find it, he returned sadly to the saint, and kneeling on the ground confessed his negligence. The saint said to comfort him, 'Do not grieve, brother, for perishable things. The skin which the ebb-tide carried away will be brought back to its place by the flood-tide after your departure.'

The same day, after Lugaid had set sail from the island of Iou, with the passing of the ninth hour the saint spoke as follows to those who stood round him: 'Let one of you go now to the sea. The skin of which Lugaid was complaining, and which the ebb-tide had taken away, has now appeared again in the place from which it was taken, brought back by the flood-tide.' Hearing these words of the saint, one lively young man ran to the seashore; and finding the skin, just as the saint had foretold, he carried it back at full speed, and in great delight handed it over in the saint's presence, to the amazement of the whole company.

These two stories told above, although they concern such small matters as a stake and a skin, are further illustrations of that association of prophecy with miraculous power which has often been mentioned. Now let us proceed to other matters.

·✝·

A PROPHECY OF THE HOLY MAN CONCERNING LIBRAN OF THE REED-BED

At another time, when the holy man was living on the island of Iou, a layman who had recently assumed the clerical habit sailed over from Ireland and came to the blessed man's island monastery. The next day he was found sitting alone in the guest-house by the saint, who began by asking him about his country, his family, and the reason for his journey; and he stated that he was born in the district of the Connachta and had endured the long labour of the journey in order to atone for his sins in pilgrimage. To test the character of his repentance, the saint brought before his eyes the hard and demanding duties of monastic life; and he promptly replied to the saint, 'I am ready for any tasks you wish to bid me perform, however hard and however lowly.'

To be brief, that same hour he confessed all his sins and promised, kneeling on the ground, to fulfil the terms of penance. The saint said to him, 'Rise, and sit down.' Then as he sat he addressed him as follows: 'You must do penance for seven years in the land of Eth. You and I, by God's gift, will live until you complete the number of seven years.'

Carpet-page from Jerome's preface: f. 2ᵛ.

The Lindisfarne Gospels, the British Library: Cotton MS Nero D iv.

Heartened by these words of the saint, he gave thanks to God, and to the saint he said, 'What should I do about a false oath that I swore? For while living in my own country I killed a man. After killing him I was found guilty and held in chains. But a kinsman of the same family, a man of great wealth, brought me timely help, freed me from the chains which held me, and rescued me from the death to which I was condemned. After my release I promised with a binding oath to serve him all the days of my life. But after I had spent some days in his service, scorning to serve a man and preferring rather to obey God, I deserted that earthly master and went away, breaking my oath; and the Lord prospered my journey, and I came to you.'

Seeing the man's great distress at these matters, the saint answered his words, as before, with a prophecy, saying, 'After completing the seven years as directed, you will come here to me during the forty days of Lent, so that you may approach the altar at the Easter festival and receive the Eucharist.'

Not to waste words, the penitent pilgrim obeyed the holy man's commands in every particular; and being sent at that time to the monastery of the Plain of Long, he completed his seven years of penance there and returned to the saint, in accordance with his earlier prophecy and bidding, during the forty days of Lent. At the Easter festival he approached the altar as bidden, and when it was over he came to the saint to ask about the above-mentioned oath. In reply to his question, the saint uttered these words of prophecy: 'Your earthly master, of whom you once spoke to me, survives, and your father, mother and brothers are still alive. Now therefore you must prepare yourself for a voyage.' And as he spoke, he held out a sword decorated with ivory carved from tusks, saying, 'Take this as a gift to carry with you, which you will offer to your master for your redemption; but he will not accept it. For he has a virtuous wife, and following her sound advice he will grant you your freedom that same day without payment of ransom, unloosing the captive's belt from your loins in the customary manner. But though released from this anxiety, you will not escape another care arising close by. For your brothers will join in pressing you to resume those duties of filial devotion owed for so long to your father, but neglected. However, you should comply with their wish without hesitation, and receive your aged father to cherish with a son's devotion. And although this may seem to you a heavy burden, you must not be distressed, as you will soon lay it down. For you will bury your dead father at the end of the same week in which you begin to minister to him. But after your father's burial your brothers will make a second urgent demand of you, that you should perform the filial duties owed also to your mother. From this demand you will assuredly be released by your younger brother, who will serve your mother on your behalf and readily take your place in performing all the work of filial devotion that you owe to her.'

After these words, the aforesaid brother, Libran, accepted the saint's gift and went his way enriched by his blessing; and on reaching his native land he found confirmation of all that the saint had prophesied. For as soon as he showed what he had to offer as the price of his freedom, whereas his master was willing to accept it, his wife opposed it, saying, 'How should we accept this that Saint Columba has sent for a ransom? We are not worthy of it. Let this devoted servant be freed for him without payment. The holy man's blessing will be of more benefit to us than this ransom that is offered.' And so her husband, hearing this sound advice from his wife, at once freed the slave without payment.

In accordance with the saint's prophecy, Libran then began to minister to his father in response to his brother's demands, but after six days his father had died, and he buried him. After the burial he was pressed to give the same devoted service to his mother, as was her due; but from this he was released by his younger brother, who came to his help, as the saint had foretold, and took his place, speaking to his brothers as follows: 'It is quite wrong that we should keep our brother in his native land, for he spent seven years in Britain with Saint Columba doing penance for the salvation of his soul.'

Then, released from all his burdens, he bade farewell to his mother and brothers and went back a free man; and coming to a place called in Irish Daire-Calcig, he found a ship under sail there putting out from the harbour, and shouted from the shore to ask the sailors to take him with them on their voyage to Britain. But they refused to take him on board and turned him away because they were not from the monks of Saint Columba. He then spoke to that venerable man, who, though far away, was yet present in spirit, as the event soon proved, 'Saint Columba,' he said, 'is it your wish that these sailors, who will not take me, one of your company, on board, should sail out with full sails and favourable winds?' At these words, the wind which was previously favourable to them swung round, more swiftly than words, to oppose them. Meanwhile the sailors, seeing the same man running in line with them by the riverside, at once took counsel together; and they shouted to him from the ship, saying, 'Perhaps it is because we refused to take you on board that the wind has suddenly turned against us. But if we invite you on to the ship with us even now, you will be able to change the winds that now oppose us to be in our favour.' Hearing this, the traveller said to them, 'Saint Columba, to whom I am going, and whom I have obeyed for the last seven years, will be able to obtain a fair wind for you from his Lord by the power of prayer, if you take me on board.' When they heard this, they brought the ship to land and invited him to join them on it. As soon as he came on board, he said, 'In the name of the Almighty, whom Saint Columba blamelessly serves, tighten the ropes and hoist the sail.' When this was done, at once the wind which blew against them was changed to be in their favour, and a prosperous voyage with full sails ensued all the way to Britain.

On their arrival in the land of Britain, Libran blessed the sailors as he left that ship, and came to Saint Columba, who was living on the island of Iou. That blessed man welcomed him gladly, and gave him a full account of everything that had happened to him on his journey, without anyone telling him: of his master, and his wife's sound advice, and how he had been freed at her suggestion; of his brothers, also; of his father's death, and his burial at the end of a week; of his mother, and of his younger brother's timely help; of what happened on his return journey; of the adverse and favourable wind; of the words of the sailors who at first refused to take him on board; of the promise of a fair breeze, and of the favourable change of wind after he was taken on board the ship. In short, everything that the saint had prophesied would come to pass, he recounted after it was fulfilled. After these words, the traveller handed over the price of his ransom, which he had received from the saint. And in the same hour the saint bestowed a name on him, saying, 'You shall be called Libran, for the reason that you are free.'

This Libran during those days took the monastic vow. And on being sent back by the holy man to the monastery in which he had previously served the Lord as a penitent for seven years, he received these words of prophecy concerning himself, which the saint spoke as he bade him farewell: 'You will live a long life, and will end this present life in a good old age. However, you will rise again not in Britain, but in Ireland.' Hearing these words he knelt and wept bitterly. And the saint, seeing his great sorrow, began to comfort him, saying, 'Rise, and do not grieve. You will die in one of my monasteries, and your part in the Kingdom will be with my chosen monks, with whom you will awake into the resurrection of life from the sleep of death.' Delighted to have received this great comfort from the saint, and enriched with the saint's blessing, he went in peace.

This truthful prophecy of the saint concerning that man was afterwards fulfilled. For after serving the Lord obediently as a monk in the monastery of the Plain of Long, for many circling years after Saint Columba's passing from the world, he was sent to Ireland, when very old, on some monastic business; and as soon as he disembarked he went over the Plain of Brega and came to the monastery of the Plain of the Oak. And there, being hospitably received in the guest-house, he was afflicted with a sickness and, after suffering for six days, went in peace to the Lord. And he was buried among the chosen monks of Saint Columba, according to his prophecy, to rise again into life eternal.

Let it suffice to have written these truthful prophecies of Saint Columba concerning Libran of the Reed-bed. This Libran is called 'of the Reed-bed' because he worked in a reed-bed for many years gathering reeds.

Carpet-page from the gospel of Luke: f. 138ᵛ.

The Lindisfarne Gospels, the British Library: Cotton MS Nero D iv.

·✝·

OF A POOR WOMAN WHO SUFFERED, AS A DAUGHTER OF EVE, SEVERE AND AGONISING LABOUR PAINS

One day, while the saint was living on the island of Iou, he rose quickly from his reading, and said with a smile, 'I must now hurry to the oratory, to pray for God's mercy on behalf of an unfortunate woman, tortured by the severe pangs of a most difficult childbirth, who is crying out now in Ireland and calling on the name of Columba here. And she hopes that through me she will be granted release from her torment by the Lord, because she is also related to me, having a father born of my mother's kindred.' Saying this, the saint ran to the church, moved with pity for that poor woman, and on bended knees he prayed for her to Christ, the son of man. After praying he left the oratory, and to the brothers who came to meet him he spoke as follows: 'Now has the Lord Jesus, born of a woman, brought timely relief of her distress, and freed her from her torment; and she has safely given birth, and will not die on this occasion.' At the same hour, as the saint had prophesied, the poor woman who called upon his name found release and recovered her health. This information was brought afterwards by some people who came across from Ireland and from the same district in which the woman lived.

·✝·

OF ONE LUGNE, A PILOT, SURNAMED TUDICLA, WHOM HIS WIFE HATED FOR HIS GREAT UGLINESS, AND WHO LIVED ON THE ISLAND OF RECHRU

At another time, when the holy man was a guest on the island of Rechru, a certain layman came to him and complained of his wife, who, he said, from hatred for him refused to allow him to enter into marital relations. Hearing this, the saint summoned the wife and to the best of his power began to reproach her for this, saying, 'Why, woman, do you try to disown your own flesh? The Lord says, *"The two shall be in one flesh"*; and so the flesh of your husband is your flesh.' She said in reply, 'I am ready to carry out whatever you require of me, however troublesome it may be, with one exception, that you do not press me to sleep in the same bed as Lugne. I make no objection to taking on the whole care of the house, or, if you bid me, even to crossing the seas, and living in some monastery for nuns.' The saint then said, 'What you say cannot lawfully be done. For while your husband still lives, you are bound by the law of the husband. For what God has lawfully joined together, it is forbidden to separate.' And to these words he at once added, 'Today let us three, myself and the husband and his wife, fast and pray to the Lord.' She then said, 'I know that it will not be impossible, that things which seem difficult or even impossible may be granted to you by God, at your request.'

In short, the wife agreed to fast with the saint that day, and her husband also. And on the following night the saint stayed awake and prayed for them. And the next day the saint spoke to the wife in her husband's presence as follows: 'Woman, are you ready today, as you said yesterday, to depart to a monastery for women?' She said, 'Now I know that your prayer concerning me has been heard by God. For the man whom I hated yesterday, today I love. My heart during this past night, I know not how, has been changed in me from hate to love.'

Not to waste words, from that day until the day of her death, the soul of that wife was inseparably bound in love for her husband, so that those rights of the marriage-bed which she had previously refused to allow, she never again withheld.

· † ·

A PROPHECY OF THE BLESSED MAN CONCERNING THE VOYAGE OF CORMAC, GRANDSON OF LETHAN

At another time Cormac, a soldier of Christ, to whom we have made some brief reference in the first book of this work, tried on a second occasion to search for a desert place in the ocean for a hermitage. After he had sailed out from land with full sails across the limitless ocean, Saint Columba during those days, while staying beyond the Spine of Britain, gave this charge to King Brude in the presence of the vassal-king of the Orcades: 'Some of our community have lately sailed out in the hope of finding a desert place in the endless sea. If by chance after their long wanderings they come to the islands of the Orcades, give strict charge to this vassal-king, whose hostages are in your power, that no harm should be done to them within his borders.' Now the saint spoke like this because he already knew in the spirit that after some months this Cormac would come to the Orcades, as afterwards happened. And because of the holy man's aforesaid charge, he was spared in the Orcades from impending death.

After the lapse of a few months, while the saint was living on the island of Iou, one day some men who were in conversation suddenly made mention of the same Cormac in his presence, saying, 'It is still not known whether Cormac's voyage was successful, or not.' Hearing these words, the saint spoke as follows: 'Cormac, of whom you are now speaking, will arrive today, and you will soon see him.' And after about one hour had passed, strange to tell, behold, Cormac appeared unexpectedly and entered the oratory, while they all marvelled and gave thanks.

As we have included a brief mention of the blessed man's prophecy concerning this Cormac's second voyage, we must now devote some words to his similarly prophetic knowledge of the third.

When Cormac was toiling for the third time in the ocean, such were the perils that beset him that he came close to death. His ship had run from land for fourteen summer days and as many nights with full sails before the south wind, in a straight course towards the northern regions, and he seemed to have sailed beyond the limit of human venture and all hope of return. And so it came about that, after the tenth hour of this fourteenth day, there arose on all sides terrors, inspiring dread almost beyond endurance; for they were confronted by some repulsive and highly aggressive little creatures, never seen before that time, which swarmed over the sea and attacked with fearsome violence, striking at the keel and sides, stern and prow with such force, that it was thought that they could penetrate the hide that covered the ship. Those who were there told afterwards that they were about the size of frogs, with extremely troublesome stings, but they did not fly, but swam; and they attacked the blades of the oars. At the sight of them, together with the other monsters which this is not the time to describe, Cormac and the sailors who accompanied him, in great fear and alarm, prayed tearfully to God, who is a merciful and ready helper in distress.

At that same hour also our Saint Columba, although far distant in body, was yet present in spirit in the ship with Cormac. At that moment, therefore, he called the brothers together at the oratory by the ringing of the bell, and, going into the church, he spoke to them as they stood there the following words of prophecy in his accustomed manner: 'Brothers, pray with all your power for Cormac, who has now sailed incautiously beyond the limit of human travel. He is now experiencing terrors of a monstrous and dreadful nature, never before seen and almost indescribable. We ought, therefore, in our minds to share the sufferings of our brother monks, placed as they are in unbearable peril, and pray to the Lord with them. For behold, Cormac, the tears streaming down his face, is praying fervently with his sailors to Christ: let us also help him with our prayers, that Christ, in pity for us, may turn round the south wind, which has blown these last fourteen days, to blow from the north. And may this north wind bring back Cormac's ship out of its perils.'

After saying this, he knelt before the altar, and in a tearful voice prayed to the almighty power of God, which governs the winds and all things; and when he had prayed, he quickly rose, wiped away his tears and gave joyful thanks to God, saying, 'Now, brothers, let us congratulate our dear ones for whom we are praying, because the Lord will turn round the south wind now to blow from the north and bring back our brother monks out of their perils; and it will return them to us here again.' And at once, as he spoke, the south wind ceased and a north wind blew for many days afterwards; and Cormac's ship was brought back to land, and Cormac came to Saint Columba; and by God's favour they saw each other face to face, to the great wonder and delight of all. Let the reader, therefore, reflect on the greatness and character of this blessed man, who had such prophetic knowledge and, by invoking the name of Christ, could command the winds and the ocean.

· † ·

OF THE VENERABLE MAN'S RIDING IN A CHARIOT UNSECURED BY LINCHPINS

At another time, when the saint was living for some days in Ireland, as he was required on some church business he climbed into a chariot which he had previously blessed, and which was yoked in readiness; but the necessary linchpins, through some careless and unaccountable mischance, had not first been inserted in the holes at the end of the axles. Now on that day it was Colman, son of Echuid, a holy man and the founder of the

monastery called in Irish Snamluthir, who was acting as charioteer in this chariot with Saint Columba. They travelled a long distance that day with severe shaking of the chariot, yet without any separating or loosening of the wheels and axles, although as said above, no linchpins held them secure; it was the grace of God alone which ensured that the chariot in which the venerable man sat proceeded safely, without any impediment, on a straight course.

Let it suffice to have written thus far of the miracles which the almighty power of God wrought through this memorable man while he was yet in this life. We must now record also a few of those which can be proved to have been granted to him by God after his passing from the flesh.

· † ·

OF RAIN WHICH, AFTER SOME MONTHS OF DROUGHT, FELL UPON PARCHED LAND BY THE GIFT OF GOD, IN HONOUR OF THE BLESSED MAN

About seventeen years ago, in the spring season, there occurred in these barren lands a great drought, continuous and severe, insomuch that the threat in the book of Leviticus, applied to transgressors, appeared to hang over the peoples. For it says: '*I will give to you the heaven above as iron, and the earth as brass. Your labour shall be spent in vain; the earth shall not bring forth her seed, nor the trees yield fruit*'; and so on. We, therefore, on reading this, in great fear of the misfortune that hung over us, took counsel and determined that some of our elders should go round the plain, recently ploughed and sown, with Saint Columba's white tunic and books written by his own pen; that they should raise in the air and shake three times this tunic, which he had worn at the hour of his departure from the flesh; and that they should open his books and read them on the little Hill of the Angels, where sometimes the citizens of the heavenly country were seen to descend to talk with the blessed man. All of this was carried out according to the plan determined; and, wonderful to tell, on the same day, the sky, which was bereft of clouds during the previous months of March and April, was suddenly covered with clouds that rose from the sea with remarkable speed, and heavy rain fell by day and night; and the land that was parched before, having drunk its fill, brought forth its seed in good time, and a most fruitful harvest that same year. And so the recalling of one blessed man's name in his tunic and books brought salutary and timely help on the same occasion to many districts and peoples.

Carpet-page from the gospel of John: f. 210ᵛ.
The Lindisfarne Gospels, the British Library: Cotton MS Nero D iv.

· † ·

OF ADVERSE WINDS CHANGED BY THE POWER OF THE VENERABLE MAN'S PRAYERS TO FAVOURABLE WINDS

Our belief in past miracles such as these, which we did not see, is confirmed beyond doubt by those of the present time, which we have witnessed ourselves. For we have ourselves seen adverse winds changed, on three occasions, to favourable winds. On the first occasion, when timbers of hewn pine and oak for a longship were being hauled over land, and timbers for the large house and also ships were being transported, we took counsel and placed the blessed man's clothes and books upon the altar, with psalms and fasting and the invocation of his name, that he might obtain from the Lord winds which should be favourable to us. And by God's gift this was accomplished for the holy man: for on the day when our sailors, with all their preparations made, intended to tow the aforementioned logs of wood over the sea with skiffs and currachs, the adverse winds of the previous days suddenly changed to favourable winds. Then, by God's grace, as favourable breezes attended them all that day, the whole of the fleet arrived successfully at the island of Iou, by long and winding courses, with full sails and without any hindrance.

On the second occasion, after an interval of some years, twelve currachs had been brought together and some oak timbers were being towed by us from the mouth of the River Sale for the repairing of our monastery. One calm day the sailors were sweeping the sea with their oars, when suddenly there rose up against us the west wind, also known as the Zephyr, and we then turned aside to the nearest island, called in Irish Airthraig, to seek a harbour in it for our shelter. But in the meantime we complained of the wind's untimely opposition, and began virtually to accuse our Columba, saying, 'Is it your wish, holy one, that this hindrance confronts us? Till now, by God's grace, we have hoped for some comfort and help from you in our labours, believing you to have great honour in the sight of God.' When we said this, after a brief pause, as it were of a single moment, behold, wonderful to tell, the adverse west wind ceased and, more swiftly than words, a north-east wind blew in our favour. Then, on the order, the sailors tightened the ropes and hoist the yard-arms, like a cross, and the sails; and with gentle breezes in our favour we made for our island that day, and travelled without effort, together with all our fellow workers who were on board, rejoicing in the transport of the logs. Our plaintive reproach to the holy man, slight though it was, brought us great benefit; and how great and special in the sight of God is the merit of the saint, whom He Himself heard in so swift a changing of the winds, is herein made manifest.

Then on the third occasion, in the summer season after a meeting of an Irish synod, we were detained by an adverse wind for some days among the people of the tribe of Loern, and came to the island of Saine; and as we waited there, the vigil of the solemn feast day of Saint Columba found us in great sorrow, as we wished to celebrate that day on the island of Iou. And so, as before on another occasion, we complained, saying, 'Is it your wish, holy one, that we should spend tomorrow, the day of your feast, among laymen, and not in your church? It is easy for you at the start of so special a day to obtain from the Lord that adverse winds be made favourable, and that we celebrate in your church the solemn rites of the Mass of your festival.' After that night was over, we rose at dawn, and seeing that the adverse winds had ceased we boarded our ships, with no wind blowing, and put out to sea; and, behold, at once from behind us the wind from due south, also known as Notus, began to blow. Then the sailors joyfully raised the sails; and so on that day, by God's gift to the blessed man, we had so effortless, speedy and favourable a voyage that, as we had previously desired, we reached the harbour of the island of Iou after the third hour of the day, and, after washing our hands and feet, entered the church with the brothers at the sixth hour, and celebrated together the sacred rites of the Mass. It was, as I say, the feast day of Saints Columba and Baithene, and at dawn on that day, as has been said above, we had sailed out from the island of Saine, very far away. Of the truth of this account given above there still survive witnesses, not two or three only, according to the law, but a hundred or more.

· † ·

OF THE PLAGUE

There is a further example of the working of his miraculous powers that I believe ought not to be reckoned as of minor importance: it concerns the plague which twice in our times laid waste the greater part of the world. For to say nothing of the other, wider regions of Europe, that is, Italy and the city of Rome itself, the Cisalpine provinces of Gaul and the provinces of Spain separated by the barrier of the Pyrenees; the islands of the Ocean, namely Ireland and Britain, were on two occasions totally laid waste by a fearful pestilence, except for two peoples, the Picts and the Irish in Britain, who are separated by the mountains of the Spine of Britain. And although among both peoples there is no lack of the great sins by which the Eternal Judge is generally provoked to wrath, yet hitherto He has shown forbearance and spared them both. To whom else, therefore, can this grace granted them by God be attributed, but to Saint Columba, whose monasteries founded within the borders of both peoples have been held in great honour by both to the present time? But what I am now going to say cannot, I think, be heard without a sigh, that there are in both countries many very stupid people, who do not know that they have been protected from diseases by the prayers of the saints, and ungratefully and wickedly abuse God's patience. We, however, give frequent thanks to God, who protects us from attacks of plagues both in these islands of ours, through our venerable patron's prayers on our behalf, and in the land of the Saxons, when we visited our friend King Aldfrith, though the plague had not yet abated and was devastating many villages in every direction. Yet both in our first visit after the war of Egfrith and in our second two years later, the Lord so protected us from danger, while we walked in the midst of this deadly plague, that not even one of our companions died, nor was any of them troubled by any disease.

Here must end the second book, concerning his miracles; in which the reader should notice that many examples, even of those that are reliably known, have been passed over to avoid wearying those who read it.

Here ends the second book.

The Visions of Columcille

The third and last book of Adamnan's *Vita Columbae* – 'concerning visions of angels' – has a more clearly discernible biographical structure than either of its predecessors, beginning with Ethne's vision of the destiny of her unborn son and concluding with Adamnan's magnificent account of 'the passing to the Lord' of Columcille. Its theme leads Adamnan to the high peaks of his hagiographical achievement, and yet also offers invaluable historical insights, most notably into the succession of Aidan and the later history of the Dalriadan kings.

Perhaps just as importantly, this third book illuminates its author as remarkably as his subject when it moves into the realm of the *Fis Adamnain*, the vision of heaven and hell which earned for Adamnan later acclaim as 'an Irish precursor of Dante'. Although these visions of Columcille suggest some of Adamnan's most significant gospel parallels, their settings are clearly rooted in the world of the Gael, even strikingly reminiscent of the graphic achievement of the Book of Kells, that masterwork of manuscript art known in the annals as 'the great Gospel of Columcille'.

The first of these visions is revealed to Columcille's mother, Ethne, who dreams 'between his conception and birth' of 'a robe of wondrous beauty' presented to her by an angel. This garment – which must invite comparison with the colourfully robed portrait page in the Book of Durrow – is swiftly taken from her, 'growing larger, so that it stretched beyond the breadth of the plains and rose above the mountains and woods with its greater stature'. The symbolism of the destiny of Columcille is clearly evident, but the Old Irish *Life* is more topographically explicit when it chronicles the same vision in terms of 'a large cloak which reached from the Islands of Modh to Caer-na-mBroc.' The translation of these place-names from the *Betha* significantly prophesies a dominion for Columcille which will reach from the islands off the coast of Mayo to Burghead on the Moray Firth.

There are two close parallels to this vision of Ethne, both of which would certainly have been familiar to Adamnan. The *Life of Ciaran of Clonmacnoise* records a similarly prophetic vision of a tree growing tall on the banks of the Shannon until its shadow falls over the whole of Ireland. Perhaps of greater import is the similarity to the angelic vision experienced by Mary before the birth of Christ and described by St Luke: 'And the angel came in to her, and said, Hail, thou that art highly favoured, the Lord is with thee: blessed art thou among women.'

Ethne's vision is followed by the first account of divine light on the young Columcille as it was witnessed by his foster-father, 'Cruithnecan, son of Cellachan, the illustrious priest', according to the Old Irish *Life*. Dr Reeves investigates the historicity of Cruithnecan with his customary tenacity but with no great success. The name is nowhere to be found in the Irish calendars, but there is a parish in Derry by the name of Kilcronaghan, which Reeves suggests might very well have derived from the Old Irish form of *cella Cruithnecain*. At the least, this episode provides us with Adamnan's provenance for the identity of Columcille's first tutor.

'From the highest place in the Kingdom of Heaven, from the glorious brightness of the Angelic state'

THE *ALTUS PROSATOR* ATTRIBUTED TO COLUMCILLE

Dawn over the Hill of the Angels, Iona.

Another vision of the youthful saint is attributed to 'the venerable bishop Finnio' – certainly St Finnian of Moville, who saw Columcille approaching with 'an angel of the Lord accompanying his journey' – and consequently provides further evidence of Columcille in deacon's orders at the monastery on Strangford Lough.

Of more substantial historical interest is the vision of St Brenden of Birr at the Synod of Teiltiu – or Teltown near Kells in Meath – which sought to excommunicate Columcille. Brenden, whom Adamnan indicates as speaking on Columcille's behalf at that assembly, sees 'a pillar, trailing fire and very bright, going before this man of God whom you despise, and holy angels accompanying him on his journey'. This remains Adamnan's only reference to the 'excommunication', but it can at least be clearly dated to the period after Culdrevny, even specifically to 563, on the evidence of its concluding statement that 'in these same days, the saint sailed over to Britain with twelve disciples as his fellow soldiers'.

Of still greater historical importance is Adamnan's substantial account of the awesome angelic vision commanding Columcille's ordination of Aidan mac-Gabran as the overlord of Dalriada. Conall mac-Comgall, who was king at Dunadd on Columcille's arrival in 563, reigned through the following eleven years, although Adamnan makes curiously few references to him. The reason for such short shrift may well be that Conall only rarely consulted the abbot of Iona on matters of state, and indeed there is no tradition of his so doing. Conall fell in battle in 574, probably at the hands of a rival dynasty of Irish settlers in the north of Dalriada, possibly even the outlaw clan of sea-raiders who clashed with Columcille on the occasions recorded in Adamnan's second book.

The choice of his successor fell to the saint, who went into retreat on Hinba to consider his decision with the benefit of divine guidance. Adamnan provides a quite extraordinary account of Columcille's being visited by an angel bearing a book of glass, in which was recorded the succession of kings, and a whip, with which to enforce that heaven-ordained royal sequence. Adamnan admits that Columcille's personal choice had already fallen on Aidan's elder brother, Iogenan, who indeed might have appeared to be the more legitimate successor. But the angel demanded that Columcille ratify the claim of Aidan, the son of Gabran and the younger nephew of Conall. The saint's reluctance caused the angel to use his whip to compel compliance and after three nights of such angelic intimidation, Columcille 'sailed across to Iou and there, as he had been bidden, ordained Aidan as king'.

It seems that Aidan mac-Gabran might have long harboured an ambition to succeed Conall. Fragments of bardic poetry suggested to Skene that Aidan fought at the battle of Ardderyd in 573, but it is certainly historically probable that he had been earlier exiled from Dalriada and sought to establish his own power base on the Firth of Forth. His son, Gartnait, became a king of the Picts – whose succession was assured through the maternal line – which would certainly suggest Aidan had taken a Pictish wife. All of which prompts the scenario of Aidan's returning to Dunadd on the death of his uncle Conall mac-Comgall, probably at the head of an impressive phalanx of fighting men, to claim the throne of Dalriada. However questionable his right of succession over his brother Iogenan – or *Eogain* in some sources – these were days of the iron sword. A warrior-king of proven qualities, with strong alliances amongst the Picts and the Britons, could well forge the Irish settlements into a powerful Dalriadan kingdom and establish himself – like Gabran – as 'king of Alba'. Such a man was Aidan, son of Gabran, and the abbot of Iona was well enough acquainted with the *Realpolitik* of his times to recognise the fact. Angelic approbation might well have been all that was needed to establish a questionable successor in Dunadd as Dalriada's greatest king.

So much for the angel's book of glass, but the scourge which he laid on Columcille prompts a somewhat different line of inquiry. Adamnan testifies that the saint bore the 'livid scar' of that whiplash to the end of his days. Such a scar would have been a familiar sight to Diormit, the saint's personal attendant, and Diormit's testimony would doubtless have been entered into Iona's hagiographical tradition. The angelic scourging might well have conveniently served to explain a scar of battle on the body of a saint, and the only occasion on which Columcille might have sustained such a scar was on the battlefield of Culdrevny. Circumstantial it may be, but the evidence of the livid scar – as the historian Alfred Smyth so cogently argues – would suggest that Columcille carried a sword as well as a psalter into that momentous conflict of the sons of Niall under Ben Bulben in 561.

At the end of the account of the ordination of Aidan by Columcille on Iona – by which act the saint blessed a line of Scottish monarchs which can be traced down through a thousand years to James VI of Scotland who became James I of England – there occurs the extract from the earlier *Life* written by Cummene Ailbe, or Cummene the White, the seventh abbot of Iona. This paragraph – inserted into Adamnan's original by the scribe Dorbbene and entered in smaller lettering into the 'A' manuscript – tells how Columcille promised their kingdom to the sons of Aidan for as long as they sustained their loyalty to Iona and also to Columcille's own Ui-Neill on the Irish mainland. This they did until the succession of Aidan's grandson, Domnall Brecc, in 630. Already a proven warrior, Domnall's military ambition was to prove disastrous for Dalriada. In 637, he allied with the cause of Congal Claen, the maternal grandson of Echoid Buide and thus his own nephew. Congal returned from exile on the British mainland and landed on the coast of Down, with an army of Britons, Saxons, Picts and Dalriadans, to lead the Cruithne in a bid for the kingship of Ulster. Congal and Domnall thus took up arms against the mighty Ui-Neill of the north under the command of their High King Domnall, son of Aid mac-Ainmure and thus blood kin to Columcille. The ensuing conflict at Mag Roth was a bloody battle of some six days' duration until, on the seventh day, Congal fell, his motley force of foreign allies broke ranks in defeat, and Domnall Brecc narrowly escaped with his skin. But Domnall had broken faith with Aidan's promise to Columcille and the defeat at Mag Roth marked the beginning of the end of Dalriada. Through the hundred years until 740 the annals record the fragmenting of Aidan's kingdom into smaller warring tribes, and more than twenty sieges of hillforts, among them the *caput regionis* at Dunadd which fell to Pictish assault.

Domnall Brecc himself continued on his ill-starred warpath for six more years after Mag Roth until he was slain in battle with the Britons of Strathclyde at Strathcarron in 642. It fell to a British bard to write his sanguinary epitaph in a fragment of battle-song:

> I saw an array, they came from Kintyre,
>   and splendidly they bore themselves . . .
> I saw great sturdy men,
>   they came with the dawn.
> And the head of Domnall Brecc, ravens gnawed it.

Adamnan apparently omitted Cummene's account of the prophecy of Columcille fulfilled at Mag Roth from his original manuscript and we owe its survival to Dorbbene. In *Iona, Kells and Derry*, Maire Herbert suggests that there had been an important revival of Columban hagiography on Iona in the early decades of the seventh century, when the Abbot Segene gathered the first-hand testimony of those surviving brothers who could recall the last years of the founder. These accounts would have provided the incomparably reliable source for the *Life* set down by Segene's nephew, the abbot Cummene, which in turn would have provided Adamnan with his principal written source.

Adamnan must certainly have drawn on Cummene for his account of the angel on Hinba and may well, as Maire Herbert suggests, have omitted the reference to Domnall Brecc and Mag Roth as no longer of sufficient contemporary interest for his

'The splendour of heavenly brightness'
St Martin's Cross, Iona.

'Behold Iona!' a blessing on each eye that seeth it'
· A BENEDICTION ATTRIBUTED TO COLUMCILLE

OPPOSITE The Abbey, Iona.

intended readership. It is thus to the scribe Dorbbene, working on Iona in the first years of the eighth century, that we owe the preservation of the only surviving evidence of even the existence of the earlier Cummene *Life* of Columcille.

The relative disposition of the references to 'Hinba' and 'Iou' in this chapter of Adamnan have prompted the very radical suggestion that Columcille might not have founded the monastery on Iona until as late as the succession of Aidan in 574. It is quite possible to read Adamnan's account as implying that Columcille's first monastic foundation in Scotland was on Hinba and only on the prompting of the angel with the book of glass did he come to the long-sacred isle of Iona to ordain Aidan as king. Whilst it is more than likely that Hinba was Columcille's first Scottish foundation, the annals are quite specific in attributing to Conall mac-Comgall the grant of Iona to Columcille. There is evidence of equal weight to be found in Adamnan when he describes the saint's vision of the ascent of the soul of Brenden of Birr as taking place on 'the island of Iou'. In Adamnan's account of that vision, Columcille is quite clearly established in a full-scale monastic settlement on Iona and yet Brenden died in 573, significantly the year before the death of Conall and the succession of Aidan.

Adamnan moves from the destiny of kings into a long sequence of visions of angels bearing the souls of holy men, of greater and lesser prominence, to their eternal reward. The passing of St Brenden of Birr – on 29 November 573, according to the calendars – is perhaps the most historically notable of these departing souls. By contrast, the Diormit 'who built himself a little monastery' is nowhere entered in the calendars. The 'holy bishop' Colman mocu-Loigse, on the other hand, does have his festival recorded at 15 May and the site of his church is marked by an old graveyard in the south of Queen's County.

Perhaps the most curiously significant of these departing souls seen in visions is that of Brito, whose name suggests a monk of British stock and whom Columcille notes as 'the first among us to die on this island.' Adamnan may well have had special reason to include this vision in the light of the sinister legend of the interment of Odhrain which has attached itself to the foundation on Iona. The Old Irish *Betha Coluim Cille* includes the story – with dark pagan overtones – of the ritual burial of the still-living Odhrain at the foundation of the monastery:

> Colum Cille said, then, to his people, It would be well for us that our roots should pass into the earth here. And he said to them, It is permitted to you that some one of you go under the earth of this island to consecrate it. Odhran arose quickly, and thus spoke: If you accept me, said he, I am ready for that. O Odhran, said Colum Cille, you shall receive the reward of this: no request shall be granted to anyone at my tomb, unless he first ask of thee. Odhran then went to heaven. He founded the church of Hy then.

The oldest burial place on Iona still bears the name of Odhrain, which might be taken to support the *Betha*'s account were it not for the fact that the dedication to Odhrain is far older than the Columban foundation. There is evidence of Christian settlement on Iona more than a century before Columcille, when both Brigid and Patrick traditionally visited Scottish Dalriada, and the dedications to Odhrain – occurring on Mull, Tiree and Colonsay as well as Iona – appear to date from this period. According to W. F. Skene, the historical 'St Odhrain' was the *Odhran* of *Leithrioch-Odhrain* or Latteragh in County Tipperary, whose death is recorded in 548 and whose festival is entered in the calendars at 2 October. Although Odhrain was an historical personality and the graveyard dedicated to him on Iona lies on the 'Street of the Dead' between the harbour and the monastery, he had no historical connection with the Columban foundation and his name is nowhere listed amongst the brothers who accompanied Columcille to Iona. It would have been wholly characteristic of Adamnan to have included the passing of 'Brito' in his *Vita Columbae* to confound any legend linking ritual 'burial alive' with the Columban foundation of Iona.

There are shades of the colourful demonology of the Old Irish hagiographies in Adamnan's story of Columcille's involvement with 'angels who made stout combat against demons' in a remote and rocky part of Iona, very probably the ruined hermitage called *Cobhain Cuildich* or the 'Culdee's Cell'. The alliance of abbot and angels drives the spike-wielding demons from Iona and their assault is redirected against the monasteries of Tiree. Although Baithene's church on 'the Plain of Long' is preserved from their onslaught, other monastic settlements on 'the land of Eth' prove more vulnerable. Any outbreak of the plague was seen as a consequence of divine wrath and an outbreak of pestilence on Tiree would have been automatically blamed on demonic assault.

There are other references to Columcille's combats with demons in Adamnan, as indeed there are in the hagiographies of other saints. Patrick did similar battle with demons on Croagh Patrick in Mayo and Cuthbert had to evict evil spirits from the island of Inner Farne before he could safely establish his hermitage there. None the less, there is nothing in Adamnan to compare with the bizarre account, quoted by Manus O'Donnell from the *Liber Lecan*, of the saint's extraordinary airborne battle with demons for the soul of 'King Brandubh':

> And they passed over Hy; and Columkille heard them while he was writing; and he stuck the *style* into his cloak, and went into battle. . . . And the battle passed over Rome, and the *style* fell out of Columkille's cloak, and dropped in front of [Pope] Gregory, who took it up in his hand. Columkille followed the soul of Brandubh to heaven. When he reached it, the congregation of heaven were at Celebration, namely *Te decet hymnus*, and *Benedic anima mea*, and *Laudate pueri Dominum*; and this is the beginning of the Celebration of Heaven. Columkille did the same as the people of heaven. And they brought Brandubh's soul back to his body again.

Further examples of angelic intervention at Columcille's behest feature in the rescue of the souls of the monks of Comgell's church at Bangor drowning in Belfast Lough, and also in the rescue of the brother falling from the roof of 'the round house of the monastery of the Plain of the Oakwood'. There may even be an interesting point of sixth-century church architecture here, because Adamnan's reference to the 'round house' might possibly refer to the round bell-towers characteristic of so many Irish medieval monasteries. These are often thought to have originated at a much later date, designed as places of safety for books and relics in the time of the Viking raids. Adamnan's reference to *monasterii culmine rotundi* has been suggested as evidence of such towers being built as early as the sixth century.

The account of Columcille's conference with 'a multitude of angels' on the small hill overlooking the monks' farmland of the *machair* on Iona is clearly intended as a hagiographical peak of the book 'concerning visions of angels'. The hill – known since as *Cnoc nan Aingel* or 'the Hill of the Angels' – would have been familiar to every member of the community and its other Gaelic name of *Sithean Mor*, 'the Fairy Hill', suggests a magical significance with its roots in Iona's pre-Christian antiquity. It is impossible to ignore the implied similarity of Columcille on the Hill of the Angels to the transfiguration of Christ as it is recorded in the ninth chapter of St Mark's gospel. On more than a few occasions when Columcille is observed by one of his monks in the presence of angels or illuminated by divine light, he charges each witness to reveal nothing of what he has seen 'during the blessed man's life'. Adamnan cannot possibly have been unaware of Christ's adjuration to those disciples who had witnessed His transfiguration: 'And as they came down from the mountain, He charged them that they should tell no man what they had seen, till the Son of man were risen from the dead.'

Similarly impressive is the following chapter's account of Columcille in retreat on Hinba and visited by 'four holy founders of monasteries'. Adamnan lists the four holy men as Comgell mocu-Aridi the founder of Bangor, Cainnech mocu-Dalon the

'The holy man was sitting in his hut writing'

The rocky mound of *Tor Abb* – 'the small hill of the Abbot' – outside the abbey was the site of
Columcille's cell on Iona.

'While the saint sat and rested there a little while, being weary with years, behold, there came to meet him a white horse, that obedient servant which used to carry the milk vessels between the cow-pasture and the monastery.'

On the vallum marking the boundary of the monastery site, Iona.

founder of Aghaboe, Brenden mocu-Alti – Brenden the Navigator – the founder of Clonfert, and Cormac the grandson of Lethan, who is nowhere in the calendars accredited with the founding of any monastery. These four 'illustrious men' unanimously invite Columcille to act as celebrant of the Mass, and while he does so St Brenden sees 'a tongue of fire, flaming and very bright, all ablaze from Saint Columba's head'. This manifestation of divine favour, even in the presence of such prominent fathers of the church, is clearly intended to set Columcille in the very first rank of saints. Adamnan's account provides one of the most vividly memorable episodes in all his *Vita Columbae* and, interestingly, an almost identical story is included in the Old Irish *Life*. There it is set not on Hinba but in the island monastery on *Rechra*, identified in this case as the island of Lambay 'in the east of Brega' near Dublin:

> Once Colum Cille, and Comgall, and Cainnech were in that church. Comgall said that Colum Cille should make the offering of Christ's Body and of His blood in their presence. Colum ministered unto them as to that. Then Cainnech beheld a fiery pillar above Colum Cille so long as he was at the offering. Cainnech told that to Comgall, and they both beheld the pillar.

Adamnan sets another of his most memorable chapters on Hinba, where Columcille is visited through three days and nights by the Holy Spirit when 'he saw many mysteries openly made manifest which had been hidden from the beginning of the world.' Columcille was anxious that Baithene should be able to join him through these days and nights of revelation, but Baithene was at that time 'on the island of Ege', or Eigg, and prevented by heavy winds from sailing to Hinba. This reference to

Baithene firmly establishes him as the *alumnus* of Columcille. This can be translated simply as 'pupil', but could also be taken as recognition that Baithene was, formally or otherwise, Columcille's foster-son. Baithene, first cousin to Columcille and certainly one of the company of twelve who came with him to Iona, was named by the saint as his own successor as abbot of Iona. 'Let Baithene write what follows,' says Columcille as he lays down his quill for the last time on the afternoon before his death. Baithene was certainly Columcille's closest companion, as Adamnan indicates by the frequency and number of his references to him, and Notker Balbulus identifies Baithene as the *familiarissimus disciplus* – 'the most favoured disciple' – of Columcille.

Adamnan chronicles a sequence of occasions when Columcille is discovered, usually in the church on Iona, surrounded by a heavenly light. These manifestations seem to have accompanied him throughout his life, from his early boyhood in the care of Cruithnecan to his later years as abbot on Iona. It might be possible to offer any number of rationalistic explanations of these apparitions of divine illumination, from psychic energy to hallucination. It is curious how Adamnan so often specifies a winter night as the occasion of their appearance, and the *aurora borealis* or 'Northern Lights' have certainly been seen from Skye. Neither was Columcille the only Celtic father to be so illuminated. Comgell of Bangor was also recorded as similarly favoured. There is indeed something especially Celtic about the whole phenomenon, as the symbolism of light throughout the Gaelic prayers and incantations of the *Carmina Gadelica* will testify.

Amongst those offered by Adamnan as witness to this luminous phenomenon is Virgno – or *Fergna Brit* – who was himself to become the sixth abbot of Iona in 605. Another witness, in defiance of the saint's explicit instructions, was the monk Berchan, and this incident carries an intriguing echo of Manus O'Donnell's version of the transcribing of the 'book of Finnian'. Berchan spies on Columcille praying in the church on Iona and surrounded by the customary divine light. When the monk is rebuked by his abbot for having 'sinned before God', Columcille adds that only his own prayers for Berchan saved him from falling dead or suffering his 'eyes . . . plucked from their sockets'. This second retribution was, of course, precisely that suffered by a similar monastic spy at Finnian's monastery when Columcille's crane pecked out his eye through the spy-hole in the door. This might just be pure coincidence, but it is difficult to ignore the possibility that Adamnan could have been seeking to reshape a traditional story in the same way as he set out to refute the legend of Odhrain with his account of Brito's soul.

Adamnan's conclusion is a detailed and elegiac account of the death of Columcille, which bears interesting comparison with the evocative simplicity of the Old Irish *Life*'s brief account of Columcille's passing:

> Now when Colum Cille came to his ending, and when his bell for nocturn was struck on the night of Pentecost Sunday, he went before the rest into the church and made prostration and fervent prayer at the altar. Then an angelic radiance filled the church around him on every side, and there the venerable old man sent forth his spirit to heaven.

By contrast, Adamnan's account is effectively an historical document, drawn from the first-hand sources enshrined in Iona tradition; and when he places the words '*with desire I have desired* to depart to Christ our Lord' in the voice of Columcille, he is quoting the opening phrase of St Luke's account of the Last Supper and leaving us in no doubt of his own assessment of the eminence of Columcille.

Adamnan's chronicle of 'the passing to the Lord of our holy patron Columba' is a deeply felt and deeply moving narrative, which speaks directly for itself across thirteen hundred years. It is a document unrivalled by any similar essay in hagiography and it stands above any need of introduction or commentary.

In the first of these three books, as has been mentioned above, some brief and concise examples of his prophetic revelations have been described, with the help of the Lord; and in the second book above, examples of miracles manifested through the blessed man's powers and, as has often been said, frequently accompanied by the grace of prophecy. This third book will treat of apparitions of angels which were revealed to others in relation to the blessed men, or to him in relation to others; and of those which were manifested to both, though in unequal measure, that is to say, to him directly and more fully, but to others indirectly and in part, that is, from without and by investigation, but in the same visions of angels or of heavenly light. These discrepancies between visions of such kinds will become clear below, where they are recorded in their places.

But now let us begin to describe these apparitions of angels from the first beginnings of the blessed man's birth.

An angel of the Lord appeared one night in a dream to the venerable man's mother, between his conception and birth; and standing beside her presented her, as it seemed, with a robe of wonderful beauty, on which fair colours, as of every kind of flower, could be seen portrayed. After a brief pause he asked for it back and took it from her hands; and lifting it and spreading it out, he let it go in the empty air. Grieving that it was taken from her, she spoke to that man of venerable demeanour as follows: 'Why do you take this delightful robe away from me so quickly?' He then said, 'It is because this cloak is so greatly honoured that you will be able to keep it no longer.'

After he said this, the woman saw the aforesaid robe gradually flying further away from her and growing larger, so that it stretched beyond the breadth of the plains and rose above the mountains and woods with its greater stature. And she heard a voice afterwards that spoke as follows: 'Woman, do not grieve. For to the husband to whom you are joined in the bond of matrimony you shall bear a son so gifted, that he will be counted as one of the prophets of God; and he is predestined by God to lead countless souls to the country of heaven.' On hearing this voice, the woman awoke.

· † ·

Of a ray of light seen over his face in his boyhood while he slept

One night, this blessed boy's foster-father, the priest Cruithnechan, a man of exemplary life, returned from the church after the service to his lodging to find his whole house illumined with a bright light; for he saw a ball of fire standing over the boy's face as he slept. At the sight he at once began to tremble, and bowing his face to the ground in great wonder, he understood that the grace of the Holy Spirit had been poured forth from heaven over his pupil.

· † ·

OF AN APPARITION OF HOLY ANGELS WHOM SAINT BRENDEN SAW TRAVELLING OVER THE PLAIN AS THE BLESSED MAN'S COMPANIONS

Many years later, Saint Columba was being excommunicated by a synod, wrongly, as became clear in the end, so venial and pardonable were his offences; and he came before the assembly that had been convened against him. When Saint Brenden, the founder of the monastery that in Irish is called Birr, saw him approaching in the distance, he rose at once, and bowing his face kissed him reverently. Some of the elders at that gathering rebuked him apart from the others, saying, 'Why, in the presence of an excommunicate, did you not refuse to rise and kiss him?' And he replied to them thus: 'If you had seen what the Lord has not disdained to make manifest to me this day, concerning this chosen one of His whom you dishonour, you would never have excommunicated him: for not only does God not excommunicate him according to your mistaken verdict, but He even magnifies him more and more.' They said, on the other hand, 'We should like to know how God, as you claim, glorifies him, whom we have excommunicated not without reason.' Brenden said, 'I saw a pillar, trailing fire and very bright, going before this man of God whom you despise, and holy angels accompanying him on his journey over the plain. I do not dare, therefore, to treat this man with scorn, who I see is predestined by God to lead the peoples to life.' At these words of his, they not only abandoned the excommunication, not daring to proceed further, but even paid him great reverence and honour.

This pronouncement was made in Teiltiu. In these same days, the saint sailed over to Britain with twelve disciples as his fellow soldiers.

· † ·

OF AN ANGEL OF THE LORD WHOM SAINT FINNIO SAW SHARING THE BLESSED MAN'S JOURNEY

At another time the holy man went to the venerable Bishop Finnio, his teacher, as a young man to an old. When Saint Finnio saw him approaching him, he saw besides an angel of the Lord accompanying his journey, and, as we are told on reliable authority, he informed some brothers who were standing by, saying, 'Behold, see now the holy Columba coming here, who has proved worthy to have an angel of heaven to share his travel.'

· † ·

OF AN ANGEL OF THE LORD WHO APPEARED IN A VISION TO SAINT COLUMBA WHILE HE WAS LIVING ON THE ISLAND OF HINBA, AND WHO WAS SENT THAT HE MIGHT ORDAIN AIDAN AS KING

At another time, when the memorable man was living on the island of Hinba, one night in a trance he saw an angel of the Lord, who had been sent to him and held in his hand a glass book of the ordination of kings. The venerable man took it from the angel's hand, and at his bidding began to read it. In the book he was charged to ordain Aidan as king, but refused, because he had more love for Iogenan, Aidan's brother; but suddenly the angel stretched out his hand and struck the saint with a scourge, and its livid mark on his side endured for all the days of his life. And he added these words: 'You must know for certain that I have been sent to you by God with the glass book, that in accordance with the words you have read in it you should ordain Aidan to the kingship. But if you are unwilling to obey this command, I shall strike you again.'

And so, after this angel of the Lord had appeared for three nights in succession, holding the same glass book in his hand, and had charged him with the same bidding from the Lord concerning the ordination of that king, the saint, in obedience to the word of the Lord, sailed across to the island of Iou and there, as he had been bidden, ordained Aidan as king; for Aidan arrived there during these days. And as he spoke the words of ordination, he prophesied concerning the future of Aidan's sons, grandsons and great-grandsons; and laying his hand upon his head he ordained and blessed him.

Cummene the White, in a book that he wrote about Saint Columba's miraculous powers, said that Saint Columba began to prophesy concerning Aidan and his posterity and their kingdom, saying, 'Believe without doubt, Aidan, that none of your enemies will be able to resist you, until first you act deceitfully against me and my posterity. On that account, therefore, give this charge to your sons, that they themselves charge their sons and grandsons and their posterity not to lose from their hands the sceptre of this kingdom through their wicked counsels. For at whatever time they do wrong to me or to my kinsmen in Ireland, the scourge that I have suffered because of you at the hand of an angel will be turned by the hand of God upon them, to their great disgrace; and their men will lose heart, and their enemies will be mightily strengthened against them.'

Now this prophecy has been fulfilled in our times in the battle of Roth, when Domnall Brecc, Aidan's grandson, laid waste without cause the province of Domnall, Ainmure's grandson. And from that day to this they have continued in subjection to foreigners, which moves the heart to sighs of sorrow.

OF AN APPARITION OF ANGELS CARRYING TO HEAVEN THE SOUL OF A BLESSED MAN, BRITO

At another time, when the holy man was living on the island of Iou, one of his monks, one Brito, devoted to good works, was attacked by a sickness of the body and brought to the point of death. When the venerable man visited him at the hour of his departure, he stood for a short time by his bed and blessed him, and then quickly left the house to avoid seeing him die; and the moment after the holy man withdrew from the house, he ended this present life.

Then, while the memorable man was walking in the courtyard of his monastery, he raised his eyes to heaven and marvelled for a long time in great astonishment. A brother named Aidan, son of Liber, a devout man of good disposition, who alone of the brothers was present at that hour, knelt down and proceeded to ask the saint to tell him why he marvelled so. The saint said to him, 'I have now seen holy angels doing battle in the air against the powers of the enemy. And I give thanks to Christ, the judge of the combat, that the victorious angels have carried off the soul of this pilgrim, who was the first among us to die on this island, to the joys of the country of heaven. But I pray you, reveal this mystery to no one during my life.'

· ✝ ·

OF THE REVELATION TO THE HOLY MAN OF A VISION OF ANGELS WHO WERE CONDUCTING TO HEAVEN THE SOUL OF ONE DIORMIT

At another time an Irish pilgrim came to the saint and stayed with him for some months on the island of Iou. One day the blessed man said to him, 'A cleric, of the people of your province, whose name I do not yet know, is now being carried to heaven by angels.' On hearing this, the brother began to search in his mind concerning the province of the eastern people, called in Irish *ind Airthir*, and the name of that blessed man. He then spoke these words: 'I know another soldier of Christ, who built himself a little monastery in the same region in which I lived; his name is Diormit.' The saint said to him, 'He it is of whom you speak who has now been conducted by God's angels into paradise.'

But this also should be carefully noted, that there were many other secret mysteries revealed by God to him, but hidden from others, which this venerable man would not allow to be brought to the awareness of men. For this, as he once told a few of the brothers, there were two reasons: to avoid boasting, and so that unbearable numbers of people wishing to ask questions of him should not be drawn to question him by the widespread fame of his revelations.

·✝·

OF ANGELS WHO MADE STOUT COMBAT AGAINST DEMONS AND BROUGHT TIMELY HELP TO THE SAINT IN THAT BATTLE

One day when the holy man was living on the island of Iou, he sought among the ravines a place more remote from men and suitable for prayer. And when he began to pray there, suddenly, as he afterwards told a few of the brothers, he saw a loathsome army of blackest demons doing battle against him with iron spikes; and it was revealed to the holy man by the Spirit that they wished to invade his monastery and slaughter many of the brothers with these spikes. But he, as one man against countless adversaries such as these, fought a stout fight, taking on the armour of the apostle Paul. And so for most of the day the battle was fought on both sides, and the countless foe were unable to defeat one man, nor had the one man the power to drive them from his island until angels of the Lord, as the saint later informed a few people, came to his support and, in fear of them, the demons were repulsed and withdrew.

On the same day, when the saint had returned to the monastery after the expulsion of the demons from his island, he uttered these words concerning that enemy host: 'Those deadly adversaries, who today by God's favour, and with the help of angels, have been driven from the territory of this little land to the land of Eth, will there make a savage assault on the monasteries of the brothers, and attack them with pestilences; and many will die of this affliction.'

This also came to pass during those days in accordance with the blessed man's fore-knowledge. And after two days had elapsed, by a revelation of the Spirit, he said, 'With God's help, Baithene has made good provision that the community of the church which, by God's will, he rules in the Plain of Long, is defended from the assault of demons by fasts and prayers; and no one there, except one man who has died, will die on this occasion.' This was fulfilled in accordance with his prophecy. For while many died of that disease in the other monasteries of that island, none but the one of whom the saint spoke died in Baithene's community.

Codex Cenannensis

The Book of Kells is the last, most splendid and most enigmatic of the three great insular gospel books. Its sumptuous blend of Irish, Pictish, Northumbrian and Byzantine graphic and calligraphic features has prompted various speculations over its origin, ranging from the Lindisfarne scriptorium to some unidentified and otherwise unproductive scriptorium in Pictland. But its Columban association initially derives from an eleventh-century annal entry of a theft. The *Annals of Ulster* at 1007 record:

> The great Gospel of Colum-Cille was wickedly stolen in the night out of the western sacristy of the great church of Cenannus – the chief relic of the Western world, on account of its ornamental cover. The same Gospel was found after twenty nights and two months, its gold having been taken off it, and a sod over it.

Thus the annalist confirms that the Book of Kells was at the monastery at Kells in the eleventh century, when evidence indicates that the Book of Durrow was in the monastery at Durrow. None the less, the evidence of their gospel texts suggests that if Kells was not transcribed from Durrow, then both were transcribed from the same exemplar. In either case both books would at one time have been in the same monastery and that monastery can only have been Iona. The dating of the Book of Kells to some time around 800 would place its creation in the period of the first Viking raids on Iona and it seems more than probable that the book travelled back to Ireland with the Iona community seeking sanctuary from the northmen at Kells in 807. It would also place the making of the book in the last years when the island of Iona still stood at the centre of the dominion of Columcille.

At that time there would have been brothers in the Iona scriptorium who had been schooled by the masters of Lindisfarne and yet working still in the ancient tradition of Irish calligraphy. The portrait of the Virgin and Child on folio 7^v (see page 162) bears such striking similarity to the same subject as it is carved on the lid of the coffin of Cuthbert that both images must have been derived from the same graphic exemplar. Similarly, the graphic themes of Pictish art might have been brought back to the island by monks who had worked east of the Spine and by the end of the seventh century Columban monks had travelled widely on the Continent, where they would have come into contact with Byzantine iconography. It is significant that the Book of Kells owes much more to the icons of Byzantium, even to the art of the Coptic fathers, than it does to any Roman inspiration. There are no representations of the Petrine tonsure in its pages and that alone would suggest that it could not possibly have been a creation of Bede's Northumbria or of any Pictish monastery under the influence of Jarrow. Iona was the place where it was made, and specifically an Iona still in the shadow of its abbot, Adamnan.

The portrait pages in the gospel of Matthew (see pages 167 and 171) and especially that in the gospel of John (see page 174) are strikingly evocative of the vision of the *Fis Adamnain*:

> Over the head of the Glorious One that sitteth on the royal throne is a great arch, like unto a wrought helmet, or a regal diadem. . . . None could tell of His vehemence and might, His glow and splendour, His brightness and loveliness. . . . Heaven and earth are filled with the light of Him, and a radiance as of a royal star encircles Him.

Here – in the words of Gerald of Wales's account of the lost gospel book of Kildare – 'you may see the face of Majesty divinely represented . . . that you would declare in truth that these were all composed by angelic rather than human artistry'.

'*Christi Autem*' – the *chi-rho-iota* monogram: f. 34^r.

The Book of Kells, Trinity College Library, Dublin: MS A.1.6.

·✝·

OF AN APPARITION OF ANGELS WHOM THE MAN OF GOD SAW CARRYING TO THE HEAVENS THE SOUL OF A BLACKSMITH NAMED COLUMB, SURNAMED COILRIGIN

There was a certain blacksmith, very devoted to works of charity and fully dedicated to all other acts of righteousness, who dwelt in the midland part of Ireland. When this man, the aforenamed Columb, surnamed Coilrigin, was brought to the point of death in a good old age, at the same hour in which he was taken from the body, Saint Columba, who was living on the island of Iou, spoke thus to a few elders who stood around him: 'Columb Coilrigin, the blacksmith, has not laboured in vain: by the labour of his own hands he has been fortunate to obtain those eternal rewards that he desired to buy. For behold, his soul is now being carried by holy angels to the joys of the country of heaven. For whatever wealth he was able to gain by the practice of his craft, he gave away as alms to the needy.'

·✝·

OF A SIMILAR VISION OF ANGELS WHOM THE BLESSED MAN BEHELD BEARING TO HEAVEN THE SOUL OF A VIRTUOUS WOMAN

At another time also, when the holy man was living on the island of Iou, one day he suddenly raised his eyes to heaven and uttered these words: 'Fortunate woman, fortunate and virtuous, whose soul angels of God are now carrying to paradise.' Now there was a devout brother named Genereus the Saxon, a baker, who while baking heard these words uttered by the mouth of the saint. And on the same day of the month at the end of that year, the saint said to this Genereus the Saxon, 'I see a wonderful sight. Behold, the woman of whom I spoke in your presence a year past is now meeting in the air the soul of her husband, a devout layman, and with holy angels is fighting for it against hostile powers; and with the support of the angels and the help of that man's righteousness, his soul has been rescued from the battalions of demons and conducted to the place of eternal rest.'

·†·

OF AN APPARITION OF HOLY ANGELS WHOM SAINT COLUMBA SAW COMING TO MEET THE SOUL OF BLESSED BRENDEN, THE FOUNDER OF THE MONASTERY WHICH IN IRISH IS CALLED BIRR, AT HIS PASSING

On another day also, while the venerable man was living on the island of Iou, he summoned his attendant Diormit, who has often been mentioned, early in the morning, and gave him this command: 'Let the sacred rites of the Eucharist be quickly made ready. For today is the feast day of blessed Brenden.' 'Why', said his attendant, 'do you command that the celebration of such a Mass be prepared today? For no message has come to us from Ireland of that holy man's death.' 'Go, even so,' said the saint; 'you must obey my order. For in this past night I have seen the heaven suddenly opened, and companies of angels coming down to meet the soul of Saint Brenden; and in that hour they illumined the whole world, shining in matchless splendour.'

·†·

OF A VISION OF HOLY ANGELS WHO CARRIED TO HEAVEN THE SOUL OF THE HOLY BISHOP COLMAN MOCU-LOIGSE

One day also, while the brothers were putting on their shoes in the morning and preparing to go to the various tasks of the monastery, the saint on the contrary gave orders that they should refrain from work that day, that the rites of the sacred oblation should be made ready, and that, as on the Lord's day, there should be the addition of a small meal. 'And today,' he said, 'unworthy though I am, I must celebrate the sacred mysteries of the Eucharist, in veneration of that soul which was carried this past night, among holy companies of angels, beyond the starry spaces of the heavens and has ascended to paradise.'

And at these words the brothers obeyed, and in accordance with the saint's bidding refrained from work that day; and after making preparations for the sacred rite, they went to the church with the saint vested in white, as on a feast day. But it happened in the course of this service that while the customary prayer, in which the name of Saint Martin is commemorated, was being chanted to a melody, the saint suddenly said to the chanters as they reached the place where this name occurs: 'Today you must chant, "for Saint Colman, the bishop".' Then all the brothers who were present understood that Colman, a bishop of the Lagin and a dear friend of Columba, had departed to the Lord. And some time later, some travellers from the province of the Lagin reported that this bishop had died on the night on which it was so revealed to the saint.

·✝·

Of an apparition of angels who came down to meet the souls of Saint Comgell's monks

At another time, when the venerable man was living on the island of Iou, on a sudden impulse he brought the brothers together by ringing the bell, and said to them, 'Let us now help by our prayer Abbot Comgell's monks, who in this hour have been drowned in the Lake of the Calf. For behold, at this moment they are fighting in the air against hostile powers that are trying to snatch away the soul of a guest who was drowned with them.'

Then after tearful and earnest prayer he quickly stood up in front of the altar, between the brothers who were also prostrated in prayer, and said with a look of joy on his face, 'Give thanks to Christ; for now holy angels, coming to meet the holy souls, have brought deliverance, like victorious warriors, even to that guest, and snatched him away from the battalions of demons.'

Virgin and Child portrait page: f. 7ᵛ.

The Book of Kells, Trinity College Library, Dublin: MS A.1.6.

· † ·

OF A MANIFESTATION OF ANGELS COMING TO MEET THE SOUL OF ONE EMCHATH

At another time, when the holy man was journeying beyond the Spine of Britain beside the lake of the River Nes, he was suddenly inspired by the Holy Spirit and said to the brothers who were travelling with him, 'Let us hasten to meet holy angels, who have been sent down from the highest regions of heaven to bear away the soul of a heathen, and who await our arrival there that we may give timely baptism to the man before he dies; for he has preserved a natural goodness through all his life into advanced old age.'

And saying this, the aged saint went with all possible haste ahead of his companions, until he arrived at the land called Airchartdan. And there an old man named Emchat was found, who heard the word of God preached by the saint, and believed and was baptised; and he at once departed to the Lord, joyful and without fear, with angels who came to meet him. Moreover, his son Virolec believed and was baptised, with his whole house.

· † ·

OF AN ANGEL OF THE LORD WHO BROUGHT SUCH TIMELY AND SPEEDY HELP TO A BROTHER WHO FELL FROM THE ROOFTOP OF THE ROUND HOUSE OF THE MONASTERY IN THE PLAIN OF THE OAKWOOD

At another time, while the holy man was sitting in his hut writing, his face was suddenly changed, and from his pure heart he uttered this cry: 'Help, help!' Two brothers standing at the door, namely Colcu, son of Cellach, and Lugne mocu-Blai, asked him the reason for this sudden cry. And the venerable man gave them this reply: 'I told an angel of the Lord, who just now was standing between you, to bring such speedy help to one of the brothers, who fell from the rooftop of the great house that is being built at present in the Plain of the Oakwood.' And the saint then made this pronouncement: 'Most wonderful and almost indescribable is the swiftness of angels' flight, equal, I believe, to the speed of lightning. For that heavenly one who flew away from us here just now, as that man was beginning to fall, came to his help as in the twinkling of an eye, and held him up before he touched the ground; and he who fell could feel no fracture or hurt. How marvellous, I say, was this most swift and timely help, which, more quickly than words, when such great distances of sea and land lay between, could be brought so very speedily.'

·✝·

OF A MULTITUDE OF HOLY ANGELS SEEN AS THEY CAME DOWN FROM HEAVEN TO TALK WITH THE BLESSED MAN

At another time also, one day when the blessed man was living on the island of Iou, he admonished the assembled brothers most strictly, saying to them, 'Today I wish to go out alone to the little plain in the west of our island. Let none of you follow me, therefore.' They obeyed, and he went out alone indeed, as he wished; but a certain brother, a crafty spy, went by another way and secretly took up position on top of a mount that overlooks that plain, wishing to find out the reason for the blessed man's solitary excursion. From the top of the mount, this spy saw him standing on a little hill within that plain, praying with hands outstretched to the sky and raising his eyes to heaven, when, wonderful to tell, behold, a marvellous sight suddenly appeared, which from his position on the nearby mount this aforesaid man beheld even with his bodily eyes; and this, I believe, was not without the permission of God, in order that the name of the saint and his honour should afterwards be made more widely known, though against his own wish, among the peoples, because of the manifestation of this vision. For holy angels, citizens of the country of heaven, flew to the holy man with wonderful speed, and as he prayed they began to stand round him, clothed in white vestments. And after some conversation with the blessed man, that heavenly throng, as if sensing that they were spied on, swiftly returned to the heights of heaven.

The blessed man himself, returning to the monastery after his talk with the angels, again brought the brothers together, reproached them sternly, and enquired which of them was guilty of transgression. They then protested their ignorance; but the guilty man, conscious of his own inexcusable fault, was unable to hide his sin any longer, and kneeling in supplication before the saint, in the midst of the company of the brothers, he prayed for pardon. The saint took him aside and, as he knelt, charged him with great menace to reveal to no man any secret, however small, concerning that vision of angels during the blessed man's life. However, after the blessed man's departure from the body, he told the brothers of that apparition of the heavenly company, with great protestations of its truth. As a result, even today, the place of that conversation with the angels bears witness to the event which occurred there by its own special name, *Cnoc angel* in Irish, which may be rendered 'the Little Hill of the Angels'.

From these examples, therefore, attention and careful thought should be given to the great and remarkable character of the sweet visitations of angels to the blessed man, often occurring on winter nights when he was awake, and when he was praying in remote places while others were at rest, which were without doubt very numerous, but unable to come to the awareness of men. Some of them, in fact, were by one means or another able to be espied by men, whether by day or by night; but it is beyond question that these were very few in comparison with those angelic visitations that could be known by no man.

This should be noted similarly of certain manifestations of light, which were observed by a few and which will be recorded below.

· † ·

OF A PILLAR OF LIGHT SEEN TO BE ABLAZE FROM THE HOLY MAN'S HEAD

At another time, four holy founders of monasteries came across from Ireland to visit Saint Columba and found him on the island of Hinba; and the names of these illustrious men were Comgell mocu-Aridi, Cainnech mocu-Dalon, Brenden mocu-Alti, and Cormac, grandson of Lethan. With unanimous assent, they chose Saint Columba to consecrate the sacred mysteries of the Eucharist in the church in their presence. In obedience to their bidding, he entered the church with them on the Lord's day, as usual, after the reading of the Gospel. And there, while the rites of the Mass were being celebrated, Saint Brenden mocu-Alti, as he afterwards told Comgell and Cainnech, saw a tongue of fire, flaming and very bright, all ablaze from Saint Columba's head as he stood before the altar and consecrated the sacred oblation, and rising upwards all the time like a pillar until those most sacred offices were completed.

· † ·

OF THE DESCENT OR VISITATION OF THE HOLY SPIRIT, WHICH ON THE SAME ISLAND REMAINED OVER THE VENERABLE MAN FOR THREE DAYS AND AS MANY NIGHTS TOGETHER

At another time, when the holy man was living on the island of Hinba, the grace of the Holy Spirit was poured out upon him in matchless abundance, and continued wondrously for three days; so that for three days and as many nights the house, its door barred, was filled with heavenly splendour, and he remained inside neither eating nor drinking, and allowed no one to approach him. From this house rays of light of immeasurable brightness could be seen flooding out by night through the chinks of the doors and through the key-holes. Certain spiritual chants also, never heard before, could be heard from his lips. Moreover, as he afterwards declared to very few, he saw many mysteries openly made manifest, which had been hidden from the beginning of the world. And all the obscure and most difficult passages in the sacred scriptures lay plainly revealed to the eyes of his pure heart, more clearly than the light of day. He regretted that Baithene, his foster-son, was not there; for if he had chanced to be present during those three days, he would have written down at the blessed man's dictation very many mysteries, unknown to other men, of ages past or future, and also some interpretations of the sacred books. This Baithene, however, was detained by an adverse wind on the island of Ege until the three days and nights of the incomparable glory of that visitation were over; and so he was unable to be present.

· † ·

OF THE BRIGHTNESS OF ANGELIC LIGHT THAT
VIRGNO, A YOUNG MAN OF GOOD
DISPOSITION, SAW COMING DOWN OVER SAINT
COLUMBA IN THE CHURCH, ON A WINTER'S
NIGHT WHILE THE BROTHERS WERE AT REST IN
THEIR BEDCHAMBERS. VIRGNO WAS
AFTERWARDS, BY GOD'S WILL, IN CHARGE OF
THIS CHURCH THAT I, THOUGH UNWORTHY,
SERVE

One winter's night, the above-named Virgno, burning with love for God, went alone into the church to pray, while the others were at rest, and there, in an annexe that was built on to the wall of the oratory, he devoutly prayed. And after about one hour, the venerable man Columba entered that sacred house, and with him a golden light that came down from highest heaven and filled the whole extent of the church; moreover, the adjoining room of that little annexe, where Virgno was trying his best to remain hidden, was flooded with the brightness of that heavenly light through the chamber's inner door, which was slightly open, filling him with great fear. And just as no one can look directly with undazzled eyes into the summer sun at midday, so Virgno, who saw that heavenly brightness, was unable to endure it, because the matchless brilliance of its radiance greatly dazzled his sight. And that awesome splendour, as of a lightning-flash, so terrified the aforenamed brother when he saw it, that no strength remained in him.

Saint Columba left the church after praying for no long time; and the next day he summoned to him the terrified Virgno and spoke to him these few words of comfort: 'You have found favour, little son, you have found favour in the sight of God this past night, by lowering your eyes to the ground in terror at His brightness. For if you had not done so, your eyes would have been blinded by seeing that inestimable light. But you must take care never to disclose this extraordinary manifestation of light to anyone during my life.'

So this memorable and amazing revelation became known to many, on the word of that Virgno, after the blessed man's passing. It was the son of this Virgno's sister, an honourable priest named Comman, who once testified to me, Adomnan, concerning this vision recorded above; and he had heard the story from the mouth of his uncle, the Abbot Virgno himself, by whom, as far as he could endure it, the vision had been seen.

OPPOSITE   Portrait page from the gospel of Matthew: f. 28ᵛ.

The Book of Kells, Trinity College Library, Dublin: MS A.1.6.

· † ·

OF ANOTHER VISION, NEARLY ALIKE, OF A BRIGHT LIGHT FROM ON HIGH

On another night also, one of the brothers, named Colcu, son of Aid Draigniche, of the race of Fechre, whom we mentioned in the first book, came by chance to the door of the church while the others slept, and stood there for some time in prayer. Then suddenly he saw the whole church filled with a heavenly light, a flash of light which, more quickly than words, vanished from his eyes. He did not know that Saint Columba was praying inside the church at that time, and after the sudden and extraordinary apparition of light he returned home greatly afraid.

The following day, the saint summoned him and most sternly reproached him, saying, 'For the future you should take care, my son, not to try, like a spy, to observe heavenly light that has not been granted to you, because it will escape you; and see that you tell no one what you have seen during the days of my life.'

·†·

OF ANOTHER SIMILAR APPARITION OF DIVINE LIGHT

At another time also, the blessed man one day strictly admonished a pupil of his named Berchan, surnamed Mes-Loen, who was studying divine wisdom, and said to him, 'Take care, my son, this coming night, not to approach my lodging according to your regular practice.' But after hearing this, he disobeyed the command and came to the blessed man's house in the silence of the night, while the others were at rest; and he craftily put his eyes opposite the key-holes to spy on him, supposing that inside some heavenly vision was being revealed to the saint, as the event proved to be true. For at the same hour the blessed man's lodging was filled with the splendour of heavenly brightness, which the young trespasser could not bear to behold, and he at once fled.

The next day, the saint spoke to him privately, reproaching him most severely, and addressed these words to him: 'This night, my son, you have sinned before God; for you foolishly supposed that your crafty spying, which you seek to deny, could be hidden or concealed from the Holy Spirit. I saw you at that hour approaching the door of my lodging and then going back, did I not? And if at that moment I had not prayed for you, there before the door either you would have fallen dead or your eyes would have been plucked from their sockets. But on this occasion the Lord has spared you on my account. But know this, that while you live in luxury in your native Ireland your face will bear a mark of reproof all the days of your life. However, I have asked and obtained this favour from the Lord, that because you are our pupil you may do tearful penance before your death, and obtain mercy from God.' And all these things so befell him afterwards as they had been foretold of him according to the blessed man's word.

·†·

OF THE MANIFESTATION TO THE HOLY MAN OF ANOTHER APPARITION OF ANGELS, WHOM HE SAW PROCEEDING TO MEET HIS HOLY SOUL AS IF IT WERE ABOUT TO DEPART FROM THE BODY

At another time, while the blessed man was living on the island of Iou, one day his holy face suddenly lit up with a wonderfully cheerful and joyous expression; and he raised his eyes to heaven, overjoyed and filled with gladness beyond compare. Then, after a brief moment's pause, that sweet and delightful feeling of joy changed to sadness and sorrow. Two men, who were standing at that time at the door of his hut, which was built on higher ground, shared his great sadness themselves, and asked him the reason for his sudden joyfulness and the ensuing sorrow. One of them was Lugne mocu-Blai, and the other was called Pilu the Saxon. The saint spoke to them as follows: 'Go in peace, and do not ask that the reason for that joy, or that sadness either, be revealed by me now.'

They wept at this, and kneeling down, with their faces bowed to the ground, they humbly begged him to allow them some knowledge of what had been revealed to the saint in that hour. Seeing their great sadness, he said, 'Because I love you, I would not make you sad. You must first promise me not to betray to any man during my life the secret of which you ask.' They at once promised readily according to his command; and after this promise the venerable man addressed them as follows: 'This present day marks the completion of thirty years of my pilgrimage in Britain. Meanwhile, for many days past I have devoutly begged my Lord to release me from my sojourn here at the end of this present thirtieth year, and summon me at once to the country of heaven. And this was the reason for my joy, about which you question me in your sorrow. For I saw holy angels, sent from the throne on high, coming to meet me to conduct my soul from the flesh. But see now, they are suddenly held back and stand beyond our island's Sound on a rock, wishing to come near to summon me from the body, but forbidden to approach closer; and soon they will return to highest heaven. For what the Lord granted to me when I asked with all my strength, that today I might pass from the world to Him, He has altered more swiftly than words, preferring rather to answer the prayers of many churches on my behalf. And to the prayers of those churches it has been granted by the Lord, though against my wish, that I should live on in the flesh for four further years from this day. This delay, so sorrowful for me, was the good reason for my sadness today. When these four remaining years in this life have ended, by God's favour I shall depart happy to the Lord; and I shall depart suddenly, after no bodily affliction, with the holy angels who will come to meet me at that time.' In accordance with these words, which we are told he spoke with deep groans of sorrow and streams of tears, the venerable man lived on in the flesh for four years afterwards.

· † ·

Of the passing to the Lord of our holy patron Columba

The period of four years mentioned above, after the completion of which the truthful prophet had long before had foreknowledge that he would end this present life, was now drawing to its close. One day in the month of May, as we wrote in the preceding second book, the aged saint, weary with years, was conveyed by wagon to visit the brothers at their work. And as they laboured in the western part of the island of Iou, he began to speak to them that day as follows: 'During the Easter solemnities, lately performed in the month of April, *with desire I have desired* to depart to Christ our Lord, as had also been granted to me by Him, if I had so preferred. But so that the festival of gladness should not be turned to your sorrow, I preferred to postpone a little longer the day of my departure from the world.'

When they heard these sad words of his, the monks of his community meanwhile became very sorrowful, and to the best of his powers he began to cheer them with words of comfort. After this, sitting as he was in the wagon, he turned his face towards the east and blessed the island and its inhabitants; and from that day to the present, as was recorded in the aforementioned book, the poisons of snakes with trifid tongues have been unable to harm either man or beast. After the words of this blessing, the saint was conveyed back to his monastery.

Then, a few days later, while the solemn rites of the Mass were being celebrated as usual on the Lord's day, suddenly the venerable man lifted up his eyes, and a flush of gladness was seen to suffuse his face; for, as it is written, '*A glad heart maketh a cheerful countenance*'. For at that same hour he alone saw an angel of the Lord hovering above, within the walls of the oratory itself; and because the appearance of holy angels is lovely and serene, and spreads joy and exultation through the hearts of the elect, this was the reason for the sudden gladness that possessed the blessed man.

When those who were present there enquired about the reason for the joy inspired in him, the saint, with an upward gaze, gave them this reply: 'Wonderful and matchless is the subtlety of the angelic nature. For see, an angel of the Lord, sent to recover a deposit dear to God, looked on us from above within the church and blessed us, and then returned again through the roof of the church, leaving no traces of so remarkable a departure.'

So spoke the saint, but none of the bystanders could understand the nature of that deposit which the angel had been sent to recover. Our patron, however, gave the name 'deposit' to his own holy soul entrusted to him by God, which, as will be described below, departed to the Lord on the Lord's night, after an interval of six days.

Now at the end of that week, that is, on the Sabbath day, the venerable man and his faithful attendant Diormit went to bless the nearby barn. After going in and blessing it, together with two piles of grain that were stored in it, he spoke these words in expression of his gratitude: 'I heartily congratulate the monks of my community, because even this year, if I have to depart from you to another place, you will have sufficient bread for the year.'

On hearing these words, his attendant Diormit began to be sad, and said, 'During this year, father, you have many times made us sad by your frequent mention of your passing.' The saint gave him this reply: 'I have a few secret words for you, and if you promise faithfully to disclose them to no one before my death, I shall be able to give you a clearer account of my departure.' And when his attendant, in accordance with the saint's wish, had concluded that promise on bended knees, the venerable man then spoke as follows: 'This day in the holy scriptures is named the Sabbath, which means "rest". And truly is today a Sabbath for me, as it is my last day in this present life of toil, and on it I keep Sabbath after my wearisome labours. And at midnight this coming night, that of the venerable day of the Lord, I shall go the way of my fathers, as the scriptures say. For already my Lord Jesus Christ deigns to invite me, and I shall depart to Him, as I say, this coming midnight at His invitation. For so it has been revealed to me by the Lord Himself.' Hearing these sad words, his attendant began to weep bitterly, and the saint tried as best he could to comfort him.

After this the saint left the barn, and while returning to the monastery sat down halfway; and at that spot a cross was later set up in a mill-stone, which can be seen today standing at the roadside. And while the saint sat and rested there a little while, being weary with years, as I said above, behold, there came to meet him a white horse, that obedient servant which used to carry the milk-vessels between the cow-pasture and the monastery. It went up to the saint and, strange to tell, put its head in his lap, inspired, I believe, by God, from whom every animal has understanding and such perception of things as the Creator Himself has bidden; and knowing that its master would soon depart from it, and that it would see him no more, it began to lament and, like a human being, to

Christ portrait page from the gospel of Matthew: f. 32ᵛ.

The Book of Kells, Trinity College Library, Dublin: MS A.1.6.

shed streams of tears over the saint's bosom, weeping and foaming profusely. When he saw this, the attendant began to drive the tearful mourner away, but the saint forbade him, saying, 'Let it be, as it loves us, let it be, that it may pour out into my lap here the tears of its most bitter lamentation. See, though you are a man and have a rational soul, you could have known nothing of my departure except what I lately disclosed to you myself; yet to this brute and unreasoning beast the Creator Himself has clearly revealed, in His own chosen way, that its master is about to depart from it.' And saying this, he blessed the horse that served him, as it turned away from him in sorrow.

Leaving that place and climbing a mount that overlooks the monastery, he stood for a little while on its summit; and as he stood he raised both his hands and blessed his monastery, saying, 'Upon this place, however small and mean it may be, not only the kings of the Irish with their peoples, but even the rulers of barbarous and foreign nations, with the peoples subject to them, will bestow great and exceptional honour. By saints also, even those of other churches, will exceptional reverence be bestowed upon it.'

After these words, he came down from the mount and, returning to the monastery, sat in his hut copying a psalter. And as he reached that verse of the thirty-third psalm, where it is written, '*They that seek the Lord shall want no manner of thing that is good*', he said, 'Here, at the end of the page, I must stop. Let Baithene write what follows.' The last verse that he wrote is especially appropriate to the saint, on laying down his office, for whom the good things of eternity will never be wanting; while to his successor, the father and teacher of spiritual children, who, as his predecessor commanded, succeeded him not only in teaching but in writing also, the verse that follows is peculiarly apt: '*Come, ye children, and hearken unto me; I will teach you the fear of the Lord.*'

After he had finished writing this verse mentioned above at the end of the page, the saint entered the church for the service of vespers on the Lord's night. As soon as this was concluded, he returned to his lodging and lay down on the bed, where by night he had the bare rock for his mattress, and for his pillow a stone, which even today stands as a kind of epitaph beside his grave. And as he lay there, he entrusted his last commands to the brothers, in the hearing of his attendant alone, saying, 'This last charge I give you, little children, that you keep between you mutual and unfeigned charity and peace. And if you observe this command in accordance with the examples of the holy fathers, God, who gives strength to the good, will be your helper, and I, abiding with Him, will intercede for you; and not only will the needs of this present life be sufficiently supplied by Him, but also the rewards of the good things of eternity, which are prepared for those who keep God's commandments, will be bestowed on you.'

Thus ends my brief account of the venerable patron's last words as he was crossing from this weary pilgrimage to the country of heaven.

After speaking them, the saint became silent for a while at the approach of his last happy hour. Then at midnight he rose up in haste at the ringing of the bell and went to the church, and he ran ahead of the others and entered alone; and kneeling in prayer he sank down beside the altar. Diormit his attendant, following later, saw from a distance in that moment that the whole interior of the church was filled with angelic light about the saint. As he approached the door, the light which he had seen, and which a few of the other brothers had also seen from a distance, quickly disappeared.

Diormit therefore entered the church and cried in a tearful voice: 'Where are you, father, where are you?' And groping through the darkness, as the brothers' lamps had not yet been brought, he found the saint lying before the altar, and lifting him a little and sitting beside him, put his holy head in his lap. Meanwhile, the assembled monks ran up with lights, and began to lament at the sight of their dying father. And, as we have learned from some who were present, while his soul had not yet departed the saint opened and raised his eyes, and looked round on both sides with a wonderfully cheerful and joyous expression, no doubt beholding the holy angels who came to meet him. Diormit then raised the holy right hand to bless the saint's company of monks. And the venerable father himself, as best he could, moved his own hand at the same time, so that, though he was unable at the departure of his soul to bless the brothers with his voice, he might be seen to do so even by the movement of his hand. And after his holy blessing, signified in this way, he at once breathed his last.

Although his spirit had left the tabernacle of the body, his face remained so flushed and wonderfully gladdened by the angelic vision that it seemed not like that of a dead man, but of one living and asleep. In the meantime, the whole church resounded with cries of sorrow.

We must not omit to mention how at the same hour the passing of his blessed soul was revealed to a saint in Ireland. In the monastery called in the Irish tongue Cloni-finchoil, there was an aged saint and soldier of Christ, named Luguid, son of Tailchan, a righteous man and a sage. Early in the morning he described his vision most sorrowfully to another soldier of Christ, named Virgno, saying, 'At midnight this past night Saint Columba, the pillar of many churches, passed to the Lord. And at the hour of his blessed departure I saw in the spirit the island of Iou, which I have never visited in the body, all radiant with the brightness of angels, and the whole expanse of air, as far as the ethereal skies, illumined with the splendour of these countless angels, who had come down, sent from heaven, to bear away his holy soul. I also heard, sounding on high, the songs of the angelic hosts, melodious and most sweet, at the very moment of his holy soul's departure among the ascending choirs of angels.'

During these days Virgno rowed from Ireland and stayed for the remaining days of his life on the island of Hinba; and he very often used to recount to Saint Columba's monks this revelation of angels of which, as was said above, he had learned for certain from the mouth of the aged saint to whom it had been shown. This Virgno it was who, after completing many years of blameless service among the brothers, completed twelve further years as a victorious soldier of Christ by living the life of an anchorite, at the place of the anchorites at Muirbolc-mar. This vision mentioned above we have not only found recorded in writing, but have also learned of it beyond any doubt on the reliable authority of some elders, to whom Virgno himself had reported it.

At the same hour also another vision was revealed in a different manner, and reported to me, Adomnan, when I was a young man, with great protestations of its truth, by one of those who had seen it. He was a soldier of Christ, very old, called in Irish Ernene, of the family mocu-Fir-roide, whose name may also be rendered 'man of iron'; and among the remains of other monks of Saint Columba he himself, also a holy monk, is buried on the Ridge of Toimm, and with the saints awaits the resurrection. He said, 'In that night in which Saint Columba passed from earth to heaven, by a happy and blessed death, I was at work with some other men catching fish, in the valley of the River Fendea, where fish are plentiful; when suddenly we saw the air illumined across the whole expanse of the sky. Startled by the suddenness of this miracle, we raised our eyes and turned them towards the east; and behold, there appeared a kind of huge pillar of fire which rose upwards in the middle of that night, and seemed to us to illumine the whole world like the summer sun at midday. And after that pillar had pierced the sky, darkness followed, as after the setting of the sun. Not only was the brightness of this memorable pillar of light seen with great astonishment by our company there, but many other fishermen also, who were fishing at different places in the various pools along that river, saw a similar apparition and were terror-stricken, as they later reported to us.' These three miraculous visions, then, appearing at the very hour of the venerable patron's passing, testify to the eternal honours bestowed on him by God. Let us return to our theme.

Meanwhile, when the matin hymns were finished after the departure of his holy soul, the sacred body was carried back from the church to his lodging, from where he had come a little earlier, whilst still living; and the monks escorted it with the melodious chanting of psalms. For three days and as many nights the obsequies were performed with due respect and honour; and when they had ended in the sweet savour of God's praises, the venerable body of our holy and blessed patron was wrapped in clean linen clothes, laid in the coffin assigned and made ready for it, and buried with due reverence, to rise again in the bright splendour of eternity.

Portrait page from the gospel of John: f. 291ᵛ.
The Book of Kells, Trinity College Library, Dublin: MS A.1.6.

We shall now describe, near the close of this book, what we have been told on reliable authority of those three days mentioned above, in which his obsequies were performed according to the custom of the church.

Now there was once one of the brothers who spoke frankly in the venerable man's presence, saying to the saint, 'To celebrate your obsequies after your death, it is thought that the whole population of these provinces will row across and fill this island of Iou.' Hearing these words, the saint then said, 'My little child, the event will not prove to be as you say. No promiscuous throng of people will be able to come to my obsequies. Only the monks of my community will perform my burial and grace my obsequies.'

The almighty power of God caused these prophetic words of his to be fulfilled immediately after his passing. For during those three continuous days and nights there occurred a great storm of wind, without rain, and such was its force that it prevented anyone from crossing the Sound by boat in either direction. And after the blessed man's burial was completed, the storm was at once stilled, the wind ceased, and the whole sea became calm.

Let the reader, therefore, judge in what great and special honour before God our patron is held, at whose prayer, when once he lived in mortal flesh, God granted that storms were stilled and that seas became calm; and again, when he had need, on the occasion mentioned above, gales of wind arose and the seas, at his will, were stirred up by the winds; but afterwards, as was said above, on the completion of his burial rites, they were changed to a great calm.

This, then, was the end of our memorable patron's life; these the beginnings of his rewards. In the phrases of the scriptures, he is added to the fathers to share in eternal triumphs, united with the apostles and prophets, and joined to the number of the thousands of white-robed saints who have washed their robes in the blood of the Lamb, and he follows the Lamb where He leads; a virgin unspotted, pure of every stain by the grace of our Lord Jesus Christ Himself, to whom, with the Father, belong honour, and power, and praise, and glory, and everlasting dominion, in the unity of the Holy Spirit, for ever and ever.

After reading these three books, every attentive reader should note how great and special was the merit, and how great and special the honour of our holy and venerable superior, so often mentioned above, in the estimation of God; how great and remarkable were the splendid visitations of angels to him; how great his gift of prophecy; how great the efficacy of his miraculous powers bestowed by God; and how great and how frequent was the brightness of God's light that shone about him while he yet lived in mortal flesh. And even after the departure of his most gracious soul from the tabernacle of the body, that same heavenly brightness, with the frequent visitation of holy angels, continues to appear to this day at the place where his holy bones are at rest; and this is reliably known through its revelation to certain chosen people.

This also was no small favour bestowed by God on that man of blessed memory; that so great was his merit, that not only throughout the whole of our land of Ireland and throughout Britain, the largest of all the islands in the whole world, was his name held in wide renown though he lived in this small and remote island of the Britannic ocean; but his fame reached even to triangular Spain, and to Gaul, and to Italy, which lies beyond the Pennine Alps, and also to the city of Rome itself, the chief of all cities. So great and special was the high honour known to have been bestowed upon that saint, among the other gifts of the divine bounty, by God, who loves those that love Him and who glorifies ever more and more and exalts with honours beyond measure those who magnify Him with the sweet savour of praises. Blessed is He for ever. Amen.

I beseech all those who wish to copy these books, or rather I adjure them by Christ, the Judge of the ages, that after carefully copying them they compare them with the exemplar from which they have written and amend them with all possible care, and that they also append this adjuration in this place.

*Whoever reads these books of Columba's miracles, may he pray to God for me,
Dorbbene, that after death I may possess life eternal.*

THE LIFE AND THE LEGACY

His grace in Hii without stain,
And his soul in Derry:
And his body under the flagstone under which are Brigid and Patrick.

Berchan's foretelling of the full habitation of Columcille

It is one of the stranger synchronicities of the history of the early medieval Church that Pope Gregory's emissary Augustine reached the coast of Kent to begin the conversion of Saxon England in the summer following the death of Columcille on Iona at Whitsuntide in 597.

The post-mortal chronicle of Columcille is no less intrigued with riddles and beleaguered by the tides of history than was his lifetime. After the spring gales across the Sound of Iona preserved the private grief of his monks through the three days of funerary rites, his remains lay in that earth for a century before they were translated into a shrine of silver and gold. The influence and importance of Iona burgeoned through those hundred years, and was somehow sustained through the centuries which followed. Multitudes of pilgrims thronged to the holy island of Columcille. The overlords of three kingdoms were borne down its Street of the Dead to lie in the Relig Odhrain. The island which had long been held sacred to the magus and the druid entered into its great age as the seagirt shrine of the Gael. It became renowned as the great centre of Celtic learning and its name was revered as far from the Hebridean seaboard as the monasteries of Bobbio in Lombardy and St-Gallen on the shores of Lake Constance.

For the Irish – and the Irish-schooled – holy men of the *peregrini Christi* who ranged across Europe, Iona was the lodestone of the 'white martyrdom' of their voluntary exile. History and legend blur in plotting the courses of seafaring saints of the Columban dominion, claiming landfalls as distant as Iceland and the Faroes for Cormac and a mythical paradise beyond the farthest horizon for Brenden the Navigator of Clonfert. If these travellers' tales became the stuff of medieval mythmakers, the most strategic outpost of the dominion of Columcille is firmly underwritten by the historical record. That outpost was the tidal island of Lindisfarne off the coast of the 'land of the Saxons' and the roots of its foundation were first laid on the day in 616 when Aethelfrith, king of Northumbria and conqueror of Aidan mac-Gabran at Degsastan, fell in battle against Edwin of Deira on the east bank of the River Idle.

After that battle, two of the sons of Aethelfrith fled to Iona in search of sanctuary. There they were educated by monks who would still remember the last years of Columcille and from there Oswald, the elder of the two, returned to reclaim his father's kingdom. A vision of Columcille promised him victory and when it was won on the field of *Hefenfelth*, he summoned a monk from Iona to bring the faith to his people. Thus it was that St Aidan came to Lindisfarne – 'a separate place near a chief city' in accordance with the Columban Rule – and from the foundation of that 'Iona in the east' sprang the 150 years of Northumbria's golden age.

For the three decades after the founding of Lindisfarne in 635, the Church and State of Northumbria recognised the island of Columcille as the fountainhead of its faith and its learning. Then, in the year 664, the link between those two holy islands was severed in the church of St Hild at Whitby. Colman of Lindisfarne was vanquished in debate with the advocates of the Roman orthodoxy of Augustine and he set out from the island monastery of Aidan, in company with all his Irish monks and some number of English brothers, to retrace Aidan's footsteps back to Iona. From there Colman journeyed on to Ireland to found his own island monastery on Inishboffin off the coast of Mayo – and thus fulfill the prophecy of Ethne's vision of 'a large cloak which reached from the Islands of Modh'.

After Colman, Lindisfarne bowed to the resolution of Whitby and, in consequence, the 'land of the Saxons' broke away from the dominion of Columcille. Eventually the ordination of Cuthbert as its bishop healed the abrasions of the divide of Whitby and provided the English of the north with a patron saint who blended Columban charisma with submission to the ordinances of Rome.

When Adamnan came to this 'land of the Saxons' it must have seemed to him that the dominion of Columcille was doomed to oblivion beyond the Sound of Iona. Northumbria was the dominant power among all the kingdoms of Anglo-Saxon England and a great centre of civilisation in seventh-century Europe – and Northumbria's obeisance was directed towards Rome. Within twenty years, the Pictish church would expel Columban monks from their footholds in Pictland and drive them back west of the Spine of Britain. Finally, in 716, more than a decade after the death of Adamnan, the community of Iona abandoned the tenacious 'ignorance' so roundly scorned by Bede and at the last accepted the rules of Rome – ironically under the guidance of Egbert, a monk of Lindisfarne.

However ignominious the decline of the ancient Celtic faith after Whitby, a far more ominous tide of history was reaching its flood in the last decade of the eighth century when the Viking longships ran their keels into the white sand of Iona. They had razed Cuthbert's Lindisfarne and plundered Bede's Jarrow. The fury of the northmen was inevitably visited on the Iona of Columcille, and the *Annals of Inishfallen* entered '*Vastatio Iae-Columkille*' at the year 795.

The 'warriors of the western sea' went on to ravage the island chain of the Hebrides and strike at monasteries off the coast of the Irish mainland. Such protection as a remote island might have enjoyed from land-based assault was worthless against the dragon-ships, and after a second raid in 802 the Abbot Cellach of Iona looked to Ireland for sanctuary. In 804 the monastery of *Cenannas* or Kells, close by Tara in the plain of Meath, was acquired for the Columban *familia*. When the northmen slaughtered sixty-eight monks in a third attack in 806, Cellach decided to transfer the foundation to Kells. It may have first been intended as only a temporary refuge but it became the principal foundation of the Columban Church, and after 807 the abbots of Kells inherited the title *comharba Choluim Chille*, 'the successor of Columcille'.

Those brothers who remained on Iona suffered the sanguinary consequences of their tenacity when the Vikings returned again and again. The maps still bear testimony to their fate when they enter the place-names of Martyrs' Bay and the White Strand of the Monks on the shoreline of the island.

Whatever actually became of the bones of Columcille is less a matter of historical enquiry than of debate between rival traditions. It would seem likely that the relics of the founder were carried to Kells in 807, but when the Vikings came to plunder the precious shrine in 825 the monk Blathmac refused to betray its whereabouts and suffered death by the 'blood eagle' for his stoicism. Some relics of Columcille were certainly in Ireland by the end of that decade because the annals record Abbot Diarmait of Kells carrying them with him on a visit to Scotland in that year. The annals record that relics of Columcille were brought to Ireland in 849 and that the 'great shrine' followed them to Kells in 878, apparently after another raid in that year.

'In Down,
three saints one
grave do fill:
Patrick, Brigid
and Columcille'

BISHOP MALACHY OF
DOWN

The traditional
burial place of
Columcille with
Brigid and Patrick
at Downpatrick.

When Kenneth mac-Alpin became king of all Scotland and the surviving Iona community transferred to Dunkeld in 849, it is claimed that Columban relics were brought there with them and even that the bones of Columcille were carried into battle at Bannockburn in the *breacbannach*, the reliquary of Monymusk. But the greater weight of tradition claims the earth of Ulster as his last resting place.

Tradition tells the tale of a Viking by the name of Mandan who stole the coffin of Columcille in the course of a raid on Iona and carried it aboard his longship in the hope of finding treasure enclosed with the saint's remains. Opening the casket to find it bereft of riches, the Viking cast both it and its contents overboard far out at sea. When the coffin was eventually washed up on an Irish beach it was given into the care of the abbot at Down where Columcille was reinterred in the tomb that held Patrick and Brigid. So much for the most spurious of folklore, and yet the obituary of Columcille in the *Annals of Clonmacnoise* affirms that his remains were 'entered in the place where the abbey of Dowen is (before the abbey was built by Sir John Coursey) where St Patrick & St Bridgett were buried before.'

Manus O'Donnell tells of a prophecy of St Patrick promising that the three patron saints of Ireland would one day lie in the same grave:

> And Padraic foretold that it should be in one tomb with him and with Brigid in Dun da Leithglas that the body of Columcille should be put after his death. And Brigid foretold this likewise.

The twelfth-century Malachy, bishop of Down, saw a vision of lines of prophecy inscribed on stone:

> In Down, three saints one grave do fill:
> Patrick, Brigid and Columcille.

Lord Grey, Deputy Governor of Ireland in the 1530s, made his own contribution to the establishment of Henry VIII as head of the faith when he put the ancient church at Down to the torch and Holinshed's *Chronicle* testifies to the iconoclastic significance of his fire-raising: 'He rode to the north and in this journey he razed St Patrick, his church in Downe, and burnt the monuments to Patrick, Brigide and Colume, who are said to have been there interred.'

The true location of saintly remains is very frequently the source of conflict of territorial imperatives. Just as Kildare has not unnaturally challenged Downpatrick's claim to be the resting place of Brigid, so have Dunkeld, Durham and Glastonbury on various occasions challenged its claim to Patrick's relics. Centuries of myth and legend have made it impossible to prove or disprove any local claim to the dust of Columcille. Whatever buildings and artefacts of the Columban church of the days of its founder might have survived the fury of the northmen, little has endured the unrelenting devastation of fourteen centuries. The great gospel books have survived to bear testimony to the creative genius of the scholars and scribes of the Celtic tradition, but they derive from a later flowering of that tradition than the time of Columcille. However inspiring the claims of the *Cathach* psalter to be the battle-book of Culdrevny, modern palaeographic scholarship throws doubt on any such provenance and qualification. The sole survivor of all the erosions of time endures as the pre-eminent material relic of Columcille for the scholar, the priest and the pilgrim. It is the tripartite masterwork enshrining his prophecies, miracles and visions set down by Adamnan mac-Ronan, the ninth abbot of Iona.

Its provenance and its inspiration are beyond dispute. The earliest surviving manuscript was written in the hand of an historically identifiable scribe, within no more than a decade of Adamnan's death and possibly even during his lifetime, and it was written on Iona in the scriptorium of the monastery founded there by the saint it celebrates. Whatever first-hand testimony was collated by Segene and set down by Cummene has not survived, but it was certainly available to Adamnan as his primary written source. The library on Iona provided him with the hagiographical classics of his time, and the *Vita Martini*, Sulpicius Severus's life of St Martin of Tours, and the *Vita Antoni*, Athanasius's life of St Antony of Egypt, were the moulds in which Adamnan cast his own text. If his sources and his models can be thus clearly identified, the question which has long attended Adamnan's *Vita Columbae* is that of why – and for whom – an ageing abbot, himself enmeshed in political and theological controversies of his own time, esteemed for the influence of his learning and yet the author of only one book in six decades, should have chosen to set down the life and works of his great predecessor at the time and in the form he did.

Unlike Bede, who was a scholar by monastic trade and the author of more than forty works before reaching the age at which Adamnan wrote his first, the ninth abbot of Iona was indisputably a writer of occasion. His *De Locis Sanctis* was the result of fortuitously accidental contact with a shipwrecked bishop from Gaul possessed of rare and precious traveller's tales from the Holy Land.

We know when Adamnan wrote his *Vita Columbae* and therein lies the first indication of his primary motive. It might not be without significance that the monks of Lindisfarne would have been preparing the early 'anonymous' *Life of Cuthbert* at much the same time as Adamnan was writing his *Vita* of Columcille. He evidently began work on his text after his return from Northumbria and had completed his task certainly by 697 and probably by 692. Although his opening sentence states that he was writing in response to 'the entreaties of the brothers', a shadow of serious doubt falls upon such a motive. The wish to comply with any such entreaties was very probably no more than a hagiographical convention. Sulpicius Severus begins his *Life* of Martin with a similar statement of compliance. There was no biographical contribution which Adamnan could have added to the Cummene *Life* and the brothers had certainly no urgent need of a new biography of the saint whose life and legend was already enshrined in their tradition. Whatever infringements of the standing of the Columban Church might have been threatened by Finnachta's political stratagems on behalf of the *paruchiae* of Patrick and Brigid, the influence of the abbot of Iona was certainly great enough for his *Cain Adamnain* to hold for the whole of Ireland, Dalriada and Pictland in 697, and by then the southern Ui-Neill had been succeeded as heirs to the High Kingship by the Cenel Connaill in the person of Adamnan's own kinsman, the *Ard Ri* Loingsech. The Irish medievalist Maire Herbert's assessment of Adamnan's achievement demonstrates how, 'unlike contemporary Lives of Patrick and Brigit, the *Vita Columbae* is not concerned with putting forward claims to status or property rights.' Adamnan's *apologia* for his unpolished prose and 'the poor Irish tongue' clearly indicate that he was not primarily addressing the Iona brothers or indeed any other community of the Irish *familia* of Columcille. It is more than likely that other immediate concerns – such as the looming controversy over the *boruma* – would have occasionally influenced Adamnan's work-in-progress in directions other than his first intent through the four or more years in which he was engaged in his task, but the frequency of the Northumbrian references and relevances throughout his pages provide *prima facie* evidence that Adamnan's principal and primary motivation derived from his visits to 'the land of the Saxons'.

The first chapter of the first book 'concerning his prophecies' is the oddly placed 'summary of his miracles' and its greater content is a lengthy account of Oswald's vision of Columcille on the eve of the battle which not only secured his kingdom but marked the starting-point of the rebirth of Christianity in that kingdom. In his last pages, Adamnan records visions of the ascent of the soul of Columcille at the hour of his passing in terms vividly reminiscent of the Lindisfarne tradition of Cuthbert's vision from the Lammermuir Hills of the departing soul of St Aidan.

Throughout my introductions to the three books, I have pointed to numerous similar indications that Adamnan was concerned to remind Northumbria of its debt to Columcille of Iona. Distressed as he must have been by the decline of the Columban tradition in Aldfrith's kingdom through the thirty years since the Council of Whitby, the abbot of Iona was also acutely aware of the ecclesiastical tides of his times. Although the divide between Celtic and Roman orthodoxies is now judged to have been of lesser consequence in the Irish *paruchiae* than Bede suggests it was in the English Church, Adamnan would have been in no doubt that adherence to the traditional tonsure and ancient calendar was isolating Iona from the wider Christian world. Loyalty to Celtic orthodoxy was perceived as no more than provincial ignorance in the view of the learned brothers of Wearmouth and Jarrow, and at the time of Adamnan's visits there those monasteries stood in the first rank of European learning. At the pinnacle of its golden age in the eighth century, Northumbria was second only to Rome as the centre of the civilised world, and the arguments of one of its principal churchmen in the person of Ceolfrith at Jarrow, however convincing to Adamnan personally, must have also presaged the consignment to oblivion of the heritage of Columcille. Thus he set out to restore Columcille's stature in the first echelon of sanctity, not simply in terms of the Irish hagiographical order, but in terms of the wider horizons of emergent medieval Christendom. The gospel references alone in his *Vita Columbae* reveal that intent quite clearly as the elevation of Columcille to the eminence of Martin of Tours, and even to that of the apostles Peter, James and John.

Maire Herbert suggests that Adamnan was writing for a readership which was 'more immediately known to him, and consisted of learned Northumbrians like Abbot Ceolfrith, men familiar with the *Lives* of the great saints of Christendom, but less familiar with a saint to whom they owed recognition'. In that suggestion lies a further synchronicity: it was Ceolfrith who commissioned the making of the magnificent gospel book of Wearmouth and Jarrow intended as a gift to the Pope and known as the *Codex Amiatinus*. In his turn, Adamnan was setting down something more than the earliest surviving biography of the medieval world. He was writing nothing less than the 'Gospel of Columcille', and he was writing it, first and foremost, for Northumbria.

It is a sad irony that his book apparently failed to reach its intended destination in the great library at Jarrow. Bede, who affords the *De Locis Sanctis* such prominence in his *Historia* – written within thirty years of Adamnan's death – makes no mention of any 'Life of Columba' from the same hand and clearly knew nothing of its existence. He does mention that 'it is said that his disciples possess some written records of his life and teaching', by which he certainly must have meant whatever he had learned from Adamnan of the Cummene *Life*, but there is no reference to anything of the exalted order of the *Vita Columbae*.

There is perhaps an element of compensation for that sad irony to be found in the 'B1' manuscript of Adamnan's text. The 'A' and 'B' versions of the *Vita* certainly derive from the same original, yet there is no surviving 'B' text of any date comparable with that of Dorbbene's 'A' manuscript. The earliest surviving edition of the 'B' recension is the 'B1' manuscript in the British Library. There is no means of knowing how many transcriptions might have been made between Adamnan's last work on his original before 704 and the twelfth-century manuscript known as the 'B1', but the contents and the calligraphy of that book indicate that it was a product of the scriptorium of the Norman cathedral at Durham, the last and greatest church of the monks of Lindisfarne.

Whether the unknown scribe who placed that text of the *Vita Columbae* on parchment – in company with hagiographies of Cuthbert and of Oswald – realised it or not, his work provides the evidence that Adamnan's book had come home at last to Northumbria.

But it is necessary to look far beyond the confines of 'the land of the Saxons' to recognise the full dimensions of Adamnan's achievement. Its impact must have been vastly greater than he might ever have imagined, because it, and it alone, shaped the tradition of St Columba of Iona for generations of pilgrims down thirteen centuries.

In the year 563, when the forty-two-year-old Columcille set forth from Ireland on his 'pilgrimage for Christ', he was indeed the founder of monasteries and a power in the lands of his own people, but if he had achieved no more than that he would have remained a relatively insignificant holy man meriting little more than his entry in the *Martyrology of Donegal*. It was in 'Alba of the ravens', the western highlands and islands of the land which was to become Scotland, that he carved out the mould into which Adamnan cast the shining legend.

The Irish tradition of Columcille has much in common with the historical figure who conquered by his prayers at Culdrevny, a warrior-saint born of the heroic sagas of the fighting Celt. That Columcille was the one so easily established beside Olaf of Norway and Magnus of Orkney in the Christian iconography of the Viking kingdoms of the northern and western isles. None of which is to impugn Adamnan's hagiography or suggest that he reworked a warlord turned holy man into a fictional myth of saintliness. He was working from first-hand accounts of Columcille deriving from the later and surely more mellow years of the first abbot of Iona, who had seen and learned and achieved so much through the three and a half decades since Culdrevny to emerge as the holy man called *Chalum-Chille chaomh* – 'Columcille benign' – in the incantations of the *Carmina Gadelica*. As much as the Old Irish *Life* reflects that persona of the warrior-saint of Culdrevny, it reflects also the Gaelic tradition of the islands and the iconography of Adamnan in the resonant lines of its closing pages:

Now there was never born to the Gael offspring nobler or wiser, or of better kin than he. There hath not come of them another who was meeker, or humbler. . . . He would chant the three fifties on the sands of the shore before the sun would rise.

'Haec sunt duodecim virorum nomina . . .'

At some point between Adamnan's completion of his *Vita Columbae* and the transcription of the earliest surviving manuscript of the 'B' text over five hundred years later, a significant list of names was added by way of appendix to the original draft as it appears in the 'A' manuscript.

> These are the names of the twelve men who sailed over with Saint Columba from Ireland, on his first crossing to Britain.
> Two sons of Brenden: Baithene, also called Conin, Saint Columba's successor, and his brother Cobthach.
> Ernan, Saint Columba's uncle.
> Diormit, his attendant.
> Rus and Fechno, two sons of Rodan.
> Scandal, son of Bressal, son of Ende, son of Niall.
> Luguid mocu-Theimne.
> Echoid.
> Tochannu mocu fir-Chetea.
> Cairnan, son of Brandub, son of Meilge.
> Grillan.

This appendix goes on to list Columcille's parents and family and to underline the blood kinship which linked the members of his monastic *familia*.

> Saint Columba's parents.
> Fedilmith, his father, son of Fergus.
> Aethne, his mother, daugher of Mac-naue.
> Iogen, Columba's younger brother.
> Also his three sisters.
> Cuimne, mother of the sons of Mac-decuil, who are named Mernoc, and Cascene, and Meldal, and Bran, who is buried in Daire-Calcig.
> Saint Columba's sisters' sons.
> Mincoleth, mother of the sons of Enan, one of whom was called Colman.
> Sinech, mother of the men of the mocu-Cein of Cul-Uisci, whose names are Aidan the monk, who is buried in Cul-Uisci, and Conri mocu-Cein, who is buried in Dairmag; and grandmother of To-chumme mocu-Cein, who weary with years ended this present life as a holy priest on the island of Iou. Amen. Thanks be to God.

The earliest 'B' text of the *Vita Columbae* is found in a manuscript volume which also includes a *Life* of Augustine of Hippo from various sources, Ailred of Rievaulx's *Life* of Edward the Confessor, and Bede's lives of Aidan, Oswald, and Cuthbert. The manuscript is written in a bold 'black-letter' hand with important passages and large decorated initial letters picked out in red and green inks. It has been dated to the last years of the twelfth century by its list of the abbots of Lindisfarne and Durham, ending with Abbot Hugo who died in 1195. Its selection of contents and dedication to an order of monks of St Augustine in Newcastle-upon-Tyne clearly indicate it as a product of the scriptorium at Durham.

The material found only in the 'B' text contains such detailed nomenclature as to indicate addition to the original at a date very much earlier than the twelfth century and to suggest Irish authorship. It is consequently far from unreasonable to suggest that these passages, and thus the other 'B' text variants, might have been added by Adamnan himself at Raphoe after his return to Ireland in 697.

Adamnan – *Vita Columbae*, f. 143.

Vitae Sancti, the British Library: MS ADD. 35110

am clare diuulgari pmuint. in
hac paruia & extrema occeani
brittannici ꝫmolatus insula-
t. ꝫ ad trigonā vsꝗ hispaniā
ꝫ gallias ꝫ vl't alpes penninas
italiam sctā puenire. ipam ꝗ
romdnā ciuitatē ꝗ cap̄ ē oniū
um ciuitatū. tantus ꝫ talis ho
nor noscibit eidem scō ml cetā
diuine donationis muñia odo
natus scrtur a deo: qui se dili
gentes amat. ꝫ eos qui eū mag
nficant laudibꝫ magis ac magis
glificās īnsus. sublimat honori
buſ: qui ē bndictus in secla aeā.

Obsecro eos quicūꝗ uoluerīt
hos describe libellos immo
potius adiuro p xp̄m iudicem
scōr. ut p̄qꝳn diligent descrip
serint ꝯferant. ꝫ emdent cū oī
diligencia ad exemplar uñ ca
rauerunt. ⁊ hanc quoꝗ adiura
tionē hoc in loco subscribant.

Dec sunt xii. uiror nōīa: qui
ꝯ scō columba de scocia p
mo eius ꝯsicu ad brittanniā
ꝯsnauigauerunt. Duo filii
brendin barchene qui ꝫ co
nin scī successor columbe ꝫ co
bthach frr eꝰ. ernam scī
auuncꝰ columbe. diormiciꝰ eꝰ
ministrator. rus. ꝫ ferhno. duo

filiū rodain scandal filiuſ bre
sail. filii endei. filiī neil luǵu
id. mocu thenmne. echoid. tho
camnu. mocufir. cecca cairna
an filiuſ branduib filiī meilgi.
Scī Columbe parētes.

edilmich p̄r eꝰ filiuſ fergu
so. erchne mr ipsiuſ filia
filii namſ. iogen gmaū frr colū
be iunior. Item tres gmane soro
res eius erumne. mr filior meic.
decuil. qui nōīantur mernooc-
ꝫ caschene. ꝫ meldal. ꝫ bran. ꝗ
sepultuſ ē in dairu calchaich.
Consobrini scī columbe.

incholech mr filior enā
quor unuſ colmaan di
cebatur. Sinech mr uiror mo
cu cein cuile aque. Quor nōīa
sunt aidanuſ monachuſ qui
sepult ē bicul uscī ꝫ chronii
moccuoein ꝗ sepult ē in daur
maig. Auia rocūmi mocu cein
qui ualde senio fessuſ p̄br.
scēs in ioua insula p̄sentē fini
uit uitam aeā. Deo grās.

Scs igitur columba erat
p̄mus doctor fidei ꝶane
cismontanis pictis ad aquilo
ne. p̄musꝗ fundator monas
tij quod in insula ꝗ tunc io
ua uocabatur: nc uero hij uo

But the most extraordinary aspect of Adamnan's *Vita Columbae* is the fact that so accomplished a work of hagiography reveals Columcille the man as graphically as it portrays Columba the saint.

The Columcille who emerges from Adamnan's pages is essentially a man of the Gael, gifted with that second sight of his kind which a hagiographer would recognise as prophecy. He has the 'seeing eye' for the natural world, bequeathed by the ancient Celtic shamans and turned to such dramatic effect in the working of miracles. He has the impetuous fire of the Celtic warrior tempered by the generosity, humanity and wry humour so characteristic of the Hebridean islander. He is a man of the book in the ancient tradition of Celtic art and Irish learning, skilled in the arts of the bard and the scribe. He is a man possessed of the full measure of nobility and courage of his ancient royal blood-line, the confidant of kings and counsellor of dynasties.

Columcille is as much a man of power as of faith and his destiny is shaped as much by the tides of turbulent times as by the path of the pilgrim. But first and foremost, he is a man possessed of a charisma so remarkable as to endure undimmed through fourteen centuries, and in that also lies the achievement of Adamnan mac-Ronan, the greatest of the successors of Columcille.

When the ferry crosses the Sound of Iona to disembark its infinite variety of passengers on to the jetty on St Ronan's Bay, those travellers are reminded by an inscription near MacLean's Cross of the observation of Samuel Johnson: 'That man is little to be envied, whose patriotism would not gain force upon the plain of Marathon, or whose piety would not grow warmer among the ruins of Iona.' Whether that impression on the part of the usually unimpressionable Dr Johnson remains true two centuries on is perhaps best not debated here, but it is certainly no small tribute to Adamnan's achievement that 'this small and remote island of the Britannic ocean' has endured into unknown centuries as 'I-Columkille' – the Iona of Columcille. The *Carmina Gadelica* includes a Gaelic rune of foretelling which seems to share in Columcille's vision of 'mysteries made openly manifest, which had been hidden from the beginning of the world':

> Seachd bliadhna romh 'n bhrath,
> Thig muir thar Eirinn ri aon trath,
> 'S thar Ile ghuirm, ghlais,
> Ach snamhaidh I Chaluim chleirich.

> Seven years before the day of doom,
> The sea will come over Erin in one watch,
> And over Islay, green, grassy,
> But float will Iona of Colum the cleric.

A Note on the Translation of Adamnan's Text

This translation of Adamnan's *Vita Columbae* has been made from the text of the 'A' manuscript in the Anderson edition of 1961. My only substantial amendment to the original text has been to restore the sentence in Book III (page 154) referring to the date of Columcille's pilgrimage to the end of the chapter describing St Brenden's vision at the Synod of Teiltiu from its clearly erroneous location at the end of the following chapter describing Columcille as 'a young man'.

I have also included two passages, the story of Vigenus in Book II (page 116) and the list of the twelve monks who accompanied Columcille to Iona (page 182), which occur only in the 'B' text and may have been added after Adamnan.

In conclusion, I must gratefully acknowledge the debt owed by any new translator of Adamnan to those eminent scholars, notably Reeves and Anderson, whose distinguished Latin editions and annotated English translations of the *Vita Columbae* have been so indispensable a source of information.

JG

A Calendar of the Abbots of Iona

563–597	**Columcille**	d. 9 June
597–600	Baithene	d. 9 June
600–605	Laisran	d. 16 September
605–623	Virgno	d. 2 March
623–652	Segene	d. 12 August
652–657	Suibne	d. 11 January
657–669	Cummene Ailbe	d. 24 February
669–679	Failbe	d. 22 March
679–704	**Adamnan**	d. 23 September

'Columcille of the graves and tombs'

'Where is Duncan's body?' asks Ross in Shakespeare's *Macbeth*. To which Macduff replies:

> Carried to Columskill,
> The sacred storehouse of his predecessors,
> And guardian of their bones.

The ancient graveyard of the *Relig Odhrain* lies to the south-west of the abbey on Iona and for centuries the rulers of kingdoms and chieftains of clans were borne from Martyrs' Bay along the Street of the Dead to lie in its sacred earth.

In his *Description of the Western Isles*, Donald Munro, Dean of the Isles, offers a sixteenth-century survey of the site:

> Within this Isle of Kilmkill there is ane Sanctuary also, or Kirkzaird, called in Erishe Releag Oran. In it are three tombs of staine formit like little chapels, with ane braide grey quin stane in the gairle of ilk ane of the tombes. In the staine of ane is written – Tumulus Regum Scotiae, that is, the Tomb of the Scottes Kings – within this lay 48 crowned Scottes Kings. The tomb on the south side has this inscription – Tumulus Regum Hiberniae, that is the Tomb of the Ireland Kings; there were four Ireland Kings in it. Upon the north side of our Scottes tomb the inscription bears – Tumulus Regum Norwegiae, the Tomb of the Kings of Norway. Within this sanctuary lye also the maist part of the Lords of the Isles, with their lynage. . . .

Two hundred and seventy years after Dean Munro, the poet Keats visited this 'most holy ground of the north':

> We were shown a spot in the Churchyard where they say 61 kings are buried – 48 Scotch from Fergus 2nd to Macbeth, 8 Irish, 4 Norwegians and 1 French – they lie in rows compact. . . . many tombs of Highland Chieftains – their effigies in complete armour face upwards – black and moss covered – Abbots and Bishops of the island always of one of the chief Clans. There were plenty Macleans and Macdonnels, among these latter the famous Macdonnel Lord of the Isles.

The great tombs of kings may have gone now, but this dark corner of the Hebrides still bears blood-stiffened testimony to Scotland's centuries of the sword. Here the remains of chieftains, kings and clerics lie beside those of Lords of the Isles and Viking warriors of the western sea: amongst them Duncan and Macbeth, successive kings of eleventh-century Scotland; Anlaf, the Norse king of Dublin who came to Iona as a penitent after his defeat in battle in the tenth century; Kenneth MacAlpin who forged Scotland from Dalriada and Pictland in the ninth century; and the royal foemen of the seventh-century battle at Dunnichen Moss, the Pict Brude mac-Bile and the Saxon Egfrith of Northumbria.

It can only have been these dark shades of the Relig Odhrain which prompted the anonymous Gaelic poet of the *Reaping Blessing*, included in the *Carmina Gadelica*, to replace the customary invocation of *Chaluim-chille chaomh*, 'Columcille benign', with that of *Chaluim-chille nam feart's nan tuam* – 'Columcille of the graves and tombs'.

The Relig Odhrain, from the Street of the Dead at dusk.

GLOSSARY OF PLACE-NAMES

The place-names used by Adamnan were either Old Irish names or his Latinisations of the Old Irish forms and scholars have been able accurately to identify in many cases the modern place-names into which they evolved. In the western highlands and islands of Scotland that scholarship has been hampered by the impact of Norse nomenclature which has very often distorted or obliterated the ancient Gaelic form. The case of the island of Hinba – discussed at length on page 122 – is the most problematic example. In addition, several other of Adamnan's place-names must remain unidentified or, at best, uncertain.

Ached-bou Aghaboe, Ossory
Ailbine Delvin, Meath
Airthir, ind East Oriel, Ulster
Airthraig Shona, island of
Aithchambas on Ardnamurchan, otherwise unidentified
Apors, Lake of Lochaber
Ard-ceannachte land of 'the race of Cian', in Meath
Artbranan, dobur of possibly Tot-Arder, Bracadale, Skye
Artchain monastic foundation on Tiree
Artda-muirchol Ardnamurchan, Argyll
Ath-cliath Dublin
Aub, Lake of Loch Awe, Argyll

Boend, River River Boyne

Cailli Aufinde unidentified
Cainle unidentified
Calf, Lake of the Belfast Lough
Cambas, monastery of Magilligan parish on the River Bann
Ce, Lake of Loughkey, Roscommon
Cell-Rois Magheross, Monaghan
Cete, Ridge of Druim-Ceatt (The Mullagh), Limavady, Londonderry
Cethirn, Dun The Sconce, near Coleraine
Clocher Clogher, Armagh
Cloin Clonmacnoise, Offaly
Cloni-finchoil Rosnarea, Knockcommon, Meath
Clota, Rock of Dumbarton Rock, Strathclyde
Cnoc angel Hill of the Angels, Iona
Coire-Salchain uncertain, possibly Salen on Mull
Colossus Coll, island of
Connachta, province of the Connaught
Corcu-Reti Corkaree, Westmeath
Crog-Reth unidentified
Cul-Drebene Culdrevny , Sligo
Cul-rathin Coleraine
Cuul-Eilne Ethne's Fold, Iona

Daire-Calcig Derry
Dairmag Durrow
Deathrib, Great Cell of Kilmore, Roscommon
Delcros unidentified, possibly in Derry

Diun, monastery of unidentified

Ege Eigg, island of
Eilne, Plain of Magh Elne on the Bann
Eirros-Domno Erris, Mayo
Elen unidentified
Eth Tiree, island of

Fendea, River River Finn, Donegal

Hinba unidentified, possibly Jura

Ile Islay
Iou Iona

Lagin, province of the Leinster
Lathreg-inden unidentified, possibly near Derry
Le, 'district named' *Fir Li* on the west bank of the Bann
Long, Plain of monastery in the south of Tiree

Male Mull, island of
Maugdorni, province of County Monaghan
Mod, River River Moy, Sligo and Mayo
Muirbolc-paradisi possibly Kentra Bay, Ardnamurchan
Mumin, province of the Munster
Nes, River River Ness

Oidech Mull of Oa, Islay
Orcades Orkney

Rechru Rathlin island

Saine possibly Colonsay
Sale, River Shiel
Sci Skye, island of
Snamluthir Snalore, Longford
Spine of Britain Grampian mountains

Teiltiu Teltown, Meath
Toimm, Ridge of Drumhome, Donegal
Trioit Trevet, Meath
Two Streams, land of Tirdaglas, Tipperary

SELECT BIBLIOGRAPHY

The Columban bibliography, as has already been mentioned here, is so vast that it virtually requires a volume of its own, and for that reason this select bibliography has been restricted to those books which we have found especially useful and most of which include their own extensive and specialised bibliographies of further reading.

Before listing those titles, it might be helpful to outline the provenance of the annal sources which have received such frequent mention in the foregoing pages. The *Annals of Ulster* are amongst the most ancient of these, deriving from the earliest medieval chronicles, including those of Iona, and compiled into their present form by Cathal Mac-Manus at the end of the fifteenth century. The *Annals of the Four Masters* were compiled from all the Irish annals available to four Irish antiquaries in the 1630s. The *Annals of Tighernach* derive from the chronicles compiled by Tighernach, a monk of Clonmacnoise whose death is recorded at 1088. The *Annals of Inishfallen* are another of the earliest surviving collections of Irish chronicles, written in different hands before the end of the eleventh century. The *Annals of Clonmacnoise* are of a later form and exist only in an English translation made in 1627 from a manuscript original which has not survived. The *Martyrology of Oengus* is a calendar of saints composed around the year 800, while the *Martyrology of Donegal* is another such calendar compiled from various sources in 1630 by Michael O'Clery, the principal editor of the *Annals of the Four Masters*. The Old Irish *Betha Coluim Cille* dates from the eleventh century, but its earliest surviving text was transcribed into the *Leabar Breac* around 1397. Manus O'Donnell's *Betha Colaim Chille* was compiled from earlier Lives and from tradition in 1532.

Adair, John, *The Pilgrim's Way: Shrines and Saints in Britain and Ireland*, London, 1978.
Anderson, A. O., *Early Sources of Scottish History AD 500–1286*, Edinburgh, 1922.
Anderson, A. O. and M. O., *Adamnan's Life of Columba*, London, 1961.
Anderson, William, *Holy Places of the British Isles*, London, 1983.
Backhouse, Janet, *The Lindisfarne Gospels*, London, 1981.
Blair, Peter Hunter, *Northumbria in the Days of Bede*, London, 1976.
Brown, Peter, *The Book of Kells*, London, 1980.
Bryce, Derek, *The Symbolism of the Celtic Cross*, Llanerch, 1989.
Carmichael, Alexander, *Carmina Gadelica*, Edinburgh, 1928.
Chadwick, Nora, *The Celts*, London, 1971.
Farmer, D. H., *The Oxford Dictionary of Saints*, Oxford, 1987.
Hale, Reginald B., *The Magnificent Gael*, Ottawa, 1976.
Henderson, George, *From Durrow to Kells: The Insular Gospel Books 650–800*, London, 1987.
Herbert, Maire, *Iona, Kells and Derry: the History and Hagiography of the Monastic Familia of Columba*, Oxford, 1988.
Lawlor, H. J., *The Cathac of Saint Columba*, Proceedings of Royal Irish Academy, 1916.
Macneill, F. Marian, *An Iona Anthology*, Stirling, 1947.
Mac Niocaill, Gearoid, *Ireland Before the Vikings*, Dublin, 1972.
Macquarrie, Alan, *Iona Through the Ages*, Argyll, 1983.
Maguire, Edward, *Life of Saint Adamnan*, Dublin, 1917.
Menzies, Lucy, *St. Columba of Iona*, London, 1920.
Morris, John, *The Age of Arthur*, London, 1973.
O'Donnell, Manus, *Betha Colaim Chille*, ed. A. O'Kelleher and G. Schoepperle, Illinois, 1918.
Picard, Jean-Michel, *The Purpose of Adamnan's* Vita Columbae, Peritia 1, 1982.
Rees, Alwyn and Brinley, *Celtic Heritage*, London, 1961.
Reeves, William, *The Life of St. Columba; written by Adamnan*, Dublin, 1857.
Ritchie, Anna, *Picts*, Edinburgh, 1989.
Simpson, W. D., *The Historical Saint Columba*, London, 1927.
Skene, W. F., *Celtic Scotland*, Edinburgh, 1876–80.
Smyth, Alfred P., *Warlords and Holy Men*, London, 1984.
Specht, Dr René, *Wie kam Dorbenes Abschrift von Adamnans* Vita Sancti Columbae *in die Stadtbibliothek Schaffhausen?*, Schaffhausen, 1988.
Toulson, Shirley, *The Celtic Alternative*, London, 1987.
Tunney, John, *Saint Colmcille and the Columban Heritage*, Donegal, 1987.
Watson, William J., *The Celtic Place-Names of Scotland*, Edinburgh, 1926.

'His grace in Iona without stain'

THE PROPHECY OF BERCHAN

The chapel on the site of Columcille's shrine against the west front of the abbey on Iona. The *Heimskringla* tells how the Norse king Magnus Barelegs came here on his Viking voyage through the Western Isles in 1098.

'It is told that the king opened the door of little Columb's Kirk there, but did not go in, but instantly locked the door again, and said that no man should be so bold as to go in the church thereafter.'

INDEX

Italic page numbers refer to illustrations.